Looking
for America

Looking
for America

*Rediscovering
the meaning
of freedom.*

DOUGLAS SIMPSON

WinePress Publishing (PO Box 428, Enumclaw, WA 98022) functions only as book publisher. As such, the ultimate design, content, editorial accuracy, and views expressed or implied in this work are those of the author.

Unless otherwise noted, all Scriptures are taken from the New King James Version, © 1979, 1980, 1982 by Thomas Nelson, Inc., Publishers. Used by permission.

ISBN 1-57921-835-0
Library of Congress Catalog Card Number: 2005911145

To the prophets of today,
the new sons of Issacar, who are again
learning to understand the times to
know what Israel should do.

Table of Contents

Introduction

As I turned to leave a late winter writer's conference in Long Beach, Washington, I heard the voice of an editor I had met there and with whom I had shared the idea of this book.

"Doug," she called out, as I turned and faced her. "Have a nice journey." I smiled and continued on.

Now I know what she meant.

In undertaking this project I had no idea just how personal it would become. This story led me to the very root of political ideology, more specifically, a root contamination that I now recognize as the ruin of great nations. Until I began, I was unaware just how much I, too, had been affected. It's not that I didn't recognize the symptoms in my own life—which allowed me to conceptualize this story in the first place—it's that I didn't realize the extent to which they reached the core of my own ideology, nor did I see how misaligned my own political thinking had become.

There are countless books that address nearly every aspect of political thought and history from both secular and Christian perspectives. Most of the books I've read do a good job of explaining the "what" of political ideology. But few ever get into the "why" we think as we do, just what it is in the human psych that shapes our conclusions about how life and government ought to be.

One book that has had a strong influence on my thinking is David Noebel's *Understanding the Times*. In his book, Mr. Noebel captures the essence of four principal worldviews that shape our political world and are the ruling governmental forces of nations today. After reading his book, I felt I was finally getting down to the nitty-gritty as to what makes the world go round. It began to stir something else in me that eventually grew into *Looking for America*. Even then, there was something still missing, something just out of reach that I could feel and sense, yet something that evaded my conscious mind. Whatever it was at first had no name or defining description. But I knew it was something that keeps us from ever arriving at real solutions in the halls of government and continues to widen the gap in our opinions one to another.

Then, as I began to pen this story about four years ago, I found the problem wasn't in my thinking so much—but in my heart. Now I know what the problem is, and that is now the purpose of this book.

Looking for America breaks one of today's cardinal clichés of secular and church thinking alike. That is: You don't mix politics and religion. But I have long disagreed and contended that – as goes the church – so goes America. In fact, I find that where we get into trouble is when we don't mix it. Although many may find it objectionable, the fact is, the principles of Christianity are the foundation of the social code for America's original charter. And I can't help but feel that what is wrong in American government today began going wrong in the church first. The responsibility has always—and will always—rest on our shoulders.

Pulpits once alive with the "flame of righteousness" that Alex de Tocqueville wrote about in his early American exposé *Democracy in America*, have today acquiesced to much the same political correctness of the times, along with every other American institution. A church that once held a nation's moral feet to the fire is, for the most part, silent today. Church marquees announce coming charity benefits, bazaars and quilting parties, but few speak to the headlines of the day.

With few exceptions, the great majority of churchgoers across the land will hear nothing on the issue of politics in next Sunday morning's sermon. This week, the halls outside the House and Senate Chamber doors of every state and our nation's capitol will be lined with representatives from literally every corporate and governmental entity conceivable. But they will see little or no representation by the Bible-believing church. Instead of confronting a government that promotes rebellion to God, much of today's church will cower from committing to battle for fear of relinquishing its beloved 501-C3 tax exempt status. And I can't help but recall that the church in Christ's day had, too, become subservient to Caesar.

In large part, the church today no longer permeates the land or the culture, which God called it to subdue. Strangely, God's people have become repulsed by politics and have handed the reigns off to a godless secular mob. And, like our secular counterparts, we have become driven by the same polls, cultural whims and myths that are the latest radio and television talk show fads. Many in the church have acquiesced to the same worldly mind-set that now treats theory as fact and the Bible as myth, keeping religion tucked neatly away in a little building on Sunday mornings.

I have found that our growing expulsion from today's public debate is due to our own apathy. Meanwhile, lurking in the shadows there is a mounting threat to the American church and freedom of worship. We are rapidly losing our ability to speak.

Politics is war and must be viewed as such. It is the war of ideologies. Held in the balance are the rights of man, of which the apex for all Americans is life and liberty. History reminds us that when politics of the legislatures fail and tyranny advances, sooner or later the final round of debate takes place on an open battlefield. So, it is essential that we begin to rediscover the price of our liberty that we received, first through shedding of the blood of Christ, and then through the blood shed by the many brave American men and women who have stood for that liberty since our beginning.

For me, the battle for America today is not about economics, equality, personal prosperity, or any other issue presented on the evening news. The true battle for the American Dream is about freedom of thought, which in my mind is the only true foundation of liberty. If this is true, then freedom of thought and freedom of worship are one and the same and the cornerstone of true liberty. Any hope we have of enduring as a free nation starts here. And if history proves correct, the day freedom of worship is lost will be the day we make our final retreat into tyranny like so many other civilizations before us. From my vantage in the political arena, that day is quickly approaching.

To many reading *Looking for America*, it might seem that I am being unduly critical of the Republican Party. That is not my intention. Although I left the party some years ago and became truly independent in my own political affiliation, I still have some stubborn lingering hope that they might somehow find the courage to at least try and live up to their own party platform. My true intention here is to call them to accountability. Because to anyone paying close attention, the GOP has yet to succeed at accomplishing anything meaningful or long-lasting when it has come to power over the past few decades. I see the Republican Party as a failed vehicle for conservatives looking to go anywhere substantive. As one state senator once said to me, "Republicans need to decide whether they want to be a party or have a party." So far, it's been the latter. Meanwhile, well-meaning Christian conservatives continue to be sucked into the black hole of spine-tingling rhetoric. There is no doubt to anyone reading this book that I would much prefer a kind of multi-party system of which the founders spoke and envisioned.

On the other hand, there is not much about the Democrat Party in this book. Practically speaking, I see very little difference in what we are getting from Republicans and Democrats today. But my own dilemma is this: I don't want what the Democrats are offering, and I can't seem to get what the Republicans are. When it comes to this unfailing love-affair the church seems to hold for the Republican Party, I'm reminded of what William Wallace told the Scottish nobles in the movie *Braveheart*, "You're so busy squabbling over the scraps from Longshank's table, you've missed your God-given right to something much better." The truth is our present dilemma has nothing to do with party politics. It's much deeper than that. The sad state of affairs in party politics is really symptomatic of something much more insidious—which is the whole reason for this book.

Understanding what is truly going wrong in the political realm today begins with our willingness to lay aside our many preconceived notions about what we may have always believed concerning the role of civil government. And it ends with our being able to see the contaminations of our own hearts, the basis for our motivations, and our willingness to change the way we think as we see the truth. Because what is really eating away at us—what is really keeping us locked in horns unable to find agreement on much of anything—is something much more personal; it is a spiritual disease that has gone undiagnosed and un-treated far too long. If truth truly sets us free, then we can only continue to be a free nation when we are truly free as individuals first. And that can only happen as we become willing to see as God sees—as best we can.

In as much as the study of history is an examination of a series of historical facts, it is more importantly an inter-pretation of those facts. To me, that interpretation can only be accurate when bumped up against God's Word. Short of that, history is merely a collection of chronological events spinning off into the universe, with little purpose. This book is my own interpretation of both events and their spiritual meaning.

Some of what you will read here is fact. Naturally, some of what is here is my opinion, experience, and in some cases, my own heart's contaminations. I leave the discovery of which-is-which up to you. I hope it will stir you to your own search for the real America and the liberty that was once ours.

So, now . . . let us start at the beginning . . .

Prologue

October 9.

Another giant wave washed over the bow nearly engulfing the tiny ship. Surely, one would expect occasional storms in this part of the Atlantic, especially this time of the year, but not like this. This storm had lasted for nearly ten days. Below top deck, the overhead hung low forcing even the shortest of passengers to crouch as they made their way to and fro. Yet, with the yawing and heaving of the ship, who would want to be walking about anyway?

As the ship would heave first to port, then to starboard, the sloshing flood of human excrement, urine, and vomit mixed with seawater moved across the deck in the opposite direction, washing between many of the crates of supplies they had carried on board. A moment later, another flood of sewage that spilled from the chamber pots would mix with more seawater pouring down the ladder and then return to the other side or, perhaps, the stern if the ship's bow happened to be rising at the same time. It continued, relent-lessly. The smell alone was revolting and merely produced more nausea among the passengers. All they could do was turn away and cover their faces. The adults sheltered the young ones.

For many, it had been days since they had gone topside, days since seeing the full light of day or inhaling the fresh, clean salty air. Food was rationed, but not in short sup-ply, for who would desire to eat in a place such as this? As each took their turn going above deck for those few brief minutes, they had to tolerate the mocking profanity of the crew toward them. But it didn't keep them from staying up long enough to fill their lungs with the clean, chilly north Atlantic air. This and a cup of fresh water would make the day more bearable. Relentlessly, the storm grew worse with each hour and day. As days passed, the ship continued toss-ing back and forth with the creaking of wood becoming ever more prominent.

If God had intended for them to make this voyage, why was He now punishing them by making hard their way? They had continued in prayer for weeks, even months on end in preparation for this journey. Were they now not in His will? If not, surely the Almighty knew it was too late for them to turn back having passed the midway point of their Atlantic crossing. Who was this God that prompted their journey, only to now bring distress and hardship upon them? Was this God's anger? Had they not heard His voice clearly?

All at once, it happened: the ear-piercing crack of wood, the thunderous shudder and the look of shock on so many faces in the dim light amidships. The frightful cries and gasps might have been heard, had it not been for the noise of the wind and waves that continued to crash against the outer bulkhead. The ship's huge oak main beam had taken far more punishment than that for which it was designed. Those sitting close scrambled to move away and out from underneath it. Wood splinters snapped, springing out from the giant mast base, and the smell of fresh wood momentarily permeated the stench of human waste prevalent only a moment before. The ship's captain was visibly shaken. He knew the fractured main beam was critical to support the mainsail mast and the completion of their journey. What could they do now?

Unknown to them, the fate of these one hundred and two passengers had been predetermined. But they now found themselves at that point of no return where God chooses to purify so many of His chosen. As William later wrote in his journal: "We committed ourselves to the will of God and resolved to proceed."

There were few options but suddenly one young man saw it. On board they had brought a printing press with its primary purpose to reproduce the Gospel for the heathens sure to be awaiting them on the other shore. But as so often happens, God has many different purposes for just one tool. Immediately, they positioned the press' heavy iron screw where it could be secured as support under the main beam. It held. Finally, further help arrived as coming days saw the return of better weather.

Yet now, with a stronger westerly flow of air and tide, it became harder for the ship to maintain its course being forced toward the distant coastline at an ever-increasing rate. Their intention was to arrive at the designated Virginia location in, perhaps, a week or ten days. But, as the days passed and the first sight of land graced the western horizon, it was apparent that to make their way further down the coastline would require the small ship to tack nearly due east for days in order to pick up its original course laid out on the charts. This would take them well beyond the scheduled arrival time; a time already putting them into safe harbor in early November. Further delay would make for a more difficult winter, with billeting and other work yet to be performed, once landing.

Although his first concern was that of his companions and their well being, it was no small matter to William that their charter required a Virginia settlement. To land anyplace above the Virginia coastal boundaries would take them out of contract with the Virginia Company of England. Without this, there were no provisional guarantees—and of most importance to William—no legal authority for them to operate under.

Following days of searching, the ship entered the quiet waters of the small harbor, lowering anchor. William gathered the elders about to deal with this most pressing matter: the now defunct Virginia Charter. William dipped his quill into the captain's inkwell and began to write:

> . . . We, whose names are underwritten, the Loyal Subjects of our dread Sovereign Lord, King James, by the Grace of God, of England, France and Ireland, King, Defender of the Faith, e&. Having undertaken for the Glory of God, and Advancement of the Christian Faith, and the Honour of our King and Country, a voyage to plant the first colony in the northern parts of Virginia; do by these presents, solemnly and mutually in the Presence of God and one of another, covenant and combine ourselves together into a civil Body Politick, for our better Ordering and Preservation . . . unto which we promise all due submission and obedience.

These were the Pilgrims, root of the past; seeds of a new nation. The search for true liberty had begun. As the hull of the longboat scraped the first rock and sand of shore and their feet touched ground, they gathered together in prayer giving a grateful thanks to the Lord for safe passage and dedication of this new land to His purposes. For centuries God had preserved this land and held it in safekeeping for a people ready to make covenant with Him. Mixed with great suffering, He would richly bless their posterity—but not without great sacrifices yet to be paid. Before the coming summer sun would set, more than half their number would perish.

PART ONE

A political campaign is an act of war. Like its military counterpart, it has opponents, a battlefield, weapons of war, strategies and tactics, and in the end—a victor. Throughout the ages all bloodshed is the product of failed political war. And to the victor go the spoils.

—Author

When compared to war—all other forms of Human endeavor shrink to insignificance.

—General George S. Patton, Jr.

Finding Cain

Counting the cars
On the New Jersey Turnpike
They've all come
To look for America . . .
All come to look for America . . .

America,
"Bookends" Album
Paul Simon & Art Garfunkel
1966

The rhythm of my tires clicking over the concrete highway joints signals my arrival into the Garden Springs area and the exits off Sunset Hill. I lower my windows a bit to let in the warm Friday evening air. The blooming lilac and pine scents of mid-May are soothing to my senses as the city lights of Spokane flicker below me a couple of miles ahead. It's always good to be home. In the darkness of my car with the backlit instruments and the passing reflective markers off to the side of the road, I realize I am not alone. *He* is with me, even now.

I can't remember exactly how many times I have driven this road to Olympia and back, but I know it must be a thousand times. *I can drive Interstate-90 blindfolded,* I think to myself as I change lanes to prepare to catch the exit up ahead. I know every rock, draw, and old barn across the basin.

It is all four-lane freeway now, but I remember the first time I drove it, as a young man of sixteen, when the old two-lane highway was anything but straight. I still think back on those warm, carefree summer days of high school, driving down the old highway playing rock and roll on the AM radio. At the age of sixteen, that was freedom to me—a car and a tank of gas.

Of all the things I ever dreamed of doing in my life, being a political strategist and lobbyist never made the list. As a young man, I wasn't even aware there was such a thing. Amazingly, I've always disliked politics and politicians. In hindsight, I now realize that the media has done that to us. Over the years, the press' contempt for public servants has removed much of the honor that was intended to be a part of public service. Today, I work with many politicians—some good, some not so good. I suppose that can be said about anyone in any line of work. But with politics, there are things that set us far apart and choke us into silence; underlying issues of the heart that divide us deeply, no longer allowing us to sit around the dinner table talking about politics—much less of politics *and* religion.

If *he* were really here today, *he* too would have a hard time.

As my car reaches the crest of Sunset hill and begins its descent into downtown Spokane, I smile, remembering the pin that Val gave me a few years before. It says: *Every so often, an innocent person is sent to the legislature.* I've found that most people going into the legislature usually arrive with the right intentions, but it's so easy to *drink funny water and get funny ideas* as I often describe it to my closest friends. If you are not strong in your core beliefs, you will most certainly drift in the heat of the battle.

Val often reminds me that people really are called and sent in life. For her part, as a senator, she should be home doing the things grandmothers do. Instead, she's made the sacrifice to serve, a sacrifice that so many men seem to have a hard time making today. She has become one of my closest friends and mentors.

As I take the Maple Street exit, I recall what I said to her then: "Val, I only wish more men were like you." She laughed. *But she has a courage I wish more men had,* I think to myself, as I begin heading up the hill toward High Drive. Fearless, Val isn't drawn in by political correctness. She isn't the smartest or most cunning legislator I've ever known, but she has the right heart—one that gives her wisdom, clarity of thought and purpose. It keeps her steady in the tough times. And when she finds herself running low, Val knows how to reach out.

I remember that phone call one year I decided to stay home from the legislature. As I came into the house, the answering machine blinked. I hit the play button, and the voice was loud and sharp. "Doug, where are you?!" Behind the frustration, I could hear the echoing background sounds of other voices over Val's phone coming from the floor of the Senate chamber. "I just took a bad vote and it's all your fault. You should be here!" Later, when I called her back, Val apologized, but reminded me how important it is for her and others to have support from the outside. She was right. But like so many others, I too was growing weary.

Val knows *him* too, even if not by name.

Smiling in the darkness of my car I think back on how this journey began. It occurs to me that if we really knew what we were getting ourselves into ahead of time, we would probably do little in life.

For me, it all began at the time of the Rodney King trial. I can still remember the two police officers who nearly carried Rodney out to speak in front of the cameras that night on national television following the rioting in Los Angeles. They did so in hopes of bringing calm to the neighborhoods. Later, I thought it strange for them to bring out the very cause of the entire fracas to call on the masses for reason. But now, immortalized in my mind are his words, his question. "Hey . . . can't we . . . just all get along?"

With that single event and question began my journey in search of an answer to Rodney's question. Why can't we get along, anyway? Just what is it that causes such division in our points of view on any given subject? What is it that is at the heart of lawlessness that saps our freedom and brings an ever increasing array of laws indicative of our growing inability to self-govern?

I remember that first trip to Olympia and the Washington State Capitol twelve years earlier . . .

. . . It was that cold pre-dawn January morning as I headed in the opposite direction leaving Spokane. The rolling hills were barren then, aside from the parched cheat grass of winter and the occasional patch of bull pines scattered here and there south of Spokane; that is, until I reached the exit at Sprague Lake. From there it flattens out, the trees disappear, and the sky grows larger over the rolling horizon. It is a foreboding time of winter, a deathly silence of cold and an emptiness of heart that is present. *It is fitting that the legislative session begins this time in January,* I think to myself.

It was there at Sprague Lake that I began to see *him* for who *he* really is. I will always remember that.

Despite having to leave home for long periods of time, I always enjoy this drive. I often take inspirational tapes or historical studies to absorb on these cross-state runs. Not only do the trips go faster, but I feel better at the other end—focused and ready for the task ahead. It's a time to think and sort through the issues. I also talk with *him,* try to understand him. *He's* had such a strong influence on my life, especially in the early days. I was so much like *him* then.

I'm a homebody. *Vietnam did that to me,* I think to myself as I reset the cruise after slowing and passing another radar speed trap. Vietnam was where I first met *his* brother, although *he* didn't impress me much at the time. I much preferred hanging out with *him.* I don't think *he* ever grew up either; that was the problem for both of us.

This trip, in early January, 1993, I'm on my way to Olympia to begin another session of working for the church. A year earlier, I had taken it upon myself to provide the church with some professional advocacy, or lobbying, as it is more commonly known. Having gained legislative experience with previous employers over the years, I saw the huge vacuum and the need for the church's voice to be heard. But I soon discovered that a large part of the church really doesn't want to be heard—and is nowhere to be found. Soon, I would find that a great deal of the church that was active in this process stood against much of what I and others believed, anyway.

When speaking to groups, Val always says: "If you knew the power I hold over your lives, you'd pay a lot more attention." Every business and organization you can think of is represented in state and federal legislatures, all but the church that is. Aside from the many faithful "kitchen" home lobbyists who courageously come to work the legislature each year—albeit with their fingers stuck in a ballooning dike—there is little or no skilled representation for the

Bible-believing churches, as we call ourselves. Nor is there much respect for the church by those who occupy the many halls and chambers of government.

He is well-represented though and I always hated *him* for it. Later, I realized that the influence *he's* had on me, *he's* had on so many others, too.

I am feeling homesick hardly before I reach Sprague Lake. The oppression sets in early on these trips. I never recognized it as oppression in these early years. All I know is that the very thought of the Capitol rotunda makes my stomach churn. It always reminds me of the first time I stood there around the gold State seal . . .

. . . It was the summer of 1968. Eighty young recruits were being officially sworn in to the United States Marine Corps. It was the first ever all-Washington state platoon—the "Evergreen State Platoon," as we were known. As we gathered around the gold seal on the floor of the huge rotunda, we took the oath by then-governor Dan Evans. The governor presented us with a miniature Washington state flag that would hang just below our scarlet and gold Marine Corps platoon flag on our guidon throughout our ten weeks of boot camp. There were five of us then, good friends joining from Spokane—cocky, full of life, so sure of ourselves and invulnerable to the world around us. Soon thereafter, we went off to war; one never returning, another without his arms, another with a mangled leg.

But at that moment in time, in July of 1968, standing there in our state's legislative building, I had no idea that twenty years later I would return to stand there again, this time engaged in a different war. That was a part of my destiny I could never have seen at the time . . .

. . . *This war was worse now*, as my mind returns to the present and I refocus on the road ahead. In so many ways, the enemy here is stronger, deadlier, more deceitful, and more determined than that earlier adversary. And now I know it is *him*. *He* is the real enemy. And I still hold out hope that in time, I might finally defeat *him* in my own life.

Just after Tokio weigh station, the road straightens out and I can see Ritzville five miles ahead at the top of one of the Palouse's many expansive rolling hills. I take out my mini-cassette recorder to make the usual verbal notes. These cross-state trips are a time when I can process all that has happened in the legislature in any given week. "Sprague Lake," I announce into the microphone. Various points along the highway always remind me of whatever issue I was thinking about the last time I passed here along my route. Usually, I can remember where I left off in my thinking on any given subject. From Tokio weigh station to Sprague Lake, I always focused on the bigger picture, rather than specific issues.

Early on, I always spent a great deal of time considering how certain biblical stories and principles related to present day America and politics. From my studies of American history, I learned that our founders did that, too. I smile as I recall that in high school my two worst subjects were history and current world problems. Now I can't get enough of either. God must have a sense of humor. I laugh out loud as I set the cruise at precisely seventy-six miles per hour. A state trooper serving in the legislature once told me that they usually will not ticket you, until you break six miles-per-hour over the posted speed limit. And I have always played the law to the limit.

On these trips I was spending far too much time with *him* and I knew it. But I needed to know and understand *him* better. I pushed the record button on my cassette recorder. "Why did God not respect Cain's offering as He did his brother, Abel's?" I asked.

I had become very discouraged in these earlier years lobbying for a church that never even knew I was there and really could've cared less. There were a few brave legislators and legislative staff, along with a handful of courageous pastors, who were aware of the assault taking place on religious liberty in America. In time they became my closest friends, a sort of camaraderie among the soldiery. Or, as is said in the conventional manner, "War makes strange bedfellows."

Several are now beginning to understand that religious freedom is the very basis—and the only basis—for true liberty. Freedom and liberty are not synonymous. Over many lunches and dinners in Olympia, we very often discussed and reaffirmed that government is not the giver of liberty. If it is, we're in deep trouble since anything the government can give, it can take away. If liberty is a natural right of man, gifted of God, then it is irrevocable, except by Him, as stated in our Declaration of Independence. It further says, "That to secure these rights, governments are instituted among men." Therefore, it is the job of government to guard liberty—individual liberty. That is the only real job of government. We can argue over the rest of it.

I often joked with friends that I was on a mission to America. But few want to go there today. I can't help but feel that the average church across the land today doesn't even see the enemy approaching—an enemy that has now advanced right into its parking lot. In these early years in Olympia, my anger was mounting against a complacent church imploded and serving itself.

But *he* knew I was there—and, yes, Cain approved of the bitterness growing in my heart.

Today in America, I find that a vast majority of Christians have come to believe that politics is a matter only "of the world," as they describe it. It's as if they've already been raptured and left the planet. *How convenient,* I think to myself, as I see the Moses Lake area coming into view over the horizon. We are forgetting that the price of liberty, to obtain and to hold it, has always been blood. And the great paradox lies in always remembering that the only way of avoiding the bloodshed we abhor is to always be willing to bleed in the first place.

Referring to today's lack of political interest by churches and pastors, I recall how a wise young friend once described it to me this way. Blaine said, "Doug, everyone has quit and is down at the corner waiting to catch the Jesus bus out of here." I laughed then, but how true, I think, as I look over my shoulder to see Harold's electric shop not far off the freeway as I approach the outskirts of Moses Lake.

Senator Harold Hochstatter: the very thought makes me smile. In all my time working in the legislature, I've never known anyone more unassuming, more down to earth, or anyone more studied in the lessons and quotations of our founding fathers. Harold is a man of history. And, not only is Harold a man of strong moral character, he *is* a character. No one I knew could drive the liberal-socialists wilder than Harold could when he stood to the floor and brought the microphone to his lips. Liberal-socialists hate common sense. But Harold was full of it—every day.

The first time I ever pulled off the freeway and visited him at Hochstatter Electric, I was struck how a man could be so salt-of-the-earth yet as stately in another way as a senator. I hardly recognized him that first time I walked through the door. He was sitting there on the phone with one foot up on an open drawer of his messy old war surplus desk. He wore dirty blue jeans, a t-shirt that was once white, and an equally dirty cap with the crown pushed in forming a dimple, which made it look silly, I thought. He and a co-worker there with him would have fit in well at any neighborhood tavern.

"Doug, how are you, my good man? Coffee's on. We were just discussing our good friends on the other side of the aisle," he would start. Harold was always up, even describing his adversaries in a positive light. I used to wonder if he ever had a bad day. *He could cheer up a condemned man*, I thought.

Harold certainly knew *him*, too. And he understood the fear Cain dispersed in the legislature. But Harold clearly identified more with Abel. Harold never grew weary in the battle. He was a man of faith.

"Don't forget this is an election year," Harold once told me when I stopped in for coffee. I had just shared a story about how one night passing through Moses Lake on my way home to Spokane I had hit—of all things—a grocery store shopping cart in the middle of the freeway in a dense fog. Harold thought that was pretty funny.

"Well, you know, Doug, I call it the political freeway out there," Harold said with a serious look on his face, yet that characteristic twinkle was still in his eye.

"The political freeway?" I inquired.

"Yeah," Harold continued. "You know in an election year, liberals always take the political freeway. On that freeway, they pass you on the right and then move back to the left." We both guffawed. He was referring to how liberals always sound like conservatives on the campaign trail, but revert to liberals after an election. After the many opinion surveys I've done, I have found that the majority of Americans have conservative roots and will "swing" that way when given enough correct information on any given issue. So, liberal-socialists have to sing the right tune in an election year when a greater number of folks are paying attention.

When Harold left the Senate after some years of faithful service to our state, his reputation lingered. In his honor, several of the staff had put together a booklet, of "Harold-ism's" including quotations and so many wonderfully simple one-liners and anecdotes that Harold always enjoyed injecting into his floor speeches. For me, there was always a comfort in hearing his voice, knowing Harold was there. He had such a way of whittling the most complicated issues down to a simple common-sense descriptive. I will never forget his analogy of how legislative bills are introduced and passed in Olympia. It was simple, he said. "It's like how we enjoy eating hot dogs, and buns. They're great, but you really don't want to know how either is made."

Senator Harold Hochstatter made way too much sense for the legislature, I thought. He told me once that they have it all wrong. Following the legislative session, lawmakers go home to show off all the bills they got signed into law by the governor as a sign of effectiveness in lawmaking virility. Said Harold, "There were over three thousand bills introduced for hearing last session. Three or four hundred of those will make it into law. That doesn't bode well for those of us who think government does far too much now and needs to be reduced." Harold said the right way would be a monetary merit system for those legislators who come home after sessions with notches on their belts representing bills and existing laws they had killed. He told me once, "Even if we pay them to kill existing laws, it will cost us far less than if they add to them." I agree.

I don't know why, but Harold brought such a sense of home and a fathering spirit to the stark marble walls and lonely hallways of the legislative buildings . . .

Oh God, I think, in a panic that takes me for a moment. *I hope you have someone to replace this blessed and loved man.*

With 147 total lawmakers, and only 105 days of session, passing three thousand bills is a tall order. Everyday, many legislators take votes on bills on the floor of the House or Senate that they know nothing about, and in some cases, have never heard of! Ask any legislator. In the case of Washington State, our legislative operating structure is very similar to that of the federal government in Washington, D.C. And a close lobbyist friend of mine once said it best when he said our founders were wise in that they shaped the bill-passing business much like a gauntlet. In this way, all bills have such a rigorous system of committee and hearing processes they have to go through, that a majority die before completing the process. Still, not enough are killed, nor are enough existing laws and regulations repealed. Such is the path into tyranny.

At the other end of Moses Lake, I continue to make occasional verbal notes on the mini-cassette, and my mind wanders back to the subject at hand of the church and why it chooses to stay far from the fray of politics. It's an ugly business. Many of my friends at home were always puzzled by my interest in the political scene. Fewer understood just what I was doing. Many others never really agreed.

"But I'm just doing what Jesus did," I would tell them. "Don't you see, Jesus was the greatest politician who ever lived?" Think about it. In Jesus' brief three-year ministry He focused on two primary targets: Caesar and His own church.

I pass the exit to George, I wonder what George Washington would think if he could visit here today and see the giant in-ground amphitheatre where many a rock concert has attracted thousands from all over the state, knowing it carries his name. On a map, George is just about as center in the state as you can get. I wonder what else he would think of America today. He would probably be shocked to find out that average Americans now pay out around fifty percent of their labor in some form of taxation. George and the other founders went to war with King George over twelve percent! A close look at history over the past century shows that we are now at least equal to, if not far beyond, the oppression the Pilgrims felt when they were compelled to leave England.

As I begin the down grade into the great Columbia Gorge, I pass the visitor's parking lot for the Wild Horse Monument on my left with its large wooden sign and an inscription carved into it. There was another inscription, too. This one was carved into the public monuments in Rome at the time of Christ, which read: "There is no other way by which a man can be saved, except by Caesar, Augustus."

Imagine that, I think, as I begin my descent into Vantage at the river. What audacity for this lowly Jew to come into this world and proclaim to Caesar, and all of civilization for that matter, "Only through the Son of God, can a man receive salvation. Only through me can he receive eternal life."

If that isn't getting in the face of government, and going straight to the top, I don't know what is. Then it occurs to me. It was His own church that sold Him over to the Romans. What did Jesus do to deserve that? He took on the two mightiest authorities in the world—Caesar and His own church. He obviously hadn't heard of political correctness.

Jesus knew *him,* too. And it was this spirit of Cain that He called out of His people, offering faith in its place.

The view of the great Columbia Gorge in either direction is so ominous from the bridge at Vantage. Having climbed the long and steep ten-mile draw from Vantage on the river, I know I've reached the top when I see the sign announcing the rest stop just ahead. This is Ryegrass, the summit of this rolling range of foothills along the Columbia River. The sign here indicates an altitude of 2,535 feet. From the peak, near the exit into the rest stop, the road immediately drops forward beginning the long and fairly steep down grade into the Ellensburg valley.

On this sunny January day, I can see the white covered top of Mt. Rainier, majestically standing proud at 14,838 feet. It is still another sixty miles to the west, but it's as if you can reach out and touch it from here. *They should have named this place Vantage*, I think to myself, *instead of the tiny town at the bridge back down on the river.* The vantage is actually here, and on a sunny day it is breathtaking. It always strikes me how things appear so much smaller looking ahead, like Rainier. From this point, if you get out of your car, you can probably see a hundred miles or so in any direction. Even Mt. Rainier, as big as it is, now seems to find its place in the larger scheme of things. *That's what happens so often in the legislature*, I think as I get back into the car at the rest stop.

Finding Cain

It is Cain again. Too often, he keeps us from seeing the bigger picture. Too often, we are unable to step back and look at the whole of things with an uncontaminated heart. We end up so "tangled up in our own shorts," as an old Marine buddy of mine used to say, that we forget what our original mission is. *That is what happens with legislators*, I think, as I see the town of Ellensburg coming into view up ahead.

It occurs to me that perhaps we need to revisit many procedures we employ in dealing with different issues in the legislature. Abortion, for example. I've begun to think that the adversary has been running a great ruse against us. In all the strife, pain, and warfare of trying to pass simple common-sense measures such as informed consent, parental consent, or partial-birth abortion bans, we somehow forget that the problem is—abortion, the murdering of innocent children. That is the bigger picture. And it's the spirit behind abortion that is the cause of it. So here we are off fighting the smaller skirmishes, hoping to get some kind of victory—anything, no matter how minute—during the frantic days of the legislature. We chip away at the fringes for a scrap—anything that we can take back home to show the troops some sign of progress in hopes of retaining their support, and to keep them from losing hope.

But the few who are involved grow weary so easily. Then we lose sight of the goal, and we continue to lose every skirmish along the way. And it never even occurs to us that we simply do not understand the problem. The problem is not abortion. The problem is Cain. The problem is what *he's* done to us. *Damn his lies and deception*, I think as I begin the descent into the Ellensburg Valley!

Things in the legislature are not how they often appear. It reminds me of something my church pastor once said in describing God's Kingdom. He said that when you ride the elevator in the Kingdom and want to go up, you have to push the down button. And when you want to go down, you have to push the up button. I laughed at the time. I think it's God's way of confusing the wise of this world. It's somewhat the same in the legislature. Only there it's used to confuse voters.

Here at Ellensburg, I pull off to gas up and get a soft drink. As I stand by the pumps waiting for the sound of the click signaling a full tank, I notice a younger woman with three young children getting gas in the next lane. She is having a hard time controlling them, as they disobey and argue with her while hanging out the car window. She seems frazzled and angry. On her bumper is a sticker that reads: "Visualize Peace." *It's a dichotomy*, I think. As I watch her, I wonder if she knows what is even going on in the world today. So many I talk with don't. But having a bumper sticker like that indicates that she must have some notion, some sense of news and information. But as I watch her relationship with her kids, it's apparent that she has spoiled them.

We are all spoiled in America, I think as I replace the gas cap and put the hose back on the pump. Statistics reveal that most young people coming out of college—much less high school today—know very little of true American history, constitutional studies, or very much at all about their country. And most of their parents are home being spoon-fed a steady diet of evening entertainment posing as news. We are so consumed by the present, we've lost our connection to our roots, and we think only as far as the next paycheck or Hawaiian vacation. We have become a nation obsessed with entertainment and toys. It's all about instant gratification; fly now—pay later. We are living in a growing age of the fast-food Burger King mentality of driving up and speaking into the menu post to hear: "Can I help you to have it your way today?" That is what we have come to expect from government today. We have turned it into an order-out window.

As I pull back onto the highway and regain speed, I notice the bumper sticker of a car on my left that reads, "Don't steal—the government hates competition." It appears that others also recognize the ballooning government we face today. Speaking to a group recently, I asked them this question. "Why does it take three different government bodies to accomplish one task?" For example, why is it necessary for the federal government to take our taxes back to DC, only to return a much smaller portion to fix our roads and highways here at home? Wouldn't it be much cheaper and more efficient to leave the money here at home with the state or the county, without paying some middleman bureaucrat back there to tell us what we already know here? Can't we figure out what is best for our road needs here without the federal government's involvement?

Education is another example. Since the federal Department of Education was born, we're all paying nearly twice as much for public schools, yet our kids are failing worse, to where we now rank eighteenth in academic achievement among the industrialized nations of the world. Are we learning anything? We must not be, because the situation only grows worse with each passing year.

I'm mindful of Adolph Hitler's remark after Austria voted overwhelmingly in 1935, (98 percent to 2 percent), to join the Third Reich. In their fervent desperation to stay out of war and avoid bloodshed, Austria ended up creating a bigger war for themselves in the end. They stood for peace, but refused to stand against tyranny. What was most telling was Hitler's remark following that infamous vote. Said Hitler, "How fortunate for us leaders that the people choose to remain ignorant."

Once I connect onto I-5 from SR-18, I will be in Olympia in a little over two hours from now—if the traffic isn't too bad. I reset the cruise and begin the gradual climb to Cle Elum and Snoqualmie Pass.

Once I asked a well-studied friend, "At what point in our history had we lost true liberty." He thought it was probably at the beginning of the 1900s, but certainly sometime after the Civil War. Back then, I was attending a weekly meeting of what we called "King's Court," a local gathering of pain-in-the-butt conservatives who met weekly to discuss issues of the day. One of our discussions had turned into what the definition of liberty truly was. It is an important question.

The final ascent to Snoqualmie Pass summit is magnificent on a sunny day like today. *The Swiss Alps have nothing on this place,* I think as I reach the top and see a few people enjoying the day on the ski slopes off to my left. I've always appreciated the feeling of freedom and exhilaration in skiing. *But is that liberty,* I wonder?

I recall something Douglas Wilson of the Logos School in Moscow, Idaho, once said while I was attending a weekend retreat called "Biography of Great American Saints." During one of the question and answer sessions, Mr. Wilson was asked a question about what he believed to be the difference between liberty—as the apostle Paul spoke about it to slaves in Rome—and the liberty that our founders sought.

Finding Cain

More specifically, he was asked if we could ever get that liberty back in this nation again. This was his answer.

"There's a difference between people who are slaves and who have been slaves for an extended period of time and are now coming to the Gospel wanting to acquire liberty and a people who [already live in] liberty and have retained it for generations and who are trying to keep from losing it.

"Paul tells the slaves that if they have an opportunity for freedom to take it. But he does not tell them to take up arms and rebel against Rome.

"Liberty always grows out of a people's understanding that [true liberty] is liberty from sin. Liberty from sin is the first step to freedom. There is no possible way that a people liberated from sin can remain civil slaves for very long. In other words, there have never been a righteous people enslaved for a very long period of time. The Gospel naturally works its way out into civil liberty. At the time of America's founders the Gospel had done just that, and these liberties were institutionalized in our founding documents, and were passed down from generation to generation. But now, [during the founding era] some people wanted to take [the founders] liberties away.

"So, the Bible distinguishes very clearly between people who are enslaved because of their sin—those who need to grow into liberty—and a people who have liberty that some other people are trying to rob them of. Our founders were not trying to fight out of slavery into liberty, but they were men who understood liberty and didn't want to have slavery imposed upon them.

"The flipside is that we do not understand liberty in America today because in our churches we [no longer] understand the Gospel. The potency of the Gospel is no longer preached from the pulpits in America. We are slaves, and the next thing we have to assert is that we deserve to be slaves—because we are enslaved by our sin.

Thus, we are not fit to be anything other than slaves. And that will continue until the Gospel of liberty is recovered in our pulpits. When that happens, which takes place over generations, then civil liberty will once again make sense to God's people."

Wilson went on to say that many of the incidents, such as Waco, Ruby Ridge, and others, while wrongfully carried out by civil authority—really out of tyranny and wrong-headedness—should be expected by a people who no longer understand the basis of their own liberty. Wilson concluded by saying that

"It is just as wrongheaded for professing Christians to believe that we can be a free people while still enslaved to our sin. As long as we are enslaved to our sin, then slaves we will remain."

It's beginning to rain—no surprise—as I take the exit onto Interstate-5 and head south through Tacoma. I'm reminded that this year the Democrats control both the House and the Senate, not to mention the governor's office. With the strong Democrat sweeps of 1992 across America, they have large majorities in the Washington state legislature. And, unlike their Republican counterparts, when they're in power the Democrats wield that power to push their agenda forward.

Democrats are much better at political warfare, and have far better generals in their ranks. Politically, they are ruthless, and they win. They know how to fight. I admire them for that. Republicans will never get into a fight that they aren't sure they can win ahead of time, and that is why they lose.

Although all of my candidates are Republican, I have had a bad falling out with leadership over my political views and criticisms of the party. I have become the Jim Rockford of political consultants, the black sheep of the Republican Party, tolerated only because I win seats for them. And like Jim Rockford, average run-of-the-mill Republicans don't like to be seen on the street with me.

It rains most consistently this time of year in Olympia, I think, as I take the State Capitol exit. With Pacific Standard Time now in effect, it gets dark early, and that darkness is rather fitting. And like the general philosophical worldview that motivates legislators, there's a dark difference that we need to understand.

The big button issues this year being pushed by the Democrats are, first of all, what I call the new Holy Grail of modern day America: public education and this year's education reform act, (House Bill) HB-1209. Second is special protection legislation for homosexuals, adding them to the growing roles of the minority class status. Unfortunately, for Democrats, this year they will seriously over-shoot the runway in estimating how many Washingtonians are true believers in their Darwinian, Utopian dreams.

I take note that already listed in the minority protection laws are Christians. We were given that protection without asking for it. By doing so, the socialists knew we would have a hard time complaining when the homosexuals came to the trough for their status. The fact is, Christians are already protected by the U.S. Constitution. Therefore, the state's minority protection class for Christians is nothing but a Trojan horse.

I cross Capitol Way and take a left turn into the parking lot, pulling into a space that was once free for capitol visitors. But since the Democrats have taken power, I must now pay for a ticket to put in my window to park in this lot. There are two reasons for this recent change, I reckon, as I fumble for coins in the rain. First, liberal-socialists will tax anything that doesn't move and license anything that does. I grin at that thought, as the machine refuses to give me the ticket or any change, and I hit the box with my fist. Finally, I get the ticket and walk back to my car. Money is the fuel of government.

The second reason for the paid parking is that folks running the show here don't want it to be easy to come down and testify at public hearings. It takes up too much time with those whose minds are already made up. *Citizen activists are such a pain in the butt,* I smile to myself as I turn and head for the campus.

Interesting how we argue today over issues long ago settled in the minds of our founders. We find ourselves in the halls of our legislatures bickering over the building blocks of freedom. That is why we can no longer move forward.

As I begin the two-block walk to the O'Brien House Office Building, I wonder to myself if Cain gave Abel a chance to say anything when he met him in the field that day and killed him. The Bible only reveals that Cain spoke to Abel before *he* murdered him.

I used to think I took Cain to Olympia with me. Now I realize *he* was waiting for me all along. But today is the first day of the legislative session. Another magic show is about to begin.

Making Hot Dogs

"The state is that great fiction by which everyone tries to live at the expense of everyone else."
—Frederic Bastiat

I pick up the hearing schedule and take my seat on the side near the window. This morning's hearing in the Health and Human Services Committee is to first hear testimony on bill funding requests for the Department of Social and Health Services. DSHS is the biggest government agency in Washington State and receives the second largest single tax appropriation, next to public education. Aside from being the second highest funded agency, it wields by far the most power over the lives of our state's families.

Over the years, it has grown into a giant social-service conglomerate, combining all sorts of adult and children services, slowly usurping the rights of parents and creating a dependency that saps independency and simply creates irresponsibility, the kind that usually ends in tyranny. Of course the question is always, which came first—the usurpation of responsibility by bureaucrats who look for ways to make for themselves secure jobs in government or the relinquishment of rights and responsibility by those who can no longer self-govern. It's the age old chicken-or-the-egg argument.

Although this is a public hearing, most of the testimony will come from government DSHS bureaucrats who are here to express the dire need for increases in funding for a myriad of reasons. I have never once heard them come in to testify that they would require less revenue from the next biennium's budget. Could that mean that the problem is going unresolved? If so, then what does that mean?

A majority, if not all, of the public testimony will come from needy people from all walks of life brought here—or encouraged to testify—by these same bureaucrats to bolster their case. Most of the needy are the worst-off in the state and line up in wheel chairs, pushed by caregivers from various hospice and charitable organizations, many of whom receive government funding.

These early days each year in Olympia are referred to as "Social Service Days" to the several government lobbyists attending, many of whom work as paid staff for the government agencies. *There is something really wrong with this picture,* I think. Through the years, many legislators have introduced bills to disallow this type of lobbying by government-paid employees. Imagine bureaucrats using your tax dollars to lobby other bureaucrats for more of your tax dollars. If citizens were really paying any attention, they would throw out those who allow it to happen.

What is worse is parading these people in front of elected representatives for the primary intention of creating guilt. It's especially hard on those legislators who genuinely care but believe that government shouldn't be in the benevolence business in the first place, that there's a correct way to deal with real needs. Secondly, many see that these people are often being exploited for the sole purpose of growing government and instituting more socialism. *Yes, there are needs,* I think, as I gaze out the window and the raindrops weave a jagged pattern down the window panes *But there is much more to it than that..*

As the sad parade begins, my thoughts wander back to Cain again, and deeper into an issue that will not come up before this committee on this day, or any other day, an issue that nobody on either side cares to address anymore. As I sit and listen, I begin growing frustrated. *This entire episode is disingenuous,* I think to myself.

The issue is this: There are many well-intentioned legislators who come here supporting government safety-net programs to help those in need. But it always seems to result into more ballooning government, with the original problem continuing to grow and go unresolved. I have a greater respect for some of these lawmakers who push to help the needy than I do for either so-called conservative or liberal elected representatives who have no real convictions about life but spend their time just trying to hug the middle of the road.

Val used to say it best: "The only things in the middle of the road in Olympia are yellow stripes and dead skunks." Some of these people have no real soul in principle or ideology. To them, Democrats or Republicans, it is only about power and prestige. Worse is the legislator who knows what needs to happen but doesn't have the courage to fight for it.

Several legislators who come here are true socialists who really believe in their heart of hearts that the state owns all material wealth and it is their job to redistribute that wealth and even the score. This has become their corporate view of mankind and life. It has attached itself to the holistic argument of what is fair in life and who gets to decide what is fair. Equity has become the new god, the new driving force behind today's legislation. *But what is it that drives this unquenchable thirst for equity,* I wonder as the hearing gets underway.

As the committee chairman calls the first person forward and the usual testimony begins, my mind drifts back to Cain again. He is here. He wanted it to be fair. It wasn't, and it destroyed two lives. I remember the first formal introduction to my great antagonist; where this debate really began for me . . .

. . . I steered the Jeep along the ocean road bordering the South China Sea complaining about something as Lieutenant Silva rode silently in the passenger seat. It was a dark, late evening as we delivered flight schedules to the Marine officer's hooches at Marble Mountain, Vietnam. The schedules assigned different crews to the various choppers that would launch the next morning in support of Marine ground troops stationed all over northern I-Corps.

I liked Lieutenant Silva. He was a good officer and fine pilot, always cheerful and considerate toward the enlisted men in our helicopter squadron. He was one of those people whom everyone liked. He listened as I went on belly-aching about something I cannot now remember.

Being in Vietnam was hell on everybody. Officer or enlisted, there was little benefit or comfort in this place. Everyone suffered equally from the merciless heat and humidity, the loneliness, the bad food, the unknown that lay ahead, waiting for incoming, and the lack of everything that waited back in "the land of the great PX," as we called it. The only real difference I recall between the lower enlisted ranks and junior officers in this place was that, when the booze finally came, we got beer; they got liquor.

I hardly stopped talking and whining long enough to catch my breath between delivery points along the way. I pulled the Jeep off the side of the road at our last stop in front of Lt. Silva's hooch. He started to get out, and then turned to me.

"PFC Simpson," he started, "Why don't you grow up? I have never met anyone who spends more time bitching and complaining than you. You're a pain in the butt, and I'm just one of many here who are tired of listening to it."

I sat in shock as he continued in a louder voice than I had ever heard from him before. "You think this world was created just for you? Is that it? What makes you so special, Simpson? How would you like it if I complained about every little thing to you constantly?" He paused for a moment, looked away, and then turned back again.

"Look, Simpson, you do good work, but I have to tell you, nobody, but nobody, can stand to be around you, for the bitching. If you don't believe it, just ask anyone, and I do mean anyone!" Lt. Silva took a breath and leaned closer. "Get this straight, Simpson. Life isn't fair! And guess what? It ain't ever gonna be! Now, for your own sake and the people around you, grow up!" With that, Lt. Silva slipped into the darkness, and I heard the screen door on his hooch squeak and slam behind him. I sat there for several minutes with the engine running, stunned.

There are mile posts in our lives that we can look back on and identify as turning points, major shifts in our thinking and attitudes about life. This was one for me. And some times we either make the shift or we die to the world around us. Lt. Silva's remarks cut through me deeply. Of all the people I knew in authority in that place, I desired his respect the most, because I respected him. As I sat there, as a twenty-year-old kid, I realized the truth the moment had brought me. And it happened quickly.

Two months later, I was called before the commanding officer. I reported at attention, not knowing what I was there for. There, on either side of the CO, stood Lt. Silva and the squadron's first sergeant—both faces blank. *Oh oh,* I thought. After being told to be at ease, the CO stood to his feet and began to read a document prepared ahead of time. I was in shock. It was a glowing meritorious citation commending me for my performance in the squadron. Immediately, he added to that the announcement that I was also receiving a meritorious field promotion to Lance Corporal. Out of the corner of my eye, I saw the smile growing on Lt. Silva's face. After leaving the CO's office, Lt. Silva caught me outside.

"Lance Corporal," he said reaching to shake my hand. "Congratulations. You deserve it," he said, then paused as I stopped and turned. "I just want to say I've never seen anyone change as much as you have these past couple of months, Simpson, and I mean that."

Three decades later, Lt. Silva and I spoke on the phone after seeing each other's name on the squadron's web site. He was now a dentist living in St. Louis. I asked him if he recalled that night in the jeep outside of his hooch. He did. I told him what a life-changer that was for me. He then replied: "Yeah, I just wish I could get my own kids to respond so well." We both laughed.

Making Hot Dogs

. . . The broken voice coming through the hearing room sound system brought me back to the present. The person testifying is crying and having a hard time. Lynn had come in and found a seat next to me. She lobbies for one of the children and family service organizations. She sees my eyes have wandered out of the room. She leans over to me and asks, "Is this boring you, Doug?"

"Yes, it is," I turn and kid her. "Very much so." She smiles. We've become casual friends, even though we disagree on many of the issues we advocate here. It often happens to lobbyists. Although polarized in much of our ideology, several chats over coffee in the cafeteria reveal sincerity in both our views and a tempered but sincere respect grows from it. When lobbying, you never know when you might find yourself in the same foxhole in the future, fused together by a common goal. That certainly is the case in this place.

The media has also done a disservice to the advocacy that takes place within the halls of legislatures across the country. They have coined the term "special interests" and use it to paint a negative image in the minds of citizens, as if these special interests are being served over theirs. The truth is every single person I know is represented by a so-called special interest. All of us belong to various groups or segments of society from health clubs to car dealers. It is these groups that come to the legislature to make our voice heard on legislative bills that are being considered, those that will affect us in some regard. Unions, medical groups, and every association in between are present. One or more of them is looking out for you in some fashion, even if you don't know it. That is the way it is supposed to be.

With that said, there is another matter: the kind of underhanded lobbying and deal-cutting that is just not right. That happens here, too. But overall, it is minor.

What a person should worry about is not the lobbyist, but the legislators—and whether or not they can be bought. One of my candidates who served three House terms here once told me, "If they can find out you can be bought, then all that's left is for them to dicker over the price." John always had time for lunch when I came around because the lobbyists knew where he stood on any given issue. You can always tell the legislator who is confused in life. He or she is the one that the lobbyists spend the most time with.

This isn't what bothers me about lobbying. What does bother me is the same kind of moral relativism that has crept into this arena like the rest of our society. Some of it is intentional; some of it is just young people coming into the lobbying business who have no real education in history, framework of good government, or strong principles. What has happened over the past decade or so is the kind of lobbying that sees into the future only as far as the end of the present legislative session. It is the same fast-food, instant-results mentality that we find so prevalent everywhere now. No one wants to wait or suffer the slightest pain for something that might possibly be better.

As the hearing drones on, it occurs to me that it was instant gratification that Cain sought from the Lord when he didn't get the recognition *he* wanted. Cain would have loved fast-food restaurants.

To many lobbyists representing a wide array of companies and associations, the game has been turned into one of just keeping government at bay for one more year, fending off one more regulation or another gnawing tax. This is especially true with many contract lobbyists—those representing a few companies as a hired gun—who are only concerned with the immediacy, rather than the long-term effects that a specific law might have on the whole of society.

Consequently, many decisions are made that may be good for their clients in the short run, but harmful to the whole of the state over the long run—and eventually even their clients. For example, if an influential lobbyist defers the pain of doing what is right over the long haul simply to avoid a short-term tax or regulation today, then he's not only hurting the people in total but his own client down the road. Often this is done, of course, at the direction of the company the lobbyist is representing. Everyone suffers equally from this desire for instant gratification today and it's no different here. What are missing here are steadfast principles that are the foundation to any long-term solutions.

In regards to lobbying and politics in general, I can't help but recall the Ronald Reagan quote when he said, "It has been said that politics is the second oldest profession. I have learned that it bears a striking resemblance to the first."

Cain wasn't interested in principle or the bigger picture. He was angry that he received no reward, and his anger blinded him from seeing down the road.

All in all, I've watched the largest of corporations in our state become short-sighted in their legislative efforts, which will come back to haunt them over time. Without any bedrock underlying principles, we are left to wander about like a boat without a rudder on a windy lake. We've forgotten that all laws stem out of foundation principles like the branches of a tree.

Some have told me I'm not pragmatic enough. Maybe so, but I think close observation of governmental direction, over the past decade or two especially, reveals that we are slipping badly when it comes to both size and scope of government, as well as our ability to do business and create wealth, uninhibited. The socialists are winning as we continue to sell out in the short run or, in the case of the church, don't really make an effort in the first place.

I've come to this Human Services hearing today, not for this part of the committee hearing on social spending but for the hearing to follow on the proposed legislation to give special class protection to homosexuals, (House Bill) HB-1343. The bill number will become etched in the minds of legislators in time, but was just assigned this morning by the bill room. But the Chairman announces that the bill will be heard in another hearing room and time because of the large number of people coming to testify. This is a hot issue among Christian conservatives and homosexual activists.

This year, for the first time ever, the homosexual community has their first openly homosexual legislator from the Capitol Hill area of Seattle. More importantly for them, he is chairman of this committee. Committee chairmen are extremely powerful and influential to what makes it out of here as law. This will be the homosexuals' best chance ever of gaining a protected minority class status, which they've been trying to obtain since 1977. Each year, they are getting closer. But, as I ponder these things sitting there, the chairman announces that the hearing has now been rescheduled. A shell game is starting, it seems.

On the more controversial issues in the legislature, often you win or lose in the media. The TV cameras and newspaper photographers show up to bring the event into the homes of thousands of people. So, it's important that you make sure you have hundreds on hand for the show, as well as to testify. The belief is, the stronger the showing, the more influence will be had on legislators who—for one reason or another—don't already have an answer to a question like this one.

I'm amazed homosexual minority status is even an issue. I certainly understand the moral issue, which is plain enough. But I'm always surprised that legislators with no strong moral base, yet conservative in their ideals about governing, don't get it. Imagine for a moment: the same legislature that used to enact laws prohibiting sodomy and homosexuality now enact laws elevating it to special class citizenship and prohibit any thought to the contrary. *We've come a long way baby,* I think as I get up to leave the hearing room.

When I've argued the point that class protection for homosexuality prohibits free thought, its proponents argue that it isn't so. They say that I and others are free to think anything we want. But I remind them that if I choose not to rent my house to them because of their homosexuality, under this new protected status, they can then sue me. If my property is now held hostage by the government in this matter, it forces me to accept their behavior. Two things are now in place. The government controls my property and my thought. The free marketplace of ideas has just been dealt a death blow.

Further, what protections do I and others of every other group not covered by this particular statute have? For example, I'm a conservative. If you are a liberal and decide not to rent to me because of my beliefs, you are free to do so, and rightly so. Constitutionally, I believe our right to discriminate is inherent in the guarantee of right of free association. See the problem here? This kind of legalizing never ends. The truth is we all discriminate for some good reasons everyday. There is a world of difference between discrimination and bigotry. Discrimination is an important factor in the free marketplace of ideas and our quest to make a better society as a whole.

The moral relativism that is behind the antidiscrimination movement of today is a threat to liberty and has no relationship with the racial discrimination of yesteryear. If it is wrong to discriminate, then it is wrong no matter what, not just for a few that some say are more worthy. At the same time, to totally throw out discrimination of any kind is to fall into this same moral relativism that claims there is no right or wrong, and that it is all up to the individual to decide. Because, if this is true and there really is moral relativism, then there really are no absolutes and, therefore, a claim that discrimination is wrong becomes invalid in itself.

If you're a moral relativist, then you believe that what is right for me may not be right for you, and vice versa. So as a relativist, you cannot find fault with my belief in my right to discriminate. If you do, then you really don't believe in moral relativism. If moral relativism is valid, then government cannot take a position either for or against homosexuality. But how can government be government and stay neutral? It must take a moral position one way or the other. So the question comes down to: how do we feel about the position government is taking?

Cain was the first moral relativist. He didn't believe that his brother's willingness to excel warranted special recognition from God. So, in order to satisfy Cain's desire for equality, we must recognize mediocrity as an attainment equal to excellence. And, in order for that to be, we must destroy the possibility of excellence. Cain murdered Abel. Moral relativism is the basis of equity and the lifeblood of socialism.

Making Hot Dogs

We have added a new commandment today, which is "Thou shalt not offend." Frankly, I think a lot of Americans just need to grow up. When I was a kid, the saying sufficed. "Sticks and stones may break my bones, but names will never hurt me."

As the Human Services hearing drones on, it occurs to me that not one person in the hearing room is testifying or lobbying for less spending on DSHS . . .

. . . Should I? Nope, better not.

I get up and leave the hearing room and head outside to the sundial to get a breath of fresh air. On a sunny day, the sundial is the place where a lot of agreements are made regarding legislative proposals between legislators and lobbyists who gather around its small garden area. I have a few minutes, so I decide to head over to the legislative building to see a staff attorney friend of mine to get the lowdown on what's ahead for the year.

It has quit raining for the moment and, as I walk, I consider this question of Cain and Abel. Outside of Eden, the story of the relationship between Cain and Abel is the first interaction we see in the Bible. Cain was the first born and was a raiser of crops from the ground, a farmer. Abel was born after Cain and became a sheepherder. When it came time to make an offering to the Lord, or tithe, as we call it today, the Bible tells us Cain did so by bringing a portion of his crop. Abel brought his offering, too, which the Bible says was the "firstling" of his flock. It goes on to say that Abel gave the "fat portion" thereof. Finally, it says that the Lord had respect for Abel and his offering, but did not have respect for Cain.

Why not? I think as I enter the side door to the legislative building and through the marble corridor.

After visiting with John, I head back to the House office building where another bill is being heard that will require children to wear bicycle helmets. I saw it on the hearing schedule and although it's not on my overall agenda for the session, it catches my attention. *Another noble cause,* I think as I approach the sundial, *for those who wish to rule over you.*

As the door opens ahead, I see Lynn coming out. She sees me and approaches me. "Why did you leave?" she asks. "There were some homeless and orphan testimonies that I was hoping you would have stayed for."

"I just had some errands to run." I could see my response didn't please her.

"Doug, you don't know what it's like for these people. They are unwanted. If the government doesn't look out for them, who will?" Anyone can see she truly cares about the needy and gives more of herself than she probably is paid to help them. But I can see it in her, too; that blindness that overtakes us without our being aware; the contamination that causes us to overrate what we believe to be right; the anger of the injustice we see. Cain did that.

I didn't respond. There was no point . . .

. . . It was a clear and distinct odor, the disinfectant cleaning fluid used for washing out the toilets and basins and mopping the floors of the large boys lavatory of Saint Joseph's Children's Orphanage. The dormitory was long and narrow, with war-surplus metal beds lined along each side in a military fashion, stopping just before reaching the lavatory at the end. From the tall ceiling, stark acorn shaped lights hung down suspended by long thin rods. An occasional crucifix graced the pale walls here and there on either side. To a six-year-old, the room was huge, and even soft voices would echo. The children were here, but the laughter was missing. All these years later, I still have an occasional dream of the sights, sounds, and smells of this place.

At six and seven years old, I was fortunate. I would only be here for a short time longer, compared to other children—some completely discarded with serious physical handicaps, many totally forsaken by their parents. Blindness, deafness, loss of limb, and many other deformities—all were represented here. I wonder now what happened to them all. This was my second orphanage since the age of two. My two half-sisters were at another Catholic home only a few blocks away, although I seldom saw them. Theirs was nicer. Mine had both boys and girls, all unwanted. Holy Names Home was for girls only and was not an orphanage but a boarding school. I always wondered why I was separated from them. My parents had long-standing marital problems. They abandoned us, too, if only temporarily.

Coming back on Sunday evenings from an occasional weekend out with my estranged family was like going to hell for a kid. I wonder now if I would have been better off never leaving for home on a weekend. Returning after a taste of home simply recreated the feeling of abandonment all over again. I passed through the large doors into the cafeteria welcomed by the cleaning smell, the other kids in one large room with an old black-and-white television set, and that horrifying feeling of loneliness. Coming back was like being punished for the same unknown crime over and over. To this day, I still cannot watch an episode of Lassie.

This was probably the first place I came in contact with Cain. I had every reason to take on *his* character and see the world through *his* eyes, maybe more so. And for years to come, I did just that.

In a drunken stupor late one evening, at the age of fourteen, my mother decided to tell me that the man I adored as my father was not really my blood father. It was Christmas Eve. Merry Christmas. But, at least, I finally knew why I was separated from my sisters in the orphanage. Although an ugly discovery, things were beginning to take shape and make sense. Nevertheless, this deepened my relationship to Cain.

Years later, even in the light of that discovery, my relationship with my father grew, and he remains my hero today. Like all boys, I wanted to be just like him. And I did just that. But God had grace for him, too, and my father would be the one who would play the most significant role in my coming into the knowledge of the Almighty. He was the father God gave me. I thank Him for it. I know a lot of others who have had it a lot worse . . .

. . . I stop off at the Capitol bill room to pick up the helmet bill. I want to read it closely. The devil is always in the details here too. Again, I head to the helmet hearing.

We don't know what Cain's early years were like. The Bible is silent on this. It appears, however, that he had a mother and father who were together throughout his childhood. So, what is *his* story? What was it that stinted Cain's vision and overtook him?

I begin to see that at the heart of the story of Cain and Abel is the choice between *fear* and *faith*. Abel gave the best he had out of faith. Abel knew where his sustenance came from and had no doubts about the future, and for this he was rewarded. Cain lived in fear. And it was fear that kept him from giving his best or being able to peer into the future and glimpse one possible outcome he couldn't see.

The Bible is chock-full of comparisons of these two distinct personalities. I have since discovered that every political ideology falls in line behind one of these two simple views of life and the world. Every system of governing ever devised—or yet to be devised in the future—is merely a natural extension of one of these two basic life positions. It is what I now call *the Cain factor.*

. . . I finish signing in to testify, only to find out the entire homosexual hearing has now been rescheduled for later in the evening in light of the apparent large amount of public testimony on its way. I turn to leave and head over to the helmet hearing.

Again, my thoughts return to Cain and Abel. During that time, there was no civil government. Biblically, civil government was not instituted until after the flood and the story of Noah. That is why God did not punish Cain for his murder of Abel by a sentence of death. Instead, the Lord drove him out from His own presence. Capital punishment was a future edict given by God only after the flood when He instructed Moses on the establishment of civil authority. *I wonder if that isn't really the definition of hell,* I think, as I leave the bill room and head down the corridor.

I walk in to the helmet hearing, which has already started. The chairman of this committee is from Spokane. Amazingly, to me, the room is only about a third full. I scanned down each page of the bill. It is proposing a state mandate requiring all children riding bikes to wear helmets.

As with the earlier DSHS hearing, testimony came from a parade of bicyclists whose children had received various degrees of head injuries from not wearing helmets while riding. Then came those who survived serious mishaps because they were adorned in helmets.

Because of my growing cynical nature, I looked around the room to see if any bicycle helmet companies were helping out here. As I listened to the testimony, it was apparent that there are plenty of good reasons to wear helmets. *It was just common sense,* I thought. My mind wandered back on my own bike-riding days . . .

. . . At eleven years old, I was riding with my sister and her cute friend, Linda. I had a crush on Linda, even though she was a year-and-a-half older than me. In those days, that was a lot of difference. I didn't care. To impress her, I was riding up ahead of them on Ash Street, doing all sorts of stunts. Look, Ma! No hands! No feet! Look, Ma—no eyes either. Kablam!

A moment later I was looking up from the ground. The pain was excruciating. I couldn't get my breath. But I couldn't grab there—not with Linda and Diane standing over me giggling. How could they possibly be laughing at a time like this?

I had run into the back of a parked car. The bike stopped, but my body didn't. My lower extremities dragged across the main handlebar capping nut. I wanted to die. My head had also hit the trunk lid. I wasn't wearing a helmet, but I should have been. As I recalled that moment, I thought that, in my case, my bike should have had a seat belt, too . . .

Making Hot Dogs

. . . Lynn taps my shoulder interrupting my daydream as she takes a seat next to me. "What are you doing in here," I ask. "Same question for you. I also see you're paying the same amount of attention in here. Off somewhere else, huh?" came the sarcastic reply. She had noticed my gaze through these windows.

"Actually, I was thinking about how we should add a seat belt amendment to the helmet bill before they pass it." She looks at me funny.

There were a lot of good reasons being presented for children, or all of us, to think about wearing helmets when we go bike riding. One reason given by the bill's sponsor, who testified first, was how much money the state would save in medical expenses it picks up for those children sustaining injuries and who can't afford hospital care, yet whose parents let them ride helmet-free. *Funny how one issue in here relates to another in the insurance committee*, I think to myself.

After ten or so people testify, all in favor of the bill, the chairman notes that there is still fifteen minutes left on the hearing schedule. He also mentions that no one has signed up to testify against the bill. He then makes the mistake.

"So, is there anyone here who would like to come forward and testify against the bill?"

One rule in politics is: never ask a question you don't already have the answer to. Immediately, his eyes catch a glimpse of me off to the side of the room. He knows me. Lynn turns her head in the other direction because she knows what's coming. I can see the look on his face as he realizes my hand is in the air. The chairman knows where

I stand on this sort of legislation, but he hadn't noticed I had slipped into the room earlier. I take the seat at the front table and bring the microphone close.

"Good afternoon, Mr. Chairman, members of the committee. My name is Doug Simpson. Although I'm a contract lobbyist, I'm here to oppose this bill on personal grounds." I feel uncomfortable already knowing that I probably didn't have any friends in the room. But that wasn't unusual. Still, you always get this feeling of eyes knifing clear through you from the back.

"Mr. Chairman, I have to admit on the surface, I feel awfully uncomfortable coming up here to testify against this bill after hearing all the preceding testimony. So I'm not going to try to deny the obvious. We're all probably better off wearing helmets. But that's just one issue. There's another issue that hasn't been discussed at all that I think certainly needs to be addressed here. It's a very simple question, really. That is—and it's a question this and every legislature must ask itself—just how much of the people's responsibility are you willing to usurp? How much decision-making are you willing to take away from parents and families? Where does this micromanaging by government stop?" I paused and put on my glasses to read a note I had written on the bill copy.

"One of the reasons given by the bill's sponsor in support of this bill is that the state will save medical expenses. Well, I have an answer for that. Those who know me know that I'm against the state being in the charity business in the first place. Or, in second place, being in the health insurance business. But, understanding that this isn't the question before you today, let me make a suggestion," I continued.

"Today, as I speak, in the other Washington, a debate is taking place on whether or not to go after missing dads who refuse to pay child support. Now, I like that idea. I like it because it puts the responsibility back where it belongs—on the people, rather than taking it away and then making the rest of us pay for their irresponsibility." The room was quiet, as I continued.

"Try this, Mr. Chairman. If the committee is dead set on running this bill out, then add an amendment to it that says 'you may or may not wear helmets or make your children wear them; it's your choice. But if you choose not to, and your child receives head injuries, the state will not pick up the tab.'" I looked up to see the chairman actually listening to see what I was saying.

"Mr Chairman, I urge you to vote no on this bill. Thank you."

With that, I was surprised to hear a sizable applause going on in the back of the room. I have no idea whether this helped or not, but the bill did die in committee.

Later, I did just a little bit of research to find out who was behind this bill. What I found was a bunch of bicycle enthusiasts out of Seattle (where helmets are required) who liked to ride out of the city on the Burke Gilman Trail to the east side of King County. From what I could tell, it irked them that people out there rode without helmets. So they had gone to the King County Council trying to get an ordinance in place to make the mandate countywide, in order to make life equally miserable for all bike riders. But King County declined and referred them to the state legislature.

In Spokane, we have the Centennial Trail, which runs all the way into Idaho. After thinking about it, I realized the same situation would eventually come to the surface in Spokane if our state decided to mandate bicycle helmets. Then Washington State's bicycle liberals will go to Congress to pass a national law mandating that all states (like Idaho where helmets are not mandated) require helmets. But then, there is Canada. And then there is the United Nations. And now we know how more and more power always shifts to the top.

Following the Health Care Committee hearing I wander over to the Capitol Grill for a quick bite and to see who is hanging out. Afterwards I will go to the Third House lounge to collect messages. Although there are only two houses of the legislature—House and Senate—the "Third House" is the term used for the corps of lobbyists here, a corps that numbers about 750, nearly five times the number of legislators who serve here. I grab an apple and take a seat to read through a few bills I picked up earlier from the bill room.

Since government is force, every law that is passed must be enforced, and enforcement costs money. It is easy then to understand that with every law that is passed there is a certain measure of liberty lost, as well as confiscation of private property through the loss of one's own wealth through taxation. Although we need legitimate functions from government at each level, we are getting far more than we need or can afford.

Val once said, "Be grateful that you're not getting all the government you're paying for." It's true. And it is one of the reasons why we always joke at the beginning of each legislative session saying, "Get the women and children off the streets and hide your wallet—the legislature is in session."

Cain wanted the same reward from the Lord that Abel received, even though he was told and knew that he didn't do as well. In Cain's mind, he gave what he thought was enough. He would have been happy had the Lord given each an equal reward. But there is also something very telling about God's character in this story that I begin to think about: *God is a respecter of those who give their best.*

Making Hot Dogs

Our task in life becomes one of understanding which view is the primary life view of the person we are in relationship with, whether it be casual or an ongoing relationship. To understand Cain is to know how to respond and act toward others. For example: if I know the person I'm talking with has a Cain-based or fear-based view, then I realize I must deal with the fear in our communication before we can make any progress or else that person won't be able to see any other point I might try to make. Fear is such a blinding agent.

Following five different legislative hearings today, I head back to my car in the visitor's lot and retrieve the parking ticket from my windshield. This is my reward from the legislature for being involved. As I get into my car, I realize Harold is right: making law is much like making hot dogs and buns. It's not a pretty sight.

In the end, in legislatures across the land, the Cain factor is becoming the primary driver of law.

A Fair Hearing

Ten people who speak make more noise than ten thousand who are silent.

—Napoleon Bonaparte

It's 7:30 A.M., and another morning of public hearings is getting underway in both the House and Senate office buildings' hearing rooms. Since the hearing on the homosexual bill has been postponed until tonight, I head over to take in the initial hearings on HB-1209, the so-called Education Reform Act. I picked up the bill from the bill room earlier and, as I scan through it, I can tell it is another attempt by the education establishment to "put a band-aid on a sucking chest wound" as we used to say in Vietnam. Even at first glance, I can tell it will further remove parental decisions from the government schools and strengthen the bureaucracy. I sit down to review it more thoroughly.

For a long time, I was as concerned as everyone about the removal of prayer, the Ten Commandments, and religious symbols from public schools and other public institutions. It only made sense, I thought, to want God as a part of our government. Many of us have fought long and hard over this issue. But the question most often asked is, "How are we ever going to get prayer back into public schools?" I don't disagree with the premise behind the question, but I'm not sure I agree with the question anymore. The U.S. Supreme Court has ruled in recent years that arguments in favor of allowing students to pray on public school campuses are correct. But what good is that if you have only a very few who want to do so? And why is that so?

In supporting freedom of worship, the First Amendment says that Congress "shall make no law respecting the establishment of religion, nor prohibiting the free exercise thereof." Over the years, since I've come to better understand civil government as God intended it—and as our founders designed it—my thinking has changed. To go further than what the Court has said and forcing prayer or religious training back into our public schools is wrong. Why? Because we are trying to religionize an institution that shouldn't even exist.

I enter the House hearing room, which is nearly standing room only. Not surprisingly, most of those signed up to testify on this bill are the bureaucrats populating the education establishment in our state. And, of course, since the Democrats are in power, this hearing will be carefully orchestrated to enhance the testimonies of the bureaucrats, beginning with the Superintendent of Public Instruction.

"Doug . . . why do you oppose the Education Reform bill." I turn to see a lobbyist for the WEA (Washington Education Association). She's noticed I signed in to testify against the measure. "Because I don't believe we need to go someplace new; I think we just need to get back to where we were." I answer. She doesn't know how far back I mean.

A Fair Hearing

We need to spend some time on this issue. Education is a matter of inheritance and the sum total of what we're going to pass on to our kids. Everything we can see in the future with our own eyes begins with the subject of education. I'm talking about public schools—or government schools, as I prefer calling them. What we've gotten away from is the old ABC's, or basic academics. Schools are changing from institutions of learning into instruments of social engineering.

By acting as the administrator of education, government is performing a function that is, in the first place, outside its biblical jurisdiction. I'm not going to argue with the person who says that children should be allowed to worship and pray to their hearts' content on public property. The question to me is should they be there in the first place?

Education of children belongs to parents, not government. It is a biblical mandate for parents that cannot be transferred to civil government. We're trying to fix something that will forever be broken. If God didn't design it, then it can't be. It's like an auto mechanic trying to tune-up a car without an engine. We keep trying to make government do and be things that it was never intended to be or do.

Therefore, the things government tries to do in the administration of schools should not surprise thinking Christians. A better understanding of the First Amendment indicates that the very nature of government is to be somewhat neutral as to religion. However, we all know that the fact is government cannot be neutral. There is no such thing, and our founders understood this. If government allows prayer in public schools, it is then proreligious. If government does not allow it, it is then antireligious. Right now, the anti's are running the show. So, how can we fix that?

"What are you doing in here," I ask Lynn, as she takes a seat next to me. "Those I work for are interested in what's going on here and want me to watch it." Everyone is here; even the business community has a stake in this bill.

The hearing gets underway and the Superintendent of Public Instruction begins her testimony after being called to the front by the Education Committee Chairman. There are no surprises in her prepared speech. I could have written it. We're merely preparing for the next century . . . we've done well but more improvement can be realized if you guys will just pass this measure (which shifts parental control to us), along with more funding of course, (because more taxes always fixes everything) . . . and so on.

It occurred to me that someone coming in from the outside would have thought that her glorious review of the present bureaucracy really made the case that reform wasn't really needed. By the time she is finished, you would think that SAT scores weren't at an all-time low.

With regard to the issue of, so-called *separation of church and state*, suffice it to say that what Thomas Jefferson was referring to—had the entire context of his remarks been shared—was that, while government must always be highly influenced by and accountable to the laws of God and the Bible, the church cannot be subject to civil authority and accountability in the same way. To that end, Jefferson said, there is a natural wall of separation between church and state. In other words, teaching in matters of religion and faith belong to the family and the church, but never civil government. Jefferson and the others had seen firsthand what happens when civil authority gets a hold of the church. The Church of England was under King George's thumb.

A Fair Hearing

Cain would have loved separation of church and state, I think as the hearing drones on with more of the socialists laying out their plan for change. *If God hadn't been around, Abel wouldn't have received preferential treatment.*

If religious teaching belongs outside government, then how can we expect government schools to teach our students religion or how to pray? Please don't misunderstand me here; given only one choice of having to have public education, I would opt for religious prayer in the classroom. But just how many teachers coming out of our colleges today would we be comfortable having teach our kids religious instruction? Knowing that education was never an intended biblical function of civil government, in my mind the rest of the argument becomes moot. There shouldn't be public schools, nor do there need to be.

For the past decade or so, Christians have argued against government schools moving toward the teaching of homosexuality as a normal, acceptable lifestyle. I have been involved in this battle for a long time. While this is a noble cause, based on the foregoing I now see the futility of that effort. The answer isn't in muscling control of public school curriculums; the answer is not to be there in the first place. And presently, we are rapidly losing our ability to leave.

Once again, government exists to uphold the morals established by law. In our case, that law is biblically based, albeit in decline. Yet, by virtue of the fact that government has been charged with the education of children puts government in a place to have to teach morals. So then, it all comes down to a matter of who, by sheer power, is running government at any given time. Whoever that is dictates what is being taught. If we now throw in the fact that a majority of Christians no longer participate in the management of their government, nor are they paying attention, we get the situation we face today with the teaching of homosexuality as a normal and healthy lifestyle.

For those who may disagree and think we should continue to assault the hill and wrestle away the reins of government, let me ask this: In this day of multicultural-ism, particularly in the arena of religions which religion are you going to teach? Which prayer or chant are you going to recite? We must understand, we've already conceded the ground on this being a melting-pot nation. With the present-day mix of religions in America, shall we have a portrait of Buddha up on the wall next to one of Jesus? Shall we allow students to be taught of all the religions providing them a smorgasbord of religious choices just before lunch break? The beginning of the First Amendment makes it clear that government cannot make any law or declaration establish-ing or elevating any religion. Like it or not, that includes Christianity. Like others, I too wish the founders would have at least chosen Christianity as the national religion, and then let us decide which religion we would follow and how we would participate under that umbrella. But they didn't do that.

Personally, I see a civil government that has taken ju-risdiction over institutions wherein it has no constitutional authority. Education is one of them. A study of how and why we came to publicize our schools—and who was behind the effort—is a good study for conservatives. We should remember scriptural governmental jurisdictional lines are there for a reason. They are boundaries to protect us.

The chairman lowers the gavel ending the first day of hearing on the Education Reform Act. As I've learned over the years, it's not what's going on in the hearing rooms that determines the outcomes of such bills; it's what is going on in the halls and the restaurants in the evenings.

"What do you think," asks a lobbyist friend as we leave the room and head down the hall. "I think the Democrats are in the majority and so it doesn't matter what I think. But I do think government is about to grow again."

I'm heading over to the bill room to pick up the transportation bills being introduced in both houses. I want to sit in on the transportation hearings. Transportation is another bastion of change in the name of socialism. After stopping by the bill room, I head down to the Capitol Grill to grab a cup of coffee and think more about this education stuff.

Frankly, with the anti-Christian influence of public schools today, I'm amazed Christian parents who want their children to grow up seeking after the things of God would allow them to attend public schools. For those who argue that our children need to be there to bring the light of the Gospel to that arena, I say that argument doesn't pass scriptural muster. Teaching belongs to adults, not children. Children are in school to learn, not to teach. They are there to learn basic academics. While certain socializing will take place in normal course, it should be secondary to the primary purpose of academic instruction. Few youngsters are prepared to bring the light into the world, especially the world today. When they come of age and wish to attend postsecondary education, that can be a different story. Even then, as a Christian parent, I would find a Christian college.

Some people may balk and say I'm dreaming—that it's just too late to return to the way things sometimes were or ought to be. To that I say we have no choice. We either begin heading back in faith, knowing an omnipresent God will be with us, or we will perish. And historical evidence is on my side.

Put another way, God has specific parameters and jurisdictions when it comes to all of His various forms of governments. He didn't leave mankind with the option of changing those jurisdictions. To do so is futile, because it will never work outside of His design, no matter how hard we try.

But it is true that I'm dreaming. I'm dreaming of rediscovering the heart of God in these matters and returning to the plan as He laid it out. Education is another example where Jesus' words to us in the Scripture, "Render unto Caesar what is due Caesar, and to God what is God's," applies. If you ask Caesar to educate your kids, then Caesar is going to educate them his way. Our founding fathers had very distinct reasons for wanting to keep government (Caesar) small and limited. And that was because of their understanding of the very specific and limited role God intended for civil authority.

The fact is, most of us are so lazy about all of this that most of the time we simply choose public education because it's the easy way out; it doesn't take any effort. The liberal-Utopians love that attitude.

The problem in public education is not the lack of prayer or religious instruction. The problems surrounding declining SAT scores, shootings, and pregnant prom queens will not be resolved by putting prayer back in our schools. It will be resolved when Christian parents reject the very notion of "public" education and leave, starting smaller, private-type education under their direct supervision, either in the home or through private cooperative means. That alone will require parents to begin taking an active role in the education of their young ones again. When a group of close friends start a school, they get to decide which religion they want to be taught, and the unbelievers can say nothing about it. Call a local PTA and discover just how many parents are involved, today. What we find is that the few who are involved tend to be already connected to the educational establishment in other ways and many times on the other side of this issue. My daughter told me of a time when she went to a PTA meeting and she was the only parent who bothered to show up!

Parents have a God-given right and obligation to follow the Lord and His teachings, and have their children do so as well. We have a further right, and further obligation, to want their basic academic instruction to include its relationship to Christianity. But at the same time, the unbeliever who pays for public schools with his tax money too, has the same right to demand that his children not be taught the same. Like it or not, that is the reality. We cannot bring people to Christ through public, institutional coercion by way of law. We need to begin to understand that it's the very ideology of public education that is the problem. Fixing public schools and adding prayer back into the curriculum is not a battle we can ever likely win, nor should we try.

What is happening in the decline of our public educational system in this country is directly linked to the same decline of strong Christian character in government. In other words, over time, as we've sent fewer and fewer Christian-principled people into public office—at every level—it only follows that the same deterioration of the public trust will trickle down through every public institution. Abraham Lincoln said it best. "The philosophy of the schoolroom in one generation will be the philosophy of the government in the next."

In the good old days, when educated Christian people outnumbered nonreligious in government, public education was not as important as a topic as it is today. Moral accountability to a basic Christian creed was still intact, so nobody was upset. Even nonreligious people seemed at peace with this basic code of society. Not so today. We've conceded the ground and are now forced to find the truth in all of this.

As a product of the public education system—coming of age in the late 1960s—I can still remember how Catholic schools, while they seemed rigid to me at the time, put out better educated kids with stronger family ties. There was an anchor of spiritual confidence given to those youngsters that I didn't receive.

Today, we see time and again how private religious school students and home-educated students are nearly always at the top of national spelling bees and other scholastic achievement. The reasons are obvious: parents who care enough to spend dollars (over and above their share of school taxes) to send their children there are going to be parents who are involved and encourage their kids. The social circus present in public schools today is not generally prevalent in private education. The odds of Sally ending up pregnant after the homecoming game are much more remote in private Christian and home school settings. The argument that private and home school kids are social misfits is unwarranted. Personally, having known hundreds in the last fifteen years, I've found that the opposite is true.

A Fair Hearing

After lunch down on the waterfront, I have the usual struggle to find parking around the Capitol. I average probably three parking tickets per week through the legislative session. I could park in a garage further away, but don't like the walk. Besides, I enjoy playing hide and seek with the meter-maids, and usually win seventy percent of the time.

The fact is, the American public school system has become a dumping ground for parents who don't—or can't care enough—for their kids. It has become a gigantic public baby-sitting service (and an expensive one at that) for parents who have chosen to focus their time and energy toward achieving the illusive new and materialistic American dream. With both parents having to work for any possibility to get there, kids now come in last in a growing majority of homes. After several decades of two-income households, we can barely do without. But we must find a way.

Consequently, schools no longer simply teach basic academics but feed the kids breakfast and lunch, counsel them, teach them about condoms, about how the world is becoming one big sports arena and that life is little more than one big athletic event. A nation that now pays its college coaches more than it pays half the remaining faculty combined has its priorities misaligned.

When a growing majority of Christian and non-Christian parents aren't paying much attention, and since the people running the institution cannot see a God-given destiny in the individual child—beyond that of getting through life with as many toys as possible—kids can't learn of their true heritage. Public schools no longer teach "why," only "what." It should be no surprise to anyone, then, that we now live in the era of "school to workforce training" as our primary goal in education. We don't educate for the purpose of critical thinking for individual achievement but, rather, to line them up as a group on the assembly line for the collective good. It is that socialist-factory mentality again, which seems the natural order to anyone without a God and or call in life.

To those who worship the environment and animals—the creation, instead of the Creator—humans are to be lined right up along side the cows and pigs at the trough. Why not? We are merely temporary inhabitants in the nonending cycle of life.

As long as we send our kids to public schools, they will be getting this mindless minutiae drilled into them—directly and indirectly. We're not showing them anything different than they already have in the world and they keep on suffering the same maladies as the non-Christian kids. Whom are we fooling? What kind of a witness is that? This is an area, again, where we need to begin to see the bigger picture. Each of us individually has a personal destiny to achieve after we discover our salvation. To step out of sin just long enough to receive redemption, only to return to the vomit like a dog and dwell therein, is idiocy. We came out, let's stay out. If we do not, then salvation was surely pointless to begin with. Consider it "spiritual commonsense." Our relationship with Christ can't be purely for our own redemption or salvation alone. It is for the ongoing redemption of the entire physical realm.

Nor is education purely for the sake of filling a spot on the employment rolls of some corporation, to purchase goods, subscribe to satellite TV, and rear another batch of couch potatoes to do the same all over again. There must be more or the whole shooting match is just a lie. There must be more. If not, then I would just as soon check out tomorrow.

I have close friends who pray with their kids daily, encouraging them to discover the specific purpose God has for their lives. They understand that the education of their kids will only have meaning when it relates to the bigger spiritual picture. Academic instruction without that correlation exists then only for physical sustenance and self-gratification and no other reason. Proverbs 29:18 reads, "Where there is no vision the people perish." Above all, we need to help our children and the coming generations to find their vision.

"Have you seen the transportation budget?"

"Nope."

"Big increases for public transit." A remark from a fellow lobbyist I pass in the hallway.

"Swell." I say.

We'll get to that later, I think as my mind returns to the topic of government education.

It is important now to address just how we can get where we need to go regarding education. It's not going to be easy.

Today, in America, there is no political lobby more powerful or influential in government than the public education establishment. Unlike the small country or town schools of yesteryear, education today is big business. So big, in fact, that it has become self-perpetuating like so many other government entities. While it certainly has direct benefit to growth of commerce and free enterprise, it overrates itself and, for the most part, no longer teaches free enterprise as a foundation for a free and prosperous nation. It has overshot the runway, so to speak, with regard to its purpose. We're not feeding it dollars for the pure sake of education anymore, as much as we are for the purpose of feeding the countless administrative types who overpopulate the educational industry as happens in governmental-socialistic enterprises.

In Washington State, nearly half of the state's twenty-four billion dollar budget goes to schools, while half of that never gets to the classroom but, instead, ends up in a top-heavy bureaucracy. During a time of unprecedented growth in public education, scholastic achievement has plummeted. There has never been a year in which I've been involved in politics when the education establishment hasn't been in our state's capitol during legislative sessions lobbying to increase government expenditures on education. This is true even at times when student enrollment has been down. Interestingly, the annual educational cost in my state is well over ten thousand dollars per pupil, while the cost in private schools is about four and a half thousand dollars, or half of that. But public education bureaucrats argue that public schools offer much more than private. While this is true to a small extent, do we want or need what they offer? Because it has gone so far beyond the scope of "basic" academics today that it is almost unrecognizable, the fact of the matter is, we can educate our kids for half the cost we pay now, and get even better test scores.

I remember clearly back in the late 1970s and early 1980s, the public outcry over the growth in cost of education. In particular, many who were never having kids were wondering why they should be required to pay the cost of education of those who did. This question gets a blank stare from a socialist, but to those who still subscribe to free enterprise (and the choice they preach) it's a worthy question. To overcome this and other objections to skyrocketing costs of public schools, the bureaucracy began opening local schools for "midnight" basketball access for anyone, including the general population. In doing so, they removed the fangs from the mouths of those snarling because they weren't receiving any benefit from their school tax dollars.

Not until we see a flood of private schools begin opening up across the land will we see any positive change in government schools. Only when parents see what they can get for their kids at half the cost will public education be forced to make any real substantive changes. It is one institution that could use a big dose of competition from free enterprise.

The socialist view of education is apparent in the unions that surround it. Endlessly in Olympia, the education lobby has come asking for more funds for better teacher pay and smaller class sizes. This has been one of the mainstays of their case for needing funding increases. But the money always seems to end up at the administration level rather than the local classrooms. Even with more than twice the funding of a decade ago, these two problems still linger. Many a lawmaker has introduced legislation to try and get a merit system of pay in order to motivate teachers and recognize good ones. But the union-socialists will hear nothing of it.

Coupled with the one-salary-fits-all mentality of socialistic unions, you find that all teachers earn basically the same paycheck (other than longevity of service or particular degrees earned). Any talk of merit pay, based upon rewarding performance and excellence in our teachers, causes the eyes of union leaders to glaze over. And with the present grading and academic degradation, it's obvious that the socialistic mentality is prevalent here, too. In order to bring about total equity of outcome, we must dumb down our entire education system to the lowest common denominator. If we don't then kids might excel, and that wouldn't be fair to the ones who don't.

To turn this ship around will require facing the wrath of one of the strongest unions in the nation today, the National Education Association (NEA), and all of its state affiliates, such as the Washington Education Association (WEA) here in our state. And don't expect these people to play fair if you talk about changing the system. They've become excellent political public relations engineers and will build the case to the general population that they "after all, are only trying to do what's best for our kids." Like so many candidates' political campaigns, they will demonize their opponents with distortions trying to make the case that they have the inside track on the Holy Grail of children care.

The movement toward "choice" in education over the past decade has gone nowhere. Voucher-type proposals have found their way to nearly all state legislative bill hoppers, only to die quick deaths under the feet of the teachers' unions. The game is really only about money and power. However, at times when an idea has grown popular beyond containment by the establishment, you find the *edu-crats* there with their version of the same proposal that keeps the new idea in their grasp.

The reason for this present reform measure, HB-1209, is that the general public is waking up to the declining academic scores. So guess who is now steering the reform bus? It is the same educational establishment who drove the first bus over the cliff. So why should we expect anything different?

Up until the early 1980s, you could not have legally homeschooled your children in Washington State. It was then that the legislature made it legal. No one has been sorrier for this than the education bureaucrats. Since then, with the high test scores coming out of home schooling, it has been all that public *edu-crats* can do to keep the lid on the embarrassment and truth of their dismal record. Even changing the curve on SAT scores several years ago to make it easier hasn't helped. The decline in testing continued. But this is the way it must be—and we must begin to see that public education cannot be fixed, prayer or no prayer.

If Christians now decide to take up the fight against this enormous educational giant, they must first recognize that they will be up against a mighty Goliath. While we've all been skipping stones across the water, the monster has been growing. With the birth of the federal Department of Education under Jimmy Carter, the key will be in education itself, that is beginning an effort to educate both Christian and secular parents who have the ears to hear about the situation.

Republicans around the campus are very upset with how the Democrats are running slipshod over them in regards to every public institution and issue, especially on education. They are getting very scrappy in their media interviews. Republicans always sound so courageous when they're in the minority.

The sky is fairly clear and it is one of those spectacular days in the Puget Sound region. It always reminds me of the 1960s television series, "Here Come the Brides," and its theme song, sung by Perry Como, "The Bluest Skies I've Ever Seen Are in Seattle." *It's true,* I think, as I come to a standstill in heavy traffic on Interstate-5, heading north. I'm on my way to Bellevue to meet with a transportation group. The Seattle region's traffic congestion ranking just surpassed Washington DC, and is now second only to Los Angeles. Citizens are beginning to take notice that nothing is being done. As I sit at a complete stop, I realize that being stuck in traffic will probably be a good excuse for being late to a transportation meeting.

The battle over transportation and, in particular, the private automobile is one of the clearest examples of the difference between how socialism and free enterprise view the world. The fight that is building across the nation is being won—slowly but surely—by the liberal-socialists as an uninformed public buys into the myths and misinformation coming their way. As one leader in transportation put it to me one day: "The public is being stuffed into a closet and fed B.S." That is the way of modern politics today. Like most issues debated here, if the public received even a large part of the true story, things would be different. But keeping the public fat, dumb and happy, and bringing more and more people onto the public rolls, is the way to political power by those who seek to rule over you.

The fight brewing in transportation is primarily over allocation of transportation spending. Should more funding be spent on public transit? (Buses, light rail, etc.) Or, should more money be spent on increasing road or lane capacity, thereby creating greater flow of traffic and less congestion?

The bill before the Transportation Committee today in the Senate is an effort to keep alive a legislature-created study organization that was recently voted down by the public for construction of a light rail system in the Seattle area. But you have to admire the tenacity of liberal-socialists who won't take no for an answer. As I take my seat, I notice that, once again, there are far more here representing the bureaucracy of public transit than the private automobile. Why? Because average Joe Sixpack is out working today, while the bureaucrats are down here using his tax dollars to slowly take away his ability to use his automobiles.

Transportation is another arena where I know if the public knew just how their tax monies were being spent—or not spent—they would certainly throw the rascals out. It is also an area in which the liberal-socialists have a plan that they'd just as soon the public didn't find out about. Their biggest fear is that you will find out.

So that I don't come across too harsh, some history is in order . . .

The federal highway act from the 1950s initiated the national freeway system we enjoy across America today. What it has done for commerce and our overall economy is immeasurable. In Washington State, the two major interstate arterials birthed from this act are I-90 running east to west, and I-5, north to south—and through the heart of downtown Seattle. Other off-shoot freeways connect in and out of I-5 feeding the many other major cities cropping out in the greater Puget Sound region.

All of these major freeways, including two major bridges connecting Seattle with the east side of Lake Washington and Bellevue, were designed to handle projected traffic up until about 1970. It was understood at the time that, if necessary, this system could accommodate traffic—under duress—up until 1990, twenty years later. It is now sixteen years later and traffic has increased far more than originally projected and now the average citizen spends sixty-six hours per year parked in gridlock on the freeways. Since 1970 in this area, only seventy new lane miles have been added.

It's true that in those early days we spent almost all of our transportation tax dollars on building highway infrastructure. But, as it goes in a free enterprise system, the public (consumers) decide by demand where the dollars go. As we arrived in the 1970s, with the completion of the two main and sub-freeway systems, those expenditures began shifting to public transit—buses, to where it's now lopsided in favor of public transit, in some cases two-to-one in dollar allocation.

Current projections are that (even with the Department of Transportation's plans) congestion will double in twenty years to where Washington State's sixty-six hours stuck on the highway will increase to 129. By anyone's thinking this is bad, but the Washington Policy Institute estimates that this congestion at today's level is costing our economy a whopping nine billion dollars a year! That's a lot of jobs and wealth. Factored out over twenty years, that means 180 billion dollars is being lost. For far less than that, we could add enough capacity to cut the time we spend in gridlock in half.

We all remember the days when bus service served primarily downtown areas and was local in nature. Not so anymore. Today, big public transit conglomerates that serve across county lines absorb a major portion of the transportation pie (sixty plus percent in King County / Seattle). The fact is, public transit has little to do with moving people anymore. If it was judged on efficiency, it would have gone the way of computer ping games.

With the cultural changes of the 60s on forward, and the advent of the environmental movement (worry over gas emissions, ozone, etc.), pressure has been coming on legislatures around the country and the nation's capital, to move away from the private auto. Remember, too, that with all the worries of the liberal-socialists that we are running out of space and other resources, the shrinking planet they envision causes them to coerce government into favoring mass transit over private mobility.

Here's what the bureaucrats don't want you to know.

In the Puget Sound region, a mere 2.3 percent of all daily trips are made on public transit. That means that better than ninety-seven percent of all trips are made by those in private autos. Up until just a few years ago, transit ridership was in decline every year for the previous twenty years. In fact, since 1900, the actual numbers of persons using public transit across America is flat—not by percentage, but by actual number of riders! All the while, we are subsidizing each ride on the bus by nearly ninety percent! That means that for every $1.00 ticket, nearly ninety cents is being paid by the taxpayers—most of whom are riding on overcapacity highways. Public transit is not paying for itself because it is not in demand. If we were to charge riders what it cost, most would rather buy a car.

As I became involved in the transportation debate, it didn't take long to figure out that it is the same old envy and strife of Cain again. It is the same have-nots after what the haves have in their quest for equality.

All of the transportation plans on the drawing board by the bureaucrats in our state's capital call for spending upwards of fifty billion dollars on transportation, and the best they can offer is that it will reduce congestion below the level of what it would be in twenty years if they did nothing. In other words, traffic congestion will double, which isn't as bad as it will be if they left it alone. Meanwhile, private plans for reducing congestion below today's levels get no hearing at all.

Few people driving the freeways today can take the time necessary to understand all of the aspects of our transportation system and the forces behind it. But for me, it didn't take long to find Cain in all of it. The stacked housing units in Moscow, the few private autos and huge amount of mass transit utilized there—out of all of it, it is easy to see the former Soviet Union's downfall.

I doubt if most people stop to think of what it would cost them personally without private mobility and their automobiles. It's not just getting to work and back, but to the soccer games, grocery store, grandma's, the mall, and weekend outings of all sorts. To an American, the car is freedom. But beyond that, what our highways and private mobility have done for our economy and overall prosperity is immeasurable.

But those who wish to rule over us are planning its demise. In Washington State, even with recent large gas tax hikes, little of those funds will be used to increase highway capacity, which is the only way we can reduce traffic congestion in any meaningful way. I told one leader that there is no question in my mind that we are fast approaching the day when the liberal-socialists controlling the legislatures will move to legislate us out of our autos. Even now, surcharges and tolls are being considered to be able to drive in different places, such as today in London where private commuters must pay a fee to enter the downtown area.

The utopia sought by the Cain crowd does not favor private mobility as an ongoing option anymore. Until such time as voters begin to study this issue and demand their legislators to refocus on increasing highway capacity, congestion will continue to grow, and our economy will suffer. Even now, companies thinking of locating in the greater Seattle area are looking elsewhere.

A Fair Hearing

Perhaps this is what the socialists have had in mind all along as a way to deal with congestion.

Myths, Lies & Media

It is the poor's contempt for money that keeps them poor.
>   —Michael Corleonni, The Godfather, Part II

Thou shall not steal
>   —The Holy Bible

T he legislative session grinds on, and there is but one week left before "cut-off"—that final moment when all bills have to clear the floor of each house or die an immediate death at 5 P.M. that day. At this point—midway through session—the bills that make it through the various committee processes, and then pass with a majority vote on the floor of, say, the Senate, are then moved to the House of Representatives and start right through the same process over again. Likewise, those bills in the House after passing move to the Senate.

Since things are on schedule, the legislature has closed down on this Saturday until Monday morning, and everyone on campus breathes a sigh of relief, heading out for a little recreation, even if only for a half day.

After unloading my bicycle and taking a ride around Capitol Lake with a friend, I head back to the house I'm sharing with two legislators. On the way, I decide to stop at the video store and pick up a movie to simply drain my mind for the afternoon. It doesn't work. As I stand in front of the rack, my eyes catch the funny looking green outfit on Kevin Costner, with his arm drawn back and fingers on a bow-string. It is *Robin Hood: Prince of Thieves*. I pick up the VHS case; grab a bag of popcorn to ruin the exercise I just got, and head out the door. I already know the story of Robin Hood, but there's always room for one more remake of this English—and now America's—greatest fable and further study of this most peculiar story.

One time, when speaking to a group of about three hundred people, I asked for a show of hands of who had never seen or heard the story of Robin Hood. Not one hand went up. It is likely that the story of Robin Hood is the most universal of generational stories passed on, or told to our kids, or one which they've seen on the movie screens. As with government schooling, this story also has a lasting effect on our world view and just how we perceive the world at large.

No less than five Hollywood movies have been made about the story of Robin Hood. It is without a doubt, the most well-known of all fables. Surprisingly, it really isn't just a fable. There is historical evidence of the Sheriff of Nottingham and a particular thief he pursued in England of old. Like other stories passed down over time, most certainly, the story has been embellished and taken on much of its character based on the wild fantasies, whims, and mind-sets of succeeding generations.

Robin Hood is the story of a man who cared so much about the plight of the poor that he formed a group of "merry men" as accomplices and then went about holding up merchants on the road or in their stores. Of course, the whole point of the story is that Robin Hood gives the money to the poor to lessen their suffering. In the one description we all know and recognize, "Robin Hood stole from the rich and gave to the poor."

Of significance to me is the fact that one of Robin Hood's merry band of thieves is a clergyman by the name of Friar Tuck. Whether or not Friar Tuck was part of the true Robin Hood story is unimportant. What is important is that in several hundred years of story-telling, this pastor became a part of it by all those telling the story. It sort of plays into the point of the story and separates what Robin Hood does from the everyday common thief who steals for his own benefit, because now he has the approval of the church. And in some ways it now even elevates him to savior status in the minds of the reader or viewer. It's not hard to believe or accept, given most people's understanding today of the job of the church, and pastors in particular, and their role in charity.

Over the years, if not centuries, the church's role has become synonymous with easing the pain and suffering of the poor and dealing with the plight of the less fortunate. Even in today's America, the myth of separation of church and state has all but relegated the church to this primary function of charity. Certainly, over time, this assumed juris-diction and new-found function of the church as a whole has helped create an adversarial relationship to the rich. And it continues to keep the church from having any real say in the civil arena today. In fact, I believe the church has abdicated its ability to be a player in politics by default.

It would be impossible to gauge the effect the story of Robin Hood has had on the country as a whole and, especially, on the American political scene. I believe its effect has been extremely significant. And I'm certain that if I asked a crowd of people how many think the story of Robin Hood is an important message in general, I doubt if very many would say otherwise.

After watching the movie, I consciously devote the entire trip back to the video store to dissecting this story so that I can better understand the truth in it. Then I realize what is happening in the movie—Cain is in it!

The many movies of Robin Hood always end with the poor being better off, Robin Hood advancing to hero status, and everyone living happily ever after. And of course, the moral of the story is that the poor are poor because the rich deprive them and it takes someone willing to take drastic measures to fix the injustice. More importantly, since society won't do anything to help their plight, this single individual takes it upon himself to risk his life to save them.

Here's the real story.

Everyone should get a stint as marketing director for a large shopping complex or spend some time in direct retail sales. It is, indeed, a learning experience on just exactly what makes the world go around, what makes America tick, and how economics truly work—regardless of governing philosophy. An average enclosed mall today may house one hundred to two hundred different stores. And one thing they all have in common is shrinkage. In a word, shrinkage is shoplifting—or stealing. So, besides the regular over-head expenses, such as labor, rent, lights, product cost, etc., merchants have to add in an additional percentage for thievery. At the time I was in retail, that mark-up was about twelve percent. That means that approximately one-eighth of my store's product is going to be stolen on an annual basis. Therefore, in order to make the profit margin required for me to stay in business, I, the merchant, have to mark up my goods by the same margin of loss: twelve percent.

When we shop, we're picking up the tab for those people who steal. Multiply that twelve percent out over the entire country, and we're talking billions upon billions of dollars lost to theft each year.

Now you may be thinking (if you truly care about the poor) that this is fine, so long as the poor are really helped; that it is a noble cause and a worthwhile motive that then justifies Robin Hood's actions.

So, did Robin Hood really help the poor? Let's find out. Here are several points to consider:

First, it is important to note that Robin Hood never really stole from the rich in the first place. Merchants I've known are rarely rich. The more successful may be fairly well off, but few are really rich in the true definition by today's standards or even the standards of Robin Hood's time. In fact, for every merchant who is successful starting a business in this country, two others go under. In Robin Hood's day, it was really not that much different. And in his day, the rich were on the inside of the moat. They were protected, just as the wealthy of today have their wealth under protection.

So, in fact, Robin Hood was stealing from the middle class. Now some of them may have been "upper-middle-class," but not rich in the same sense as most often perceived today. I've often said that some people's definition of rich would be anyone that has a dollar more than they do.

Second, the story of Robin Hood never really gives the reader or moviegoer enough information. For example, it would be virtually impossible for Robin Hood with his small band of accomplices to meet all the needs of all the poor. How much would he have had to steal to meet all of the needs of all the poor throughout the land? Or even those within living distance of the village of Nottingham? Can we assume that there is no way possible that Robin Hood could have met all of the needs of even one poor family, much less all the needs of all the poor? Let's assume that even some of the poor would have declined to take stolen merchandise on moral grounds. That's not a wild assumption by any stretch.

Now, in order for any merchant—in Robin Hood's day or today—to make a living he has to make a profit. No matter the system of government, be it socialistic or capitalistic, production and distribution of goods has to be profitable, or the producer and distributor cannot stay in business. It is a simple fact. In the shopping center business, for example, if you have nine women's apparel stores, they must stay competitive or they can't stay in business. This principle then requires that they must sell their wares and services at the most competitive price, and the merchant who sells the best product and service at the best price will always rise to the top.

If I'm one of those merchants and you are another, and you lower your prices because you found a more efficient method of operation, or added some other enhancement, then I had better at least match it or I won't be able to stay in business. All of this to say that, for the most part, profit margins are slim. If someone is stealing from me, I either have to mark up the costs of my products to make up for the shrinkage or I can't stay in business.

When those who are not on the take from Robin Hood go into town to shop, they now have to pay twelve percent more for products because Robin Hood stole from those merchants. Do you see it? Someone has to pay for stealing—or in this case, for what the poor are getting from Robin Hood. Worse yet, even those who are on the take from Robin Hood are losers. As I noted, he couldn't possibly have addressed or provided for all of their needs. And he certainly didn't make them rich; he merely met their minimum needs in a particular area. So, when they go into town to purchase something they need that Robin Hood couldn't provide, they still have to pay the twelve percent mark-up to the merchants who were robbed somewhere on the highway. In effect, they are now paying back what Robin Hood stole!

It gets worse.

How did Robin Hood eat? Not one movie or story I've ever seen about Robin Hood indicated that he was rich or self-sufficient—beyond that which he stole. In other words, Robin Hood has to take a cut in order to stay in business. He has to eat himself and feed his merry men. Even if he has some other means of employment or wealth, he still has to be paid for his time and the labor cost of his merry band of thieves. Therefore, not all of the twelve percent he is taking even gets to the poor. Some portion has to be retained in order for Robin Hood to stay in business. Let's say it is one-quarter of that twelve percent. That leaves nine percent that is actually getting to the poor. But when they go into town to make other purchases, they are paying twelve percent more. So, in fact, it is costing the poor more in order to keep Robin Hood in the thieving business. The truth is, Robin Hood is not helping the poor at all; he is only hurting them more than if he had done nothing at all. There is still more here.

Contrary to all the stories and movies out there today, most business people are not greedy, uncaring crooks. Statistics show clearly that even in light of the tremendous amounts of taxes utilized in government charity programs, most charity still comes from the private sector. People from all walks of life, including merchants—even the rich—do care about the poor and less fortunate. But I can't help believe that merchants of Robin Hood's day were getting hardhearted because of Robin Hood's thievery. In other words, I'm sure they became a lot less charitable as they continued getting ripped off, regardless of the noble cause.

There are two false assumptions in the story of Robin Hood. The first is that no one but Robin Hood cared—or currently cares—about the poor. Common sense dictates that this is simply a lie. It is no different today. The poor do not need Robin Hood. Even if they did, the foregoing shows that, in reality, he wasn't helping them, he was hurting them worse.

The second assumption—and really the major point—is that we as Americans are teaching our kids by the telling of this story that it's OK to steal, so long as you believe the cause is just, to take from someone else's labor for what you deem a moral cause. It's OK to steal and break the law—even God's law—if you think the end justifies the means.

Robin Hood was a thief, no better or no worse than any other thief. He was a lawbreaker. He broke the law of God and a civil law of man that was based on that higher law. He ended up becoming a middleman who merely increased the plight of the poor and made a living for himself in the process. Robin Hood simply consumed another slice of the pie without producing or contributing to increasing the size of the pie. This is the true story of Robin Hood that we need to teach our kids.

The story of Robin Hood also teaches us to hate the rich, to hate the very thing that we would all like to be, to reject one part of the American dream we all seek. Robin Hood is the story of government welfare, benevolence programs, and many other noncharitable government expenditures we see today across the land. Government in America today is the Robin Hood of yesteryear. In it is the same faulty assumption that if the government doesn't meet the needs of the poor, or take on many other tasks, no one else will. It is a fabrication to increase the power and scope of government.

Finally, assuming that benevolence is the job of the church, rather than government, as long as we force people to go to Caesar for help, then we invite Robin Hood to come and steal from us. We keep the lie alive and we further violate one of the immutable laws of God. In this case, Exodus 20:15 says, "Thou shalt not steal." There are no commas or buts. There is a period after the word "steal." Not one of us, or civil government, can add to or twist that commandment. If you take from the labor of another without his or her consent, even if you think and believe it is for a worthy cause, it is stealing. Even if done by a legislator, it is stealing none the less. Charity belongs to the individual, not to any other entity.

Psalm 94:20 says this: "Can wicked rulers be allied with you, those who contrive mischief by statute?" In other words, God will have no fellowship with rulers who legislate against His laws.

I've come to believe that Cain likely felt the same way about Abel as Robin Hood felt about the rich.

The truth is that Social Service Days in Olympia each year are a travesty. On those days, we turn government into a feed trough, a place where we insult and degrade the poor and needy even worse by making them line up at the trough to get a ticket on the gravy train that does not exist. We make them render to Caesar. It's embarrassing to many of them and a game to pile tremendous guilt on those legislators who would vote against social service type programs recognizing it as a nonlegitimate jurisdiction of civil government. And, might I say, in many cases to get votes for some candidates who want you to believe they're compassionate. God's commandment to us is, thou shalt not steal. When are we going to quit justifying lawlessness by making exceptions to God's laws? Sometimes I think the truth is that we justify it because we really don't want to take our own responsibility for charitable needs. Robin Hood was a thief and a lawbreaker, not a hero. And it's as simple as that.

The totality of what Robin Hood has really done for America is to simply make it OK for government to steal.

When James Madison penned the first draft of the new American Constitution for the Constitutional Convention in 1787, he did so with the understanding that government's reach into our personal lives and wealth should be limited. The founding fathers understood and history has proven that the best chance the poor have of reaching prosperity is through less government—or Robin Hoods—in their lives. Following the convention in Philadelphia, a further statement of government's limitations was demanded by some of the states before they would ratify the new Constitution. In order to more clarify those limitations, the Bill of Rights, or the first ten Amendments, was drafted and presented to the states. In particular, it was the Tenth Amendment that "bound government in chains," as Thomas Jefferson said, and limited the scope of civil government. It reads: "The powers not delegated to the United States by the Constitution, nor prohibited by it to the States, are reserved to the States respectively, or to the people."

Since there was no mention of any benevolence or welfare program or any jurisdiction given to the federal government to spend tax revenues on such programs, this amendment then prohibits it. Obviously, over the course of the past century especially, this has been largely ignored by those well-intentioned but misinformed legislators—some who wish to buy your vote. Certainly, this amendment didn't prohibit the states from creating welfare programs if they chose to do so. But there was a common understanding at that time that charity and social programs were not the jurisdiction of government at any level. This is more evident by the fact that no state had any form of benevolence programs at the outset.

There was so much hope among conservatives across America following the 1994 Republican sweeps that the pendulum would swing back in the direction of limiting the things government does, especially on the federal level. One of the things done by the new Republican-controlled Congress was to pass a House Rule where all proposed legislation must have a rider attached explaining what constitutional provision gave the bill authority. Unfortunately, most of the bill sponsors simply listed that authority as the "*promoting the general welfare*" clause of the Constitution. Nobody has ever challenged it. If they did, and studied the history, they would see clearly that this clause never had anything to do with the largesse type of benevolence programs the feds are involved in today.

The story of Robin Hood has been one of the most harmful stories ever sold to the American public. In referring to the Republican congressional budget once, Vice President Al Gore commented that the budget was nothing but taking from the poor to give to the rich: "Robin Hood in reverse," as he put it. The fallacy here is found when you ask the simple question: how can you steal from someone who doesn't have anything to begin with or from someone who has only what you've given them?

Government bureaucrats and career politicians love the Robin Hood story because it advances their goal of convincing Americans that it is all right for them to take (steal) from one person to give to another. It is justified by the fact that the goods are going to the less fortunate. But, as I have illustrated earlier in dissecting this story, it is more about setting in place a self-serving bureaucracy that produces nothing of any real value. Nor is it a legitimate function that wouldn't be met if governments weren't doing it in the first place. It amounts to nothing more than redistribution of the wealth. All they need to do is continue creating class division and teaching your children to hate the rich in their quest to ever-expand the powers of government.

There are some other fundamental problems I have with this story.

First of all, we need to make up our minds whether stealing is right or wrong. If it's wrong in the first place, then justifying it on social grounds doesn't cut it.

Secondly, the fact is that by the best estimates I've seen, a mere twenty-seven cents out of every government dollar intended for the needy ever gets to them. (Some studies show as little as three cents.) The remaining amount goes to support the system of bureaucrats and middlemen, which is what the real intention is anyway. Wouldn't it be more effective for you and me to give directly?

In addition, the fact is they're not taking from the rich anyway. They're taking from the middle class. Every major study undertaken has shown that the rich are seldom harmed by increases in taxation. Besides, the rich own but a minute percentage of our total national wealth anyway. If we continue to make it impossible to get rich in this country, what are your kids going to aspire to?

"Social responsibility" belongs to us, our families, neighborhoods, and communities. That's where the efficiency is, as well as the accountability. The reason why everyone is calling for welfare and social program reform is because the government system has failed miserably. I contend that is because we have broken the first principle: it is wrong to steal from the rich or the poor—or anyone in between.

Government is extremely inefficient even when it is efficient. There are always layers of bureaucracy that must be fed. One time when illustrating this to a civics class I was instructing, I called on two volunteers. I had one young man stand at one end of the stage and a second young man stand at the other end. I told the fist young man that he was Citizen A, and the other Citizen B. I told the class that I would function as the government in a simple charity transaction. I then explained to Citizen A that his friend, Citizen B, was down on his luck and needed a helping hand. I told him to take out a dollar bill and give it to Citizen B, which he did. We all agreed that Citizen B received one dollar. I asked Citizen A who he thought Citizen B was now accountable to. He answered that it was he, Citizen A, who he was accountable to. Then I had him take the dollar back and return to his position. I explained to the class that this is the way charity and benevolence was intended to work:

each of us helping another directly, and accountable one to another.

Then I illustrated the government way. I then had Citizen A hand me the dollar, since I was now taxing him for it, and walked over to Citizen B. I asked the class how much I was to give him. They all said one dollar. I handed him about twenty-seven cents. "That," I said, "is how much he gets after the government takes out for administration and program costs." Then I asked, "Who is Citizen B now accountable to?"

A further problem in this transaction is this: when we are beholding to the government for sustenance of any kind, then we have to conform to whatever the political correctness is in that particular government at the time. In the case of Citizen B today, if he is opposed to homosexuality, then the gag rule is in effect. He must dance to that piper.

There is envy in this story of Robin Hood. It is the same thing that motivated Cain. And in his case, it developed to hate, strife, and eventually murder.

It is odd that socialism or the ideal of total government ownership of all property and wealth would have much appeal if a person would consider just two things. First, socialism's own history and track record as a ruling philosophy over the past century. Second, a look at the very nature of the philosophy is telling. The operative ways of socialism foster the very dilemmas its proponents seek to resolve. For example, by taking over the job of benevolence, socialists promote irresponsibility in the arena of charity. Why would they do this, unless it is really about power? Where is the efficiency of government in the benevolence business? If I know the government is doling out money that it has taken from me, I'm a lot less likely to give graciously on my own. And this is playing out in America today.

How can government be benevolent? People are benevolent. Government cannot love or hate. It is not a person, it has no feeling. If someone makes the argument that it is "we the people," then my answer to that is that the people may love, institutions do not.

There are many stories or fables like the story of Robin Hood that have affected our worldview in America today. But that is just one aspect. Liberal-socialism operates on fear and feeling. Capitalism and free-enterprise operate on faith and trust. The story of Robin Hood is one to play on people's pity and to weaken their resolve against doing something they have a natural aversion to, namely stealing.

Michael Medved, in his look at the movie industry in *Hollywood vs. America*, shows clearly that things have changed in fantasyland. No longer is Hollywood in the business of reflecting the culture in America; they are now out to design it. Unfortunately, it appears they have a ready and willing population. Mr. Medved says that this manipulation of the American public is intentional. Such, was the case with Robin Hood and a thousand other movies.

There is little time in the legislature for entertainment. Yet, in many of the rooms throughout the capitol, televisions are on and tuned to the various news programs in case any legislator is about to be sliced-and-diced by some reporter.

"What's the matter?" I ask one legislator friend as we board the elevator to the ground floor of the House Office Building. "The TV covered my bill but made it look just the opposite of what I'm trying to do," came his reply. It's not unusual to hear this.

Looking for America

Probably nowhere in America is the manipulation of the American mind more prevalent than in the mass media culture of network television news and major urban local television news. Having spent years in radio and television broadcast, I can assure anyone that all media is biased—because everyone is biased. And the worst lie is always by omission. Consider for a moment that in a thirty-minute TV news cast, only eighteen minutes is dedicated to news. Twelve minutes of the half hour goes to station promos and/or advertising. In today's news, a greater portion of those eighteen minutes are dedicated to the more sensational style stories, if they can be found. The media knows that what most Americans want today is to be entertained. We now live in the days of the modern "gladiator," much like during the time of Rome.

There is tremendous competition in the media, as there is in any business. The most profitable part of a TV station is its news programs where a larger audience frequents and a very substantial advertising rate can be demanded. For a local TV station, its local news is usually the biggest earner for the station. For networks, its evening news is much the same, as they charge enormous rates for commercials in the half-hour news programs in the evenings, and now mornings—not to mention the growing evening "news magazine" programs, such as ABC's *20/20* or NBC's *Dateline.*

Newspaper readership in almost every major city has been in steady decline over the past couple of decades. Even with their declining readership, they can still pack a wallop in delivering the news. With the many choices people get now, via cable and satellite television and radio, or the Internet for example, this trend will continue.

News is big business. I've found that it is the natural inclination of the media to find fault. There are several reasons

108

for this. First, the fame and prestige of being a broadcast personality, a columnist, or political reporter gives an air of superiority with what they write or say. After awhile, many of these people—like some of the politicians they despise—begin to think they have the corner on truth.

Second, is what I call the Woodward-Bernstein syndrome. During the Watergate era of the early 1970s as these two *Washington Post* reporters, Bob Woodward and Carl Bernstein, and others in the media went after President Richard Nixon, the feeding-frenzy eventually grew into a new type of investigative reporting that remains with us today. The media has also learned that an accusation of wrong-doing today is as good as a conviction in the minds of the reader. And, of course, truth—or lack thereof—is all in how the story is constructed. As I've said, the most common lie is born out of omission. If you leave certain facts out of a story, it paints an entirely different picture of the truth. It never ceases to amaze me, as a political consultant, how different reporters and political writers twist the truth in this manner, all according to their own biases.

In 1982, seven people in the Chicago area collapsed suddenly and died after taking Tylenol pain capsules that had been laced with cyanide. These victims were the first to die in what became known as "product tampering." The poisoned capsules, which had been placed on shelves in six different stores by a person intent on killing innocent people at random, prompted the government to institute the safety mechanisms now prevalent in every consumer product on the shelves across America today. From medication containers to food products, tamper-proof seals and construction protects consumers from worry as to product tampering. This is not all bad certainly, but not without a cost, a cost borne by consumers reacting to an overabundance of fear.

Ever since Watergate and the Tylenol tampering, the media has known it can easily shape public opinion and drive forward an agenda. It can also train a coming generation into a particular political bent using the same technique. Much of the debate of environmental policy has been fear based in the media allowing the liberal-socialists to pile on more and more stifling regulations that now threaten to destroy the goose that lays the golden egg.

Finally comes the issue of modern day education of young people entering the media. Most are coming from public funded secondary education institutions that teach from a liberal-socialist bent, which tends to skew the final copy of the story presented to the public. It is not balanced, as they want us to believe. Every human being is biased and thinks, speaks, and writes from the perspective of those biases. Anyone who professes—as many do in the media—to being unbiased, is either stupid or living in a bubble. It cannot be so. I'm writing here from a bias. Our biases are born purely out of our past environment, education, and life experiences.

In the same vein of media bias, one of the growing phenomena of our media culture today is the live court TV. Although some programs of this nature existed even dating back to the 1970s, I think it was the O.J. Simpson trial that brought it to the forefront.

I don't believe I have ever seen a greater mockery of the American judicial system than what we witnessed in this "made for TV" trial. It seemed apparent to me that the goal of the defense was simply to take the jury's eye off the ball and to get them confused and unfocused. The tool in this case was the race card played to the hilt in the court of public opinion, and thus, it truly became a trial of Detective Fuhrman—who lied and simply made matters worse.

I have several attorney friends but have yet to find one who believed from the outset that O.J. Simpson would ever be convicted. Now I know why—because they know the system. We are no longer out to achieve justice, but to find every kind of device with which to manipulate a jury. I used to have this naive idea that a main objective of trial defense was to ensure that defendants' rights are upheld—to make sure that the accused is not railroaded into conviction by angry mob mentality. I don't believe that is the case with this trial. Had O.J. Simpson been a pauper, do you think the defense would have worked as hard to cook this stuff up?

However, another thought comes to mind. Along with the jury, I wondered if the defense could have done any less than convince the American public of Simpson's innocence. In any case, it probably became as much of a spectator sport as it ever was a trial. Two teams on the field, with large coaching staffs, TV cameras, commentators, odds makers, souvenirs—and fans. As we watched the injustice of injustice mounting, we were left rooting for a team mostly, with little more than fleeting ideas of restitution for two people "butchered" by a madman.

There was another mockery.

You may recall that hot summer night in Los Angeles, California. It was the summer of 1993. It was high-speed vehicle pursuit, in which four LAPD officers finally cornered the car trying to elude them. How could we ever forget? A man standing in a nearby yard captured the scenes on a home video camera, and you and I were treated to scenes of a brutal beating of Rodney King, followed by the ensuing several-month trial of the four officers for the charge of brutality. And finally, that fateful jury decision of acquittal.

The night following the verdict will also remain imprinted on our memories . . . the special news reports showing multiple fires shooting into the sky, the countless smashed store windows, and even other motorists being pulled from their vehicles and beaten.

Finally, on the second night of the rioting, whom do they bring out to stand before the TV cameras and call for an end to the riots? They bring Rodney King to the microphone.

"Hey . . . can't we just all get along?"

Today, the spirit behind what Rodney King said that night I believe has permeated our culture and the church. It has totally crippled us and it has made us impotent when it comes to dealing with the issues at stake outside of these walls.

"Hey . . . can't we just all get along?"

It didn't start with Rodney King and his statement. That was merely the culmination of years and years of the culture in America being molded by an unrighteous generation that really began in the 60s, and a neglectful church. Coming of age in the 60s, I can remember clearly the rebellion that swept the land promoting "free love," "Do your own thing" . . . and the worship of the god of peace. Today, the spirit of that seed planted then has reached the fullness of its fruit. Behind Rodney's question is really this: all cultures, all religions, all lifestyles, all views and opinions, can reside together in harmony.

I have these recollections of the Coke commercials in the late 1970s when this movement was getting into full swing. Do you remember this one: "I'd like to buy the world a Coke . . . and furnish it with love . . . and to sing in perfect harmony."

The primary objective in any situation today has become simply to get along, to make peace at any and all cost. In other words, peace is the goal. Peace has become the god of our times. We might be comforted to find out that the United Nations passed a resolution about five or six years ago outlawing war. Now, because of this resolution agreed to by treaty by the United States of America, the U.N. is the only entity left with the legal right to declare war.

Is it true? Is there nothing worth fighting for anymore? Is there not a cause?

Today, the message to the "right wing" church from the homosexual community is, "Hey, why can't you people just live and let live? Why can't you just leave us alone. Why can't you just get along and quit causing problems." But is that the agenda? Is it all about just getting along with the homosexual community? For twenty-nine years in Olympia bills have been submitted to give "minority status" to homosexuals. It has happened in a lot of places already. Do we really believe they just want to get along? That's what the media is telling us. And it's become one of the reasons why conservatives are hated by the media. In their view, we can't just get along.

Jesus in Matthew 10: 34, said, "Do not think that I came to bring peace on earth. I did not come to bring peace but a sword. For I have come to 'set a man against his father, a daughter against her mother, and a daughter-in-law against her mother-in-law'; "and a man's enemies will be those of his own household.'"

The message here is clear; we have been called to separate ourselves from those things that are in direct conflict with the Lord of Hosts. The reason why "we can't just all get along" is because God has called us to a higher standard, by which we are obligated to divide right from wrong. In other words, He will not tolerate any less. It is the church's obligation to call the world to accountability.

Cain and Abel were both biased. Cain believed in equality or, more likely, equity of outcome. Abel simply believed—and that faith caused him to be the best he could be.

The next time, when watching the news, look to see who is simply telling you the latest news compared to who is selling an ideology through the use of omission of fact or the coercion of fear.

All of this is not an indictment on freedom of the press, or even the merits of the responsibility that goes with news reporting. What it is, is an indictment of each of us and our own responsibility to stay informed by gathering the news from different sources. In this way, we can develop a studied view and become educated to the facts, remembering that everything we absorb in the world around us must be compared and examined through the microscopic view of God's Word. Short of that, it cannot possibly be conclusive in our search for the truth and, in fact, leads us to misinformation.

There are those who are calling for regulating the press. I do not concur. Again, this brings in the power of government and a censorship that, in the end, will jeopardize liberty. What I do call for is for each of us to become re-sponsible about what we consume in the media. The church seems to be content on merely being careful not to watch "R" rated movies, not realizing that the same dangers exist every night on the evening news. A lie is a lie no matter what the source.

The Road to Serfdom

"God creates dinosaurs . . . God destroys dinosaurs.
God creates man . . . man kills God . . . Man creates
dinosaurs."

—Jeff Goldblum
Jurassic Park

I remember another time on this road, State Highway 2. It was the summer of 1971. I had been home from Vietnam only a few months and was serving out the last year of my four-year hitch in the Marine Corps at Whidbey Island Naval Air Station.

Occasionally I would take a weekend drive across the state to my father's home in Spokane. This particular weekend it was a hot Friday afternoon. The drive east on Highway 2 toward Waterville and the winding road up through Pine Canyon, on through the great coulee to its immediate east, was always a spectacular part of the drive. Some scientists say this huge half-mile-deep gorge, two miles across, was caused by ceaseless erosion from a trickling stream or river that ran through it over a period of sixty million years. The song on the radio as I drove through the bottom of the gorge fit the magnificent scenery—and the theory. It was Crosby, Stills, Nash & Young: Woodstock. I loved the music, but paid little attention to the lyrics in those days.

"We are stardust
We are golden
We are two billion year old carbon . . ."

If I had listened closer at the time, the words wouldn't have meant anything anyway. The only thing they meant to me at the time was music to party on. As I drove east through the basin of this mighty expanse, I had already gone through a six-pack of beer and was starting in on the second. I drove a lot like that in these days, trying to wash away memories of Vietnam and the girl I had lost before going there.

Now I just wanted a good time. It was shallow thinking, but I had not yet come into the knowledge of God. And I took pride in the fact that I could drink most of my friends under the table. Consuming a case and a half of beer in an evening was not unusual, and I could still function afterwards. Never mind that my mother was a raging alcoholic who would die a year later at the young age of forty-five. Fresh home from the war, I was already doing all I could to break her record.

A friend whom I flew with in Vietnam, also stationed at Whidbey, would sometimes drive with me. We often stopped in Waterville at the local tavern to add to our load, always on the lookout for a good fight with some hippies we might run into. It wasn't political or war-related in those days. We didn't care about that. We just didn't like them.

The Road to Serfdom

"We are stardust
We are golden
We are caught in the devil's bargain . . ."

At the time, I couldn't have cared any less whether the earth was sixty million years old or six days old. The only number *six* I cared about at the time was in *six-pack*. My mind returned to the present as I started up the grade on the opposite side of this gigantic gorge.

Cain had a strong grip on me then. Trying to reconcile lost friends, burying the younger years—all needed his perspective for survival. Cain's view is a very simple one. He is a seeker of fair-play and equity—the only producers or definition of true justice in his mind, and the only one the human mind can truly comprehend.

One worldwide government made perfect sense to me then, and I would preach it loud over a brew or two in the tavern. It was simple and didn't need much thought. A strong hand of government could settle all disputes and keep wars from taking place. *I can buy that,* I would think as I tipped back another bottle.

Today, I see the formation of this gorge as an argument worth the debate. With the eruption of Mount Saint Helens in 1980, scientists discovered that gorges, such as this one, can be carved in a matter of hours and days, in what are now referred to as "catastrophic" geological events. The Saint Helens eruption changed the way any credible scientist now views geological history. And now it's pretty much a given that the great Grand Canyon was not caused by the trickling of water over an incomprehensible period of time but caused in much the same way that the new large gorges around Mount Saint Helens came into being—by a thundering thousand-foot deep cascading flood of mud and rock moving along at over a hundred miles per hour. That sounds like God to me. Why take sixty million years to do what can be done in a few minutes, I always say.

The thing I find disturbing today is that the scientific community, along with academe, no longer has the courtesy to use the term "*theory*" when they make scientific claims that cannot be proven. Recently, in one court decision, a federal judge ruled against a family who sued to force their school district to, at the very least, use the term "*theory*" when teaching evolution to their children.

Cain would have made the same decision. He would have had to in order to build his case, too.

It is not fact that a river eroded this gorge over a period of sixty million years. It is theory—and recent happenings make it a very shaky theory at best. For one, no one was there to see it happen and testify to it. We now know most assuredly, it was likely created in hours and days, much the same as the Saint Helens gorges, which are nearly identical.

For another, many scientists today are viewing *carbon dating*, as faulty at best in determining geological age. Some scientists now claim that this catastrophic flood that I'm passing through now happened around the time of Noah, just a few thousand years ago, which certainly supports the biblical thesis. It now makes sense. In either case, at some point in time, every person must choose between these two views. A friend of mine once said to me that all science, left to man and his own devices, outside of any biblical influence, is purposed only to confirm the *non*-existence of God. I've found that to be true. *For as the heart believes, so the mind will follow,* I think, as the warm breeze reveals the scent of the orchard fields up ahead.

Conversely, other scientists who truly believe in the existence of the Creator say that, as they study earth sciences, they can see that all of science itself confirms God's existence in every element they study, which again confirms the biblical thesis. It is human nature to always search for the answer that supports my own presupposition. But, it is faith that opens the door to seeing. The world says that *seeing is believing*. But the Bible tells us that *believing is seeing* —in order to see the truth, we must first believe it.

Cain couldn't do that. And he couldn't stand that Abel could. I guess it comes down to what it is you're looking for. Our worldview has everything to do with what we discover in life.

I turn down the music as I pull into a gas station near the top of the east side of the gorge. Several motorcycles and rough-looking riders are sitting on or standing around their Harleys drinking beer as I shut off my engine. I remember those days. The truth is it was fun. But, in my life, it produced nothing fruitful, only chaos and death. But almost anyone who ever lived on the other side has to be honest enough to admit, there is an attraction to that simple way of living. Partying as a way of life is fun. But it's a dead end. The price is much higher than the benefit. That's another good element of free-enterprise—the ability to see if you got what you paid for. Nevertheless, as I watch them I find an envy growing in my heart.

As I get out of the car, I notice they all have the old, very short Marine Corps *high-and-tight* haircuts like I was wearing in 1971 when I used to stop here. Back then, they were all wearing long hair. Today, mine is longer and theirs is short. Go figure.

After getting a good stiff diet soda, I get back in the car and onto the highway. My mind returns to the lesson . . .

It's very important for liberal-socialists to get rid of troublesome words like "*theory*" in public discourse. Because, if they are unable to do so, then it lends credence to God's existence and the debate goes on. For them, having government as an ally in this effort is a must. Public policy then creates an atmosphere wherein only their side of the debate receives exposure and becomes reality. Since government determines what is taught in public schools, this becomes all important in their understanding of so-called "separation of church and state".

As I continue the drive east, I consider the following questions:

> Dinosaurs roamed the earth sixty million years ago—fact or theory?
> The ozone layer is in serious depletion—fact or theory?
> The reason for this is the usage of fossil fuels—fact or theory?
> The earth is approximately two-and-a-half billion years old—fact or theory?
> Mankind evolved from the ape—fact or theory?
> The Bible—fact or theory?

It seems that somehow we've managed to get things turned around today, so that science has become fact and the Bible has become theory. In the world's view, the first four items are fact, not theory. The last one to them, the Bible, is theory or, perhaps, fable. To those of us who believe—supposedly—the first four are theory and the last one, the Bible, is fact, even though we refer to it as "theology." But the required ingredient for it to become fact—is faith. I say supposedly because I'm really beginning to wonder if the church as a whole hasn't begun to buy into the secular world's view, as well.

Coming up on my left is the turn off to Banks Lake, a man-made lake formed as backwater to the Grand Coulee Dam. The great Columbia River, largest in North America, is another natural wonder. *Its gorge is another testament*, I think to myself, to that sudden flood that passed through here just a few thousand years ago. As awesome as the dam itself is in size and power, it pales in comparison to the creation around it. As I pass a semitruck-trailer and return to the right lane of this old two-lane highway, I can't help but think of another part of the Grand Coulee story.

The dam was one of the 1930s New Deal work projects from the Roosevelt administration. In addition, it became the birth of the Columbia Basin's Federal Reclamation Project. There is no denying that this huge irrigation project utilizing waters from the Columbia River turned much of the former near desert into fertile farmland I'm now passing. This is one of the examples used by the socialists to make their case that this land should all be public, not private.

To socialists, all resources belong to the whole of society, whether it is air, water, or land. Therefore, no single person should profit more than anyone else. Of course, that dismisses the factor of individual labor and effort, as well as who owns that labor. That's where the trouble always begins for them. In order for the socialist worldview to pass muster, individual drive, ability, and initiative has to be consumed by the whole. The socialistic worldview sees only the corporate or whole view. It does not see the individual, other than as a piece of the whole. I see now that this is where the argument always gets tangled until no one wants to discuss it. It becomes one of those chicken-or-the-egg debates that seems to have no end—no end perhaps, until you see it from God's point of view.

It mattered not to Cain that Abel had given a better offering than he. In his view, he had complied with the requirement and had brought his offering to the Lord. Cain couldn't see that, to the Lord, it wasn't the gift he gave that was the issue. It was a matter of his heart. All Cain knew is that God did not look upon him with favor, as He did Abel. Abel gave joyfully from his heart, giving the best he had. Cain gave out of reluctance. It is never what we give; it's our heart that is in question.

Another debate that has been silenced is whether the giant public-works projects of the era really contributed to the economic recovery of the Depression. Or, did they prolong it? In his book *How Capitalism Saved America*, author Thomas J. DiLorenzo builds a case and draws the conclusion that the New Deal crippled capitalism and prolonged the Depression. DiLorenzo writes, "In reality, FDR's economic policies made the Great Depression much worse; caused it to last much longer . . . and established interventionist precedents that have been a drag on economic prosperity and a threat to liberty to this day."

DiLorenzo is a professor of economics at Loyola College in Maryland. According to DiLorenzo, had it not been for World War II, the Depression would have likely lasted much longer. Unemployment five years after the start of Roosevelt's New Deal remained equally high.

"Despite doubling federal government expenditures from 1933 to 1940, the creation of dozens of new federal programs, and the direct employment of some ten million Americans in government 'relief' jobs, the economy was basically no better off in 1938 than it was in 1933," DiLorenzo goes on. "Indeed, it was precisely *because* of all these programs and expenditures that the Great Depression dragged on until after World War II."

Remarkably, the professor states, "The average rate of unemployment from 1933 to 1940 was 17.7 percent—more than five times the 1929 level." Things had not improved even after implementation of Roosevelt's New Deal.

Working at a small town radio station in the early 1970s, I had just cleared the news from the UPI wire teletype machines, which are obsolete today. Although I certainly don't remember all the words of the story, I do remember the gist of it. The story declared that we were running out of fossil fuels. Within weeks or months, the story pushed all other news to the back burner, as Americans were treated in every newscast with the sad supposed reality that we were in a serious situation—our gasoline was running out.

Those my age to about ten years younger can remember the lines waiting for gasoline. The images on television of lines a mile long in Los Angeles—waiting. The gas prices went from around forty-four cents a gallon to seventy-five to eighty-five cents a gallon almost overnight. How could we have been so far off? How could we have missed this calamity? Who wasn't minding the store? Was it the oil companies? Was it the government? Who forgot to check the dipstick to see how much we had left?

The interesting thing I remember about the "crisis," as they referred to it, was that from that very first story that I read on air, we were being told that we had been warned for years of the pending shortages by officials that had told us of this situation some ten or fifteen years prior. So just how was it that none of us saw it coming? Well, I know for a fact that in that radio station I had never seen a story on the fuel shortage before that summer day in 1974.

It's important to note in this particular story that they weren't saying that we were having a production problem in which they couldn't keep up with demand. Nor were they saying that we better get it together now because in the next few years we were going to run out. No. What all the stories were firm on at that time was that we were running out then—right at that time. There was not enough fuel to get us through the present demand or into the future. Those who recall that time will remember that was when we ended up with gasoline rationing, remember?

There were Congressional hearings where they dragged in all the oil executives and all the government experts. And out of all of it came reams of new regulations, laws, and government control in this arena of fuel supplies. Not to mention 55 mph federal speed limits. The feds could do that because they had taken our money from here, sent it back for our interstate freeway system, and now controlled much of the thoroughfare in our own states. So, what's the point of all of this? What's this got to do with politics?

It is this. We began making laws and regulatory decisions based, not upon fact or even good science, but upon theory. In this case, out and out lies and fabrications. In fact, several years later a lawsuit was settled between the federal government and the oil companies for an amount of about $2.5 billion dollars because of fraud.

However, you can't always operate only on fact. Sometimes it's necessary to plan for the unseen or prepare for things. Defense would be one of those things. Or, another example would be Y2K. Was it fact or theory? In the case of the huge concern over the potential consequences surrounding Y2K, most now believe that the resulting preparation was prudent and lent itself to avoiding those consequences. I was one of those running around talking to people about preparing for it. And I certainly believed it was going to be more than it turned out. Surprisingly, even the media said in the end that had we not all prepared for it, had computers not been updated, it could have been the disaster we planned for.

Regarding the first five theories I mentioned above, I used to say it doesn't really matter—sixty million years versus 6,000. But it does matter. It matters because if we operate on the theories of the world, then we're back to worshipping the creation rather than the Creator. Our faith then shifts from the Creator to the creation. The decisions made legislatively and governmentally then are made from idolizing the creation and man's view, rather than on the facts and faith of a Creator.

Someone recently asked me a question about whether or not I felt America is in decline or just ebbing and flowing. I think my initial response had to do with the old frog in the boiling pot of water. If you put him in the water when it is room temperature, then gradually turn up the heat, he doesn't notice the temperature is rising until it's too late and he's become paralyzed and then cooked by the boiling water.

But I began to think about that question a lot over the coming days. And I began to ask if whether or not we are declining over the long haul or whether we are just in a temporary valley. I think the answer to the question lies in two areas.

First, history in America certainly, but really in world history and in the study of other nations and civilizations, which have had their ups and downs.

Second, God's Word tells us that "the prudent man sees what is coming and prepares for it." We haven't been preparing very well and have seriously neglected our obligation to our country and the political arena.

My thoughts drift back to one recent church sermon in which my pastor was discussing God's grace and the difference between a person who was capable of extending grace to people and another type of person who was unable to do so. To illustrate, he had titled his sermon "The Yes Face, and the No Face."

It was actually a simple analogy of the difference in how each of us views the world each day and our basic outlook on life. I was struck how his sermon applied to political and governmental worldviews as well, even though he did not see it from that perspective. At the time I had been reading the story of Cain and Abel in Genesis 4. As he spoke, I saw a startling picture I had never seen before. For me, this sermon caused me to stumble onto a very simple picture of how I view the political struggle in the world today.

Every day when we awake there is only one of two attitudes we can choose that day, or one of two faces we can put on. And it goes beyond just grace. They are the only two choices God gave us in Scripture in which to base our belief system and tackle the issues of life. The entire Bible is chock-full of comparisons of these two attitudes. Interestingly, every political worldview falls in line behind one of these two simple choices. That is the choice between *fear* and *faith*. Every single day we make this choice.

The Road to Serfdom

I want to spend some time on this issue because, to me, it is an overwhelming principle pertaining to not only governmental issues but to life in general. When we as Christians understand this simple principle, we are then capable of identifying which attitude is coming at us in any given situation or from a person we're dealing with. We are then able to understand how to respond and act.

As mentioned earlier, there really are only two governmental systems available to man, free enterprise/capitalism (private ownership, liberty, and freedom) or socialism (state ownership, restriction, and loss of liberty). Although our adversary always wants to paint a picture of many choices or variations, it always comes back to these two. No matter how you cloak it or what color you paint socialism, in the end it is still socialism, still despotic, still repressive, and still a government of man created out of fear.

As I've spent time in the election campaign and legislative business, I've come to recognize where the liberal-socialists come from in their opinions and the way in which they approach issues. In almost every instance, I can predict how they will vote and why, or what tactical position they will take in a race for public office, for example.

The struggle between pro-abortion and pro-life factions is a good example of the two choices of faith and fear and how the liberals see the world. When Margaret Sanger began Planned Parenthood in the early twentieth century, she and other socialists of her time lived in fear of world famine and shortage of resources. They saw the increasing threat of overpopulation and were afraid. To them and those lacking faith, world resources were already in short supply and would soon reach critical mass. Coupled with their bitterness toward the wealthy, they chose the "no" face. A study of Sanger's life is a biography of a woman who had no faith in God or man, and lived in fear every day. Thus, abortion as a means to begin population control (and especially of particular classes) took on its public organizational form. Prior to that time, America had no organizations openly promoting abortion and birth control.

At the time of Sanger, it took approximately forty-five percent of the population to feed the other fifty-five percent. Outside of faith, there was no way Margaret Sanger and the other socialists of her day could have seen the coming technology on the horizon that would allow only two percent of the population to feed the other ninety-eight percent. Only faith could have seen this through trust in God.

Faith requires that we arise each morning knowing that we cannot see beyond our own lives and capacity, nor can we choose to violate a commandment of God (thou shall not murder) in order to assuage our fears. Much like in the story of Robin Hood, we violate immutable laws of God (murder of innocent humans) for a moral cause we believe superior (avoiding overpopulation), because we can't see the future clearly, due to our own lack of faith.

Ironically, today we find ourselves right back in the same place facing the same fears of overpopulation and shortage of resources as in Sanger's time one hundred years ago. Nothing has changed on the planet but the players. Those who have on the "no" face today are crying out in fear. To them, those of us wearing the "yes" face don't live in a realistic world. Although we don't always see it, people of faith continue to believe that God has a plan for any situation. I believe history is on our side. Murdering the innocent unborn is simply a lack of faith.

The debate over the environment is another hot issue today and another example of the way in which the liberals win the issue with voters, once again through their use of fear. They tell people that their opponents—usually conservatives—don't care about the environment. They take that approach after years of media onslaught building a case that the ozone layer is in depletion, the oceans are dying, or the rivers are all polluted by corporations that don't care.

After building a ship of fear, they put their opponents into it and sink it with the help of a leftist media. They then take the high road of a political savior, morally superior to their opponents. As an aside, they and their cohorts in the mass media no longer have the decency to use the word theory anymore when stating fearful claims about various issues like the ozone layer or discussing the age of the earth. They don't want people to know that there are just as many credible scientists with opposing views on a great many of these issues. Like many people, we will look for the information that best supports our viewpoint. In their case, a failing environment moves an unwitting population toward more government socialism.

Regardless of the issues, it's the process of creating fear that is winning the majority of elections today. If I can convince you that my opponent doesn't want you to drink clean water, breathe clean air, or have healthy fish to eat, then I can receive your vote. It's a loser's game because the majority of voters are voting against someone, rather than for someone. Out of fear, people are not voting the best choice, just against what they perceive as the worst. Thus, even the way in which candidates receive votes is now out of fear, rather than faith.

Amazingly, voters respond first to fear. That happens the more we succumb to a fear-based societal outlook. As a political consultant, I can tell voters that my candidate's opponent is a bad guy in some way or another. He's going to tell you he's a good guy in some way. But if I can raise your level of fear and doubt about him, then I can get you to vote for my candidate—not out of faith—but out of fear. It's an ugly way to win an election.

This past election, after understanding this more clearly, I began rallying my candidates around a new message, a message of hope and faith. In our printed materials, we would make statements that basically said: "You don't have to give up better roads for a healthy environment . . . or trade more taxes for better jobs. In America, we can have both! In America we've always had the faith that we can find a way. It's in our time-tested American ingenuity and faith in one another that will find a way."

This approach makes an opponent attack faith with more fear. As that happens, the lines and attitudes are drawn more clearly for the voters to see. Today, more than ever, people want hope. Through this approach, I believe people can see the truth of what's going on.

Fear must always be subdued by faith or tyranny will reign. It is a matter of biblical historical fact. If you don't have faith in God, you cannot possibly have faith in man, because there is no civil-governmental system able to satisfy man's hunger for equity and justice outside of the government of God. Democracy only works in the presence of a set of bedrock undying principles. To have faith in democracy without a never-changing standard as a foundation is to put credence in mob rule and faith only in man.

When our founders created our American system of civil government, they did so understanding this principle and designed it with their understanding of God's government in mind.

Faith requires a trust that God is in control. Fear says I do not trust Him and that I'm going to be in control, even if it means violating His laws and statutes. This road always leads us down the path of socialism and destruction. Fear always sees with the physical eyes in any given situation. Faith sees where the physical eyes cannot.

The "no" face goes way beyond the issue of a lack of faith. It is also shows a tremendous lack of knowledge about the God of the creation. In the Scriptures, we have many examples of one of the chief characteristics of the Father. It starts in the beginning, in Genesis, 1:22 and 28. After having created every living thing, God tells both beast and man alike, to go and multiply—or increase—and fill the earth. To multiply—that is a primary characteristic of our God. He is a God of increase. Whether it is children, or whether it is every leaf on a tree that comes into bloom in the spring, God is about increase and multiplying life itself. He is life—and He wants to multiply! That's why He spends so much time in the Bible talking of "lineage" and of all the generations linked together. Seeing and understanding this simple but awesome characteristic should build our faith and give us confidence in the future. Yet, fear is such a strong weapon and motivator of the enemy.

Our founders feared government because of their understanding that it couldn't be anything other than tyrannical. They knew that by its very nature, government was socialistic and intended to be so. Civil government as a tool of God provides man with the only things he can understand outside of faith. By faith we can see equality doesn't always mean evenly distributed wealth or justice. Without faith, that cannot be understood. Then civil government gives us what we demand, which is nothing but tyranny clothed as security.

On the ladder of governments, civil law was intended by God to be the last rung. It was the one form of government He intended to be ruthless, the last arena to corral man's disobedience. As man chooses to turn from faith and disobey God's statutes, civil government increases in order to subdue man. Call it God's fail-safe method of reigning in man's insatiable appetite for rebellion.

Without faith, man can only comprehend justice in the context of absolute division of property and edict. Our founders knew that civil government was an instrument of God, with its sole purpose having to do with punishing those who operate outside the laws of God. Beyond that, our founders had little desire for it, aside from the order it would bring to society in this same regard. It was their understanding that man was to serve God and His laws to reap the blessings and benefits of His government. Short of that, we are relegated to the pains of tyranny.

Our founders also knew that the scope and power of civil governance would increase as the people began arising each day choosing fear instead of faith; choosing to put on the "no" face. In other words, the more people would turn from God and the faith He requires, the more they would submit to civil authority. Civil government, or the government of man, is tyrannical. The mercy of the court can only extend as far as man's faith in Christ behind that court, because in Christ is the only place in which true mercy can reside. As that faith and understanding of the true mercy of Christ wanes, so does man's ability to dole out true mercy. That's why, throughout history, governments outside of Christianity have fallen to tyranny.

Not surprising, lacking faith, voters respond first to fear. That happens the more we succumb to a fear-based societal outlook.

I love Cain. I understand him. I was him, so very long ago. I wish I could reach out to him, make him understand what it was that caused him to fall short of God's reward. I want him to know that God didn't love him less than his brother. Cain, can you hear me now?

To repeat, there are really only two governmental systems available to man, free enterprise/capitalism (private ownership, liberty and freedom), or socialism (state ownership, restriction and loss of liberty). Show me a person who believes in socialism and I will show you a person who really does not have an understanding of God, the Father. Today, in America, socialism threatens to destroy the very foundation on which our greatness was built. Socialism stands against the Lord Jesus Christ. It was not socialism that brought us to the blessings we've known. It was an unencumbered free enterprise system that caused the greatest amount of individual incentive that did that.

Not just one or two scriptures taken out of context can build any case for socialism, which has been tried so many times. It really is that simple. Socialism is despotism in its worst state as feared by our founding fathers. This was the "leveling" they described, which we now refer to as "socialism" that they feared and the cause for them to build safeguards into our Constitution against it.

The most common Scripture used in selling socialism by the church is Matthew 19:21, ". . . go and sell your possessions and give to the poor, and you shall have treasure in heaven; and come, follow Me."

This has probably been one of the most misused verses in the Bible when it comes to those "equality monks" who want to socialize America. To them, this is the heavenly license to take from one pocket and put into another. Don't be fooled; whether a burglar does it in the night or whether it's a legislative body, it is thievery just the same. A Scripture that tells another story is found in John 12:8, "For the poor you always have with you . . ." This is a strong indication that Jesus saw something else in the war between the haves and have-nots. That is, benevolence belongs to the individual, not any other entity. When it comes to specific jurisdictions, benevolence is not a job of the state.

Further evidence can be found in Jesus' challenge to the Pharisees when confronted with whether or not a person should pay taxes. ". . . render to Caesar the things that are Caesar's; and to God the things that are God's" (Mat. 22:21). Jesus was merely telling them that God has specific jurisdictions laid out in the way He divided responsibility. Taxes were not a thing Jesus was concerned with. He knew that was a function of civil authority. He also knew that civil authority falls under God. He was not going to be trapped into letting them off the hook on supporting the costs of civil government. Civil government is a God ordained entity. But, as with all forms of government, it has very specific limitations of jurisdictions.

The truth is, we can sit and trade Scriptures all day long to build a case for any kind of government we desire. However, when one takes into account the whole personality of God as revealed through the Bible as a whole, you begin to understand the way in which He intended the various governments to operate. Benevolence belongs to you and me—no one else!

I had an interesting discussion with my senior pastor some years ago concerning our church's benevolence board. It has long been held by many that benevolence belongs to the church corporately. So, if Mrs. Wilson's husband dies and she has finds herself without any money to get by, the church steps in and helps her out. But I contend that benevolence belongs solely to the individual. The money that comes into the church is to be used for the advancement of the Kingdom in the propagation of the gospel—taking the good news throughout the world. To take those funds and use them for individual purposes, no matter how noble, is an improper jurisdiction. To me, it's as the same as taking back sacrifices from the temple of God because we see a need for it elsewhere.

In actuality, this is exactly how socialism began taking root in America. I'm convinced that the tendency for civil government at any level to begin acting as a welfare office first started in the church. In other words, had the church not started doing the same thing, the government would have not done it. It first began in the church.

Taking from one person's pocket to give to another in our society is nothing but a cop-out on our personal responsibility to be charitable to those in need.

I believe that any Christian with an intimate relationship with the Almighty and who has read, even studied, the Scriptures cover to cover, must come to the conclusion our founders did—that capitalism or free enterprise is the best worldly system man can devise, as well as the system that can best serve all peoples, rich or poor. It is the system that offers the greatest opportunity for poor to become rich. That's why in America today our poor are comparatively rich when compared to the majority of the world.

Today in America, we seldom hear the term "socialism" anymore. The reason is simple—the very word carries with it a negative connotation of the worst kind. The average American voter no longer understands the term, nor realizes our present day sinking into the socialistic abyss. In order to understand socialism, we need to understand both its history in combination with human characteristics present in all of us. When seen in the full light, it should scare the freedom-loving individual.

Interestingly, since the McCarthy era of hunting down Communists, socialism bashers have gone into the closet. That's unfortunate. It's time to come back out. The hunting is good in America today.

The illusion out there today is that you can mix these two systems. But where the Devil has a goal of overcoming freedom and liberty with tyranny and despotism, socialism has an equal goal. Many Christian socialists are well-meaning people with honorable intentions. However, they are misled and being used by an insidious enemy. Overruled by their God-given sense of compassion, and bitterness against those who they've judged as not charitable enough, they fall into the trap of "equality" and fail to understand the true nature of God that stands in opposition to socialism, equity and state benevolence.

It's in this regard that we begin turning over every governmental function to civil authority. Even now, with federal legislation offering to reaffirm freedom of religion, we see government poking its nose into areas that the constitution declares out-of-bounds. It's in this assumption that civil government rules over all that caused our founders to break away from King George. The state had inappropriately made the Church of England the national religion. When that happened freedom of religion was lost and the story of the pilgrims (separatists and puritans) became reality.

I think we became satisfied with the prosperity we achieved in this country, not aware of the bountiful prosperity God had beyond that. If we hadn't become willing to let government take more and more of our productivity from us for bureaucracy instead, what might have we achieved?

There is a wretchedness creeping into capitalism today in America that threatens to be its downfall. At the least, it is now causing government to take more control in the marketplace. It is in the conduct of our dealings with each other. After faith, there still is a way in which we must deal in the marketplace for capitalism to be successful and benefit the most people. I used to wonder why Mexico and other countries weren't successful, even though they were Christian-based, as we are.

In other cases, such as social-welfare programs, it is always arguable that the service is: 1) not a proper jurisdictional function of civil authority (both constitutionally and biblically); 2) can be done more efficiently in the private sector; and 3) has failed miserably in alleviating the problem it was created for.

The Rose Garden

We Don't Promise You a Rose Garden
                    —U S Marine Corps recruiting poster

I died in 1968. I distinctly remember the day and the hour. I had just boarded a Greyhound bus and sat looking out the window at my father who had come to see me off. It was 9:30 A.M., July 12th. Dad was standing outside waving goodbye as the bus pulled out of the terminal in Spokane, Washington, heading for Seattle and, eventually, Marine Corps Recruit Training Depot in San Diego, California. I had left Dad many times before—for hours—even days. At first, this departure would seem no different.

My life came to an abrupt end in that moment, yet I would fail to see the death or be able to mourn the loss for years to come. Little did I know at that exact moment, on that hot July morning, that this bus was doing nothing more than taking away my body to another world in which it might begin to live again. And no matter how hard I would try over the next year or more, I would not be able

141

to revive the young boy who died in Spokane that early midsummer morning.

The following day, along with seventy-nine other young boys mostly, eighteen and nineteen years of age, I began my initiation into one of the world's most elite men's clubs, the United States Marine Corps. Nine weeks of the most grueling training one can imagine, Marine Corps boot camp is a legend. It is a system strong on tradition and proven methods of transforming immature boys into responsible fighting men. And even ex-Army members I knew who later crossed over to join the Corps confirmed this in comparing the Corps' rigidity and intense discipline to that of the Army. The Marine Corps has resisted every political effort in the days since to soften and feminize its methods.

Yet, it was not too many years ago when I finally figured out just what else really went on in San Diego that summer. For us arriving that late evening in July, it had not changed from how the late Leon Uris described it in his World War II Marine Corps epic, *Battle Cry:* buses pulling through the gates of the recruit depot and into the parking area of the receiving barracks; voices rising, then fading all in unison as the busses pass, "YOU'LL BE SORRYEEE!" Then, just as Uris wrote, "The gates of mercy closed behind them."

What you really die to, in the Marine Corps, are your old ways of thinking and functioning. Because of the very nature of warfare and combat, there is a strict uniformity required in order to maintain discipline and achieve automatic and absolute obedience to command. It is certainly a necessary element in winning battles. There is no place for argument and negotiation in the Marine Corps. A couple of the things they yell at us in boot camp: "You had better get your heads and butts wired together, maggots!" and "You will learn that there is a right way, a wrong way, and the Marine Corps way."

The Rose Garden

We learned the Marine Corps way.

The whole point of boot camp was to completely retool a man to conform to a specific pattern, an exact replica of the other men around him. There is no place for individualism in the Marine Corps. There can't be. And, considering its mission, that's the way it should be. I liken it to how I always enjoy rebuilding car engines from the ground up. The Marine Corps, from the moment you stepped off the bus, broke you down, stripped you of all individualism, false pride, and any other unnecessary baggage. They then spent the next nine long, hard weeks rebuilding you their way. It was like taking an ordinary 302-V8 Ford engine and turning it into a high-output screaming machine that would turn on and off with their key. That was their objective. They would constantly scream at us, "You can't do the Marine Corps any good if you're dead." I always appreciated that one. Or, another one of my favorites: "Pay attention here and you might live through Vietnam. Let the other SOB die for his country; we want you alive!" I liked that one, too.

Military is as an efficient way of life as anyone could possibly imagine. Once you passed the test of boot camp and infantry training and were allowed into the brotherhood, life was easy for the most part—at least until Vietnam. But, war aside, the nice thing I found about military life was the socialism. I liked it. In a larger sense, I didn't have to think for myself in the same way I have to in civilian life. In the Marine Corps, all your major life decisions are made for you: where you will live, what you will do, how much you will earn. Everything is exactly the same, base to base, unit to unit, man to man. You got the same government-issued uniforms, the same amount of space in your living quarters, the same bunk and bedding, the same food, and you got to take showers in one big room along with hundreds of other guys who looked the same as you—short hair and all. No waste of water here. And—what every real socialist would like the most—no personal automobiles. We all rode standing up, crammed into real cattle cars that had not even been hosed out before they picked us up. So, no waste of fuel here, either. They always told us that if the Marine Corps didn't issue it to us, then we weren't supposed to have it.

In retrospect, this Marine Corps boot camp model of life is as socialistic as it gets. And it should be. Military is government. Besides their existence for national defense, the Marines are the strong arm of government (more accurately that of the President, as it is written in their original charter). They are called out to wage physical warfare whenever political warfare fails. The Marines didn't promise us a rose garden—and they delivered!

The very definition of government is force. Every law and statute passed must be enforced. To govern means to confine, to constrict, and to stop. And, of course, that is the same purpose of the military. The US Marine Corps' mission, along with the other branches of military, is to force the national will on others who threaten our freedom. It really is as simple as that.

To the true socialist, government is military. To them, the most strict and stringent government would eliminate the need for military in the conventional sense. That's why true socialists despise the military. In their utopian dreams, like Marx and Engels they envision the perfect government. One that is essentially the very same picture of Marine Corps boot camp: a national police force that forces the will of socialism and equity on all peoples of the world.

Make no mistake; that is what the United Nations is all about to them. It is not the forum to sit around and discuss common problems, as most of us thought. Few people know that the UN of today is a living, breathing nation unto itself.

Equality and equity are the primary goals of both socialism and communism—the natural and eventual extension of socialism. But in all our quest as humans to achieve these goals, no one has stopped to figure out 1) if it is even achievable or 2) if it should even be the goal. That isn't to say that fairness and justice aren't worthy goals. But it is our misunderstanding of justice that haunts us and keeps us as societies forever running in circles trying to achieve the unachievable. As we've confused the term justice with equity, we've turned justice into something it is not.

Cain didn't seek fairness or justice with the Lord; he sought equity. Cain's complaint to the Lord stemmed from his own inability to accept inequality and the inequity of treatment he saw in that brief exchange—even though he made the choice to give less than his best. Moreover, he looked outside himself to fix the blame.

Free-market government, the economic governing philosophy which our founders selected, requires a minimal amount of civil law, free from encumbrances, so that it can function as intended. That was one of the reasons why the Tenth Amendment to the US Constitution came into being—to limit the powers of government. No economic system or governing philosophy is without imperfections and inequities. But today we've turned equality and equity of material as well as outcome into a god. The fastest way to kill it or render capitalism worthless is to begin regulating it and micromanaging the economy that it produces. In our haste to create perfection in a world that was actually created to be imperfect, we destroy the very concept that can bring about the most prosperity of any system—and, in reality, the best for the most people.

I'm beginning to see that we seek the impossible in our quest for equality and try to create rights that we have no right to. So many in our country today are running to the government asking for special treatment based on some drummed up ideal of a right that they created on their own and then found a willing media to beat the drum for them. We need to inform people again that government doesn't bestow rights, it protects them. It merely grants privileges, according to the wishes of the majority. Rights only come from God.

Is God equitable? According to scientists there are no two grains of sand on the beach alike, nor two snowflakes. No two people are exactly alike, not even twins. No two people ever had exactly the same life, trials, victories, or experiences. No two days of weather have ever been exactly the same. Every molecule in the solar system changes tonight, so that it is not the same tomorrow. Nothing is the same. Nothing is equal—not in weight, shape, size, or quantity. Therefore, what is equal?

One of the hardest things for people outside the faith to understand is this most important fact of inequality. Even in the church many of us point to disasters, sudden deaths, accidents in the family, or horrible atrocities to conclude that God doesn't exist. Somehow we've drawn the assumption that "a real God could never allow those things to happen." So, what we've done is to confuse justice with fairness. The character of God I've come to know is just and fair but only in keeping with His plan for my life and my overall destiny. He's going to do whatever is necessary—good and bad—to ensure that I reach that destiny. My problem is I always associate bad things with the Devil, and believe that God holds the same view of life that I do. Life is probably more sacred to Him than to me, but I'm now coming to believe He views it differently. If He viewed it the same as you and I, then atrocities wouldn't happen. But they do.

Let me explain. In our natural instinct for survival as animals, we fight for our lives. As humans, we add to that natural instinct the value of our lives from our own ability to reason. In other words, we love others, memories, things, and life in general. And the greatest fear of death, I think, is in losing those things, loved ones—all mixed together with the fear of the unknown. A dog doesn't know that one day he will be dead, but I do.

Somehow, at my age now, I understand and see a God who loves life far more than I can ever imagine. As I've begun to understand so very little of His character, I can't help but believe that for those who love Him there is a life much greater on the other side of the veil. For me, if I didn't have a confidence in this, I would very definitely be hanging out with the "eat, drink, and be merry" crowd on a permanent basis. As far as the atrocities go, Vietnam taught me than you can leave mighty quickly. Or, with some serious diseases you can suffer for a long period of time. Either way, in the larger picture it's not very long. Yes, it is unfair. It is unjust to us. He is God, not me. He has reasons for things, as I've discovered, that I will likely never understand here on earth. And I do keep in mind that He caused His own Son to suffer immeasurably for me.

What I am going to share here is an understanding that I believe is absolutely essential for any American to understand and believe in order reach maturity and have any kind of meaningful walk in life. Without comprehension of this information, everything else I will share afterwards will be lost. This is simply the biggest stumbling block of probably any person. I sincerely believe that those who can hear this word and receive it, for them it will change their entire outlook on life. And it will completely change their view of politics and the entire world around them. It is, by far, the hardest thing in life I've had to grasp and accept. And it is also the thing Cain missed.

To begin, it is important to lay the groundwork with four principles of the "fairness doctrine."

1. Life isn't fair.
2. Life isn't going to be fair.
3. Life was not intended to be fair.

And finally,

4. God actually intended that life not be fair.

I need to spend some time on the last. The dictionary's most common word used in the definition of fair is "equitable," described as "superficially true or good." In Noah Webster's 1828 dictionary, he said that the word fairness *implies* equity. What that means is that being fair is not a guarantee of equality or equity. I think this part of the definition says that Noah also knew that there was no such thing as equality too.

> Equitable also implies justice, *but less from the standpoint of a rigid code of rules than from a sense of what is in the best interest of all concerned in a given issue. It therefore may imply justice tempered by reason or compromise.*

This is enlightening. In essence, fairness merely implies justice, and then only in terms of balancing by way of compromise in order to achieve equity. To fully understand the point I am building here, we need to also look up the meaning of justice. You see, most of us confuse the two as meaning the same thing. But let's look at Noah Webster's 1828 again:

> Justice—1a. The principle of moral rightness; equity. b. Conformity to moral rightness in action or attitude; righteousness. 2. The upholding of what is just, fair treatment and due reward in accordance to honor, standards, or law. 3. Something that is just or due. 5. Conformity to truth, fact, or sound reason.

Now, to get the total picture we need to go one step further and see if we can get a better view of the difference between *fairness* and *justice.*

To begin with, I believe that fairness, as we think of it today, is a view of man. Justice is of God. We need to know the difference. As we just discovered, the best term for fair is equity. And equity essentially means equal amounts of everything for everybody, which is what we are striving for in this country every day. But it will never come to pass, because God won't allow it. He did not intend it that way.

What God is concerned with is justice and what it means to each of us as individuals. God's justice is not equity. It is, in my opinion, what each of us is due according to His purpose for each of our individual lives.

Now I need to stop here and interject something else important to this fairness doctrine.

Let me give you a couple of examples: First, I have a nephew named Ryan who is now thirty-seven years old and was born with such serious birth defects that he is blind, deaf, dwarfed in size, and nearly totally physically dysfunctional. And no matter what we do as humans, Ryan will never know life as most of us know it, which certainly seems totally unfair. But the question is: how can we ever make it fair for him? Can we give him a court settlement, of say, fifty million dollars to make it fair? Would that even make it equitable in terms of human fairness? Will his life then be as rich as any one of us? Of course not. Am I then saying that we should give up trying to make things fair? Of course not.

Today in America, as individuals, we have entered the age of the victim society, which is what Cain had become in his transaction with the Lord. As is obvious by the current state of affairs, we are adding legislation by the bushel, striving to make things fairer. But are we ready to see the truth? The truth is, the more we try to make things fair through human means, the more they continue to be unfair, and sometimes get increasingly unfair.

One of the worst things that I see happening today in corporate America is the major corporation's very definite shift toward what I will call "socialistic-capitalism." It is the unionization that has taken hold of the remaining industries left in the US. Boeing would be an example. Here is, in my opinion, the best airplane manufacturer ever, with the corporate officers looking on society as a workforce rather than a social people. For example, in 1999, the Boeing company endorsed the state legislature's proposed school-to-work education thinking. It sounds great but, in my mind, they were only looking on their needs as a corporation leader, rather than what this type of public policy represents.

In essence, the problem with school-to-work is that it merely teaches the student just enough to get a job, as if that is all there is in life. It doesn't put the emphasis on basic academics or on the problem-solving type of education our young people used to get. It's the view that all people are merely a herd of bodies that will fill a position on some assembly line. Now if this sounds a little off the chart, I suggest a look at Japan's work force and what has happened there over the past thirty years because of this same view of education and life. Their families are in ruin, with suicides epidemic. That's what Japan's school-to-work education has done for them.

The movie *Network* from the mid-1970s is an example of what happens when corporate America begins operating in the same mental framework of socialism; that is, social focus redirected to the corporate level instead of the individual. The movie was based on how television networks live and die on the viewing ratings that are given to them by the Nielsen ratings, derived from ongoing viewer research. In this particular case, the network portrayed in the movie had found a news anchorman who, while brilliant in some sense, had overloaded on the news and stress and began going mad. Much to the delight of corporate management, Howard Beal, attracted a wide and excited audience as he would rant and rave his way to a blackout at the end of each broadcast. His eyes would roll back in his head, and he would literally pass out backwards in front of the cameras.

Eventually, Beal began to spread the gospel of freedom and democracy by telling his viewers that they needed to turn off their TVs and go to the window and yell: "I'm mad as hell, and I'm not going to take it anymore." He was basically promoting rebellion to a corporate world that no longer recognized the individual.

Finally, in a desperate move to rein Beal in, and retain their corporate advertisers that Beale is beginning to rail against, the network president gives probably the most rousing sales speech I have ever heard.

To set the stage for his pitch to his anchorman, Mr. Jensen closes the drapes in this large boardroom and stands at one end of a long boardroom table lined with chairs and tiny lights at each placing. He places Howard Beale at the other end and brings the lights down, so that only the small lamps that line the table give off their mystic light into the room. Jensen leans forward looking down the full length of the table at Beale at the other end and, in the half-light, he speaks in a loud and very commanding voice.

> You have meddled with the primal forces of nature, Mr. Beale, and I won't have it. Is that clear?! You think you have merely stopped a business deal—that is not the case! The Arabs have taken billions of dollars out of this country, and now they must put it back. It is ebb and flow, tidal gravity, it is ecological balance.
> You are an old man who thinks in terms of nations and peoples. There are no nations! There are no peoples! There are no Russians! There are no Arabs! There are no Third Worlds! There is no West! There is only one holistic system of systems, one vast and immune, inter-woven, interacting, multivariant, multinational dominion of dollars! Petrodollars, electrodollars, multidollars, reichmarks, rins, rubles, pounds and shekels! It is the international system of currency which determines the totality of life on this planet. That is the natural order of things today. That is the atomic, and subatomic and galactic structure of things today. And you have meddled with the primal forces of nature, and you will atone!"

He pauses for a moment—and speaks normally with a question to Beale,

Am I getting through to you, Mr. Beale?

You get up on your little twenty-one inch screen and howl about America and democracy. There is no America. There is no democracy. There is only IBM, and ITT, and AT and T, and DuPont, Dow, Union Carbide, and Exxon—those are the nations of the world today. What do you think the Russians talk about in their councils of state, Karl Marx? They get out their linear programming charts, statistical decision theories and minimax solutions and compute the price-cost probabilities of their transactions and investments just like we do. We no longer live in a world of nations and ideologies, Mr. Beale. The world is a college of corporations, inexorably determined by the immutable by-laws of business. The world is a business, Mr. Beale. It has been since man crawled out of the slime, and our children will live, Mr. Beale, to see that perfect world in which there's no war or famine, oppression or brutality. One vast and ecumenical holding company, for whom all men will work to serve a common profit, in which all men will hold a share of stock, all necessities provided, all anxieties tranquilized, all boredom amused. And I have chosen you to preach this evangel, Mr. Beale.

As the scene switches back to Beale's face, his eyes are wide open, as if he's just seen the Second Coming. After a moment of silence, Beale speaks.

"I have seen the face of God!"

Terrified, Beale is pressured and forced by Jensen to continue preaching about dehumanization and the death of democracy. He returns to the airwaves to preach Jensen's corporate truth, championing corporate rather than individual human rights. That night on the network news, following his on-air introduction, Beale starts reversing his previous ranting and concludes with this:

Because in the bottom of all our terrified souls, we know that democracy is a dying giant, a sick, dying, decaying political concept, writhing in its final pain. I don't mean that the United States is finished as a world power. The United States is the richest, the most powerful, the most advanced country in the world, light-years ahead of any other country. And I don't mean the Communists are gonna take over the world because the Communists are deader than we are. What is finished is the idea that this great country is dedicated to the freedom and flourishing of every individual in it. It's the individual that's finished. It's the single, solitary human being that's finished. It's every single one of you out there that's finished, because this is no longer a nation of independent individuals. It's a nation of some two hundred odd million transistorized, deodorized, whiter-than-white, steel-belted bodies, totally unnecessary as human beings and as replaceable as piston rods. Well, the time has come to say, "Is dehumanization such a bad word?" Because good or bad, that's what is so. The whole world is becoming humanoid, creatures that look human but aren't. The whole world, not just us. We're just the most advanced country, so we're getting there first. The whole world's people are becoming mass-produced, programmed, numbered, insensate things . . .

Interestingly, from that time forward, the ratings for the Howard Beale show begin to fall, now that he has alienated his viewing audience by preaching about the meaningless of their individual lives, and about "dying, democracy, and dehumanization." The corporation eventually hires hit men to kill Beale on air.

This is easily the most accurate description of socialism I have ever come across. When people lose sight of any meaningful purpose for their life as an individual and are only able to see it from the corporate-socialistic whole,

154

then that is the end of the individual. No one is more pro-business or *laissez faire* than I am in economic or political philosophy. But this view of the corporate world preached by Howard Beale is more accurate of the world we live in today than we would like to believe. It is the new type of corporate-socialism that we see, as opposed to the days of the Bolsheviks and the type envisioned by Karl Marx earlier.

What I see at work in the world today are two distinct different socialisms. First, is the more idealistic, which is the Karl Marx version, wherein individual human rights are the supposed focus. That is also the socialism sought by the 60s era hippie movement. Then there is this new type of corporate socialism (realistic versus idealistic), where those in power are honest enough to see and admit that the natural end of any socialism is a total corporate worldview where the individual becomes extinct and swallowed into the whole.

Both, however, eventually lead to communism, as pointed out by David Noebel in his book, *Understanding the Times,* wherein he describes at length the four major and distinct political and philosophical worldviews. What we face today, however, is that corporate-socialism will eventually transform into civil-socialism, then totalitarianism, because that is the natural ebb and flow of which Mr. Jensen spoke.

On the other hand, I must stick up for corporations—and really all business—to say that we are pushing them to the door of socialism by turning them into tax cash cows. A story on NBC news began by the announcer stating that a recent study of corporate America revealed that "they are not paying their share of taxes." He added that their failure to do so was ". . . legal, but is it fair?" First of all, says who? Who says they are not paying their fair share of taxes?

Once again, here is a hate-the-rich story that fails to tell the truth by omission. In the first place, corporations are owned by people—you and me. If I'm going to invest in stocks, then I want them to be profitable. When they make money, so do I. Secondly, when corporations do well, it stirs the economy and creates jobs, which benefits everyone, even those not holding stock in the company. Finally, when we tax various entities, like businesses, we're taxing ourselves. The reason is that, once again, to stay in business, the corporation must make a profit. When they are taxed, like any business they have to raise their prices for their products. Then you and I pay that tax for them in the form of a higher price. The fact is, there isn't a tax out there that you and I don't pay. As the saying goes, there's no such thing as a free ride.

But what we have here is another media-driven, liberal-socialist ruse that teaches us to hate the rich and business because—even though it's not true—somebody may be getting something we are not. In essence, we are being told that we're being cheated. So what do we do when we hear stories like this? What do we say? We say, "Well, the government should tax them more. Yeah, that's it. Tax them!" Unfortunately, this is the same old shell game of taxation to see this week under which shell will we find the most taxation, and it's exactly what they want us to say and feel. You and I pay every tax there is. If we scream for business to be taxed more, we just taxed ourselves and grew government one more time.

What is especially important to recognize going on today is how the liberal-socialists sell their wares as in the story above. They use Cain to do it. They use fear. As with

Cain, their fear is not having enough to sustain them in the future, and it leads to envy and strife.

Hate is what is propelling so many of the Muslim countries to turn against America. But hate almost always begins with envy. If you can't have it—whatever it is—and you view the world the way Cain does, you will eventually hate who has it. As stated earlier, it is the eternal story of the haves and the have-nots.

Another way socialism is sold to us is by using the poor as a battering ram to our wallets. No matter how much we dislike it, as Jesus told us, the poor will always be with us. No matter what system of government men may choose, no matter what method we devise to make it otherwise, we can never totally eliminate poverty. The closest we will ever come to doing it is when we begin to take the responsibility of charity on individually in our own families, with our own friends, and then with the strangers in our neighborhoods. The government makes a terrible nanny. One on one—that is the answer and the intention of our Father in heaven. As humans we are inherently lazy minded, self-centered, and the ultimate buck passers who will naturally defer to someone else to take care of the needs. When we succumb to that mode of living, we invite the path of bureaucratic government that always leads to tyranny.

Poverty does not come from a social stigma or a particular governmental system. Capitalism does not create poverty or a greater class disparity claimed by so many socialists. The truth is, poverty comes primarily from a mind-set that is opposite the fundamental requirement of faith. That is not to say that every poor person or family necessarily created his or her own situation or need. What it does mean is that, in God, all persons have their own individual maze wherein they must defeat the foes which are determined to keep them bound by that spirit—including poverty.

If we read His Word correctly, it is plain to see that our Father wants His people to prosper. Socialists teach us that the only true humbleness is being poor. They point to Scriptures taken out of context to convince us that unless we give away all our private wealth, there is no heaven for us. But it is just as plain to see that God does not set up "equality" among the population of the earth. Granted, there are—and will always be—social inequities about which man can do nothing.

Socialism can never solve poverty or inequity. The sales pitch is, with the kind of equality socialists envision each of us will drive a Mercedes. But the reality is that when incentive is killed, property is confiscated, and individuality is swallowed by the corporate, we will all be driving beat up old Chevy Vegas—or, worse, riding the public buses that, by then, will be equally run down.

I have long understood that mankind has a destiny. But that destiny is both individual and collective. And it is my belief that it is first individual before it can be collective. As I discuss at length in the next chapter, in many ways the primary difference between the Old and New Testaments in the Bible lies in the difference of that focus. In the Old Testament, God seems to deal with His children more as a group and as nations, with much of His dealings coming through those He had chosen for leadership.

In the New Testament, we learn of a Christ, the Son of God, who came to save all mankind, but as a *personal* Savior. The new emphasis was now on the individual. It is also the primary focus and basis for American government, unlike any government before. I believe that this single point is one of two of the most important factors in our nation's rise to unprecedented prosperity and power. Free marketeers see the power of the individual; socialists see the equity of the group. And each worldview is focused as in the following:

Capitalism
(Free-Market)

Focus is on:

- Individual
- Private Ownership

Socialism
(Total State Regulated & Owned)

Focus is on:

- The whole group
- Public Ownership

Our founders understood this key difference of governmental focus and established for us a nation whose primary governing foundation was seeded in self-government by individuals. They knew that any short- and long-term success of this great governing experiment was predicated on the ability of each person to live within the confines of moral virtue established in the Bible, each according to his own virtuous restraint and then each according to his own abilities and desires, tending to his own property. Socialists hate it when it's shown that our founding fathers tied our government together with the Bible. James Madison, architect of the Constitution, said it this way:

> We have staked the whole future of American civilization, not on the power of government; far from it. We have staked our future on the capacity of each and every one of us to control ourselves, to sustain ourselves according to the Ten Commandments of God.

Under our present form of government—at least that which was established in our founding era—the following was the hierarchal structure understood by the founding fathers:

God's governmental hierarchy:

GOD (Headship of Christ)   Power flows down

SELF government

FAMILY government

CHURCH government

CIVIL government   ↓

This was the way that, biblically, our founders envisioned all of it working correctly. And, this was the biblical structure they modeled our government after in a working sense. In this order, power and authority flows down from God, to the individual first, then the family, the church, and finally civil authority. It was their understanding (as Madison spoke of above) that civil government would be the least needed form of government for man, if the hierarchy here was adhered to.

True socialists—who are generally unbelievers—can only see the authority of Caesar. Therefore, what they and the Cains of today seek is a total reversal of this hierarchy to reach their goals. Thus, it would now look like this:

Man's governmental hierarchy:

CIVIL government

CHURCH government

FAMILY government

SELF government

GOD (Headship of Christ)

Power flows down ↓

In this hierarchy, which has been seen many times throughout history, the power flows down again and places God at the bottom of the power structure. This is certainly the way it was at the time of Christ under Caesar's rule. Notice, too, that it is important for the church to be just under civil government in authority but over the rest of the hierarchy. This is the way it was with King George and the Church of England when our founders made the decision to separate from Britain.

Certainly worth mentioning is the fact that throughout history, whenever God's hierarchy has been in place, the people bask in liberty. Whenever man's scenario is in place, the people are in bondage as were the Israelites under the Pharaoh. Further, the only time in the history of man that

God's hierarchy was understood and set as the foundation of governing structure was at America's founding. It is the express objective of the non-believers, in essence, to become God themselves. As quoted from the inscription in the first chapter, Caesar saw himself as God and claimed the throne unto himself. He declared that a man could only be saved through the state. Even in a democracy the same can be true, as legislatures can trample the rights of men just as easily as any dictator.

Put simply, the more godly the government, the more liberty the people will have. The less self-governing we are, the more civil government we will get and the suppression of liberty. The founders knew that the real job of government was to suppress those who would violate the rule of law. In addition, the question arose in discussions between the founders as to how you can make a government that was created to suppress, limit, and contain not do so in the marketplace. That is why they wrote the Tenth Amendment into the Bill of Rights, to specifically prohibit the federal government, especially, from getting into jurisdictions it didn't belong.

This is not a new battle we're in. It's always been going on. It is the age-old strife that asks who mankind will worship: Caesar or an omnipresent God. Or as Bob Dylan sang so many years ago, "You're gonna have to serve somebody, Well, it may be the Devil or it may be the Lord, But you're gonna have to serve somebody."

Even atheists are worshippers of man while they reject God.

Thinking back again to my time in the Marine Corps, it was easy to get up in the morning and have someone else tell me what to do. I didn't have to think too hard then. That is why we sometimes daydream of being kids again when life was easy and fun. But to be free men and women requires individual effort and a raising of the bar. I don't want to depict a bad image of the military, nor am I saying you don't have to think. You do, but it's much more routine and less about creativity, and more about drilling and discipline and training over and over again. As a lower enlisted man, you pretty much did what you were told until achieving some advancing rank, like corporal or sergeant.

I mentioned earlier that we don't hear the word socialism much anymore. I believe that is because those on the left—with the help of the leftist media—would really rather the word vanish from the lips of Americans. You won't be thinking about a misery quite the same if it doesn't have a name for it. And, misery loves company. As of this writing, liberal-socialists are now trying to rename liberalism, because of the bad connotation that it has been associated with it for so many years. So, today, the new word is "progressive." But, as it's said, a rose is still a rose by any other name.

Liberal-socialists cannot believe that their ideologies can't ever work. To do so would be an admission that there is a God. If there is no God, then equity is an achievable goal. Therefore, what some other socialist did that failed has no bearing on the next attempt. That is why I was skeptical when the media announced that communism was dead at the fall of the Soviet Union. It is not dead. And as long as the mind-set of Cain is present in the world, socialism will be alive and on the move.

In the end, the whole of the mission of the true liberal-socialist is to alleviate the inequity they see in the world, the unfairness. However, like Cain, their motive is not pure and outward, as they would have us believe. As with Cain, it is born of envy.

In the previous chapter, I discussed Margaret Sanger and the motivations behind her drive toward abortion and creating Planned Parenthood. To her, and the fellow socialists, the world is shrinking. If you watch the news and read much of newspapers, the mantra from the left that drives them to take America down the path of socialism is their innate fear that we are running out of everything. To them, all of our resources are in short supply—water, air, food, ground—everything. If you listen and look closely, you can see and feel the fear in what they are saying. This coming famine and shortage of resources they envision is not only based on faulty science and shaky theory, but history proves that it isn't so.

Perhaps the Marine Corps boot camp is a pretty good view of life in general. The night we checked into boot camp, as our heads were shaved, our civies packed up and shipped home, we all became very equal. After that, what happened to us was up to the individual—but always keeping our buddies in mind.

I am not an anarchist. I truly understand the necessity of civil order and government. I remember a week I spent in Taipei decades ago when there were no traffic lights or traffic cops at intersections. Pedestrians, cars, buses, and bicycles would all come to an intersection at the same time and scream, honk horns, and fight their way through. There is a necessary order that government brings to society.

In the end, I think what the liberal-socialists are really after is to keep everyone stuck at the starting gate.

PART TWO

Whatever else history may say about me when I'm gone, I hope it will record that I appealed to your best hopes, not your worst fears; to your confidence rather than your doubts. My dream is that you will travel the road ahead with liberty's lamp guiding your steps and opportunity's arm steadying your way.

—President Ronald Reagan

The Marketeers

I have little interest in streamlining government or making it more efficient for I mean to reduce its size. I do not undertake to promote welfare for I propose to extend freedom. My aim is not to pass laws, but to repeal them. It is not to inaugurate new programs, but to cancel old ones that do violence to the Constitution, or that have failed in their purpose, or that impose on the people an unwarranted financial burden.

—Barry Goldwater

I start up the parking ramp and into the garage, finding a parking spot as close to the mall entrance as I can. This is Bellevue Square in Bellevue, Washington, the premier shopping center in the northwest. As I cross the skywalk and enter through the second floor doors, it is all very familiar to me. I entered these doors on a daily basis many years before while working for Kemper Freeman, Jr., serving as director of marketing for the center. I had worked for Kemper previously during the late 1970s managing his radio stations in Spokane.

Looking for America

This morning, I'm on my way to have breakfast with Kemper. The garage is all but empty at this early hour. It reminds me of the fact that it takes about sixty-thousand customers a day to make this place work. What guarantee is there that they will show up again tomorrow or the next day, I wonder, as I cross the street to the restaurant?

I smile as I pass a store on my left that I used to deliberately avoid when coming to work in the mornings. The merchant in this store at that time was as difficult as any I ever had to contend with. Although he and his wife were good people, from the day he opened his unique pewter gift shop in Bellevue Square, Jim began to frown. Many times I walked by his second level store, and saw him standing outside with his arms crossed, a scowl on his face, almost daring someone to come into his store. He was so sure that he wasn't going to get any customer traffic and business that he seemed determined to make it so. It was not unusual for me to get calls on a daily basis from Jim giving me the count on people passing his store. "Where are the customers, Doug?" He would snarl into the phone. He was a good man, but there was something that kept him blinded from the opportunity before him.

As marketing director of the new Bellevue Square in the early 1980s, it was my job to coordinate the advertising and promotional needs of the individual stores with that of the shopping center as a whole. At the time—and to this day—Bellevue Square is one of the leading centers in the nation, oftentimes ranking in the top ten in terms of dollars-per-square-foot sales. Of all the things in my career, I learned more from this job about free-enterprise, capitalism, entrepreneurialism, and the true American spirit than from any other.

The Marketeers

First to arrive at *Eques,* I take my seat in the little cove area often reserved for Kemper. The elegance of the surroundings of this restaurant is echoed in the richness and quality of the entire Bellevue Place and Bellevue Square. In Spokane, we have NorthTown Mall. It is nice, but the difference between its construction in appearance, and that of these Bellevue centers, is the difference between a folding lawn chair and a finely crafted wing-back.

"Heeeey, Doug." Kemper arrives and greets me in his trademark fashion. He may be a wealthy and powerful man, but Kemper Freeman is as down to earth as anyone you will ever meet. He comes from the old school that says that your word is as good as a contract. Having worked for him for eight years, I believe he is the most honest man I've ever known in business. He works at least, if not more hours, than those he ever asks any of his employees to do.

"Had that motorcycle out lately?" Kemper asks. Kemper loves to work hard. But he loves to play hard, too. And any business meeting with Kemper usually never gets underway until a half-hour or so after discussing the latest technology on the market or the newest Harley motorcycle—the things he connects with real life. He is one of the most personable people you will ever meet.

At any time in Bellevue Square, there are as many as fifteen to twenty women's apparel stores, ten-plus men's apparel stores, fifteen or so jewelry stores, ten to fifteen eating establishments, several each of candy stores, cookies, art, kitchenware, and any number of gift stores—not to mention three major department stores. Viewing from the larger picture, as marketing director, it was easy to see a stark difference between those who were successful and those who weren't, and why that was so.

Looking back now, I realized Cain was here, too. And, although I didn't recognize it at the time, this is where I first saw him in everyday life at work. In retrospect, he was easy to spot in a place like this where you almost have to work hard to be unsuccessful. Bellevue boasts the highest per capita income level of any city in the state and one of the highest in the nation. Out of ten or so jewelry stores, for example, there might be one or two who just can't seem to make it, regardless of their location or other variables. Overtime, I began to see how the Cain factor has influenced some of these merchants' outlooks and, thus, the outcomes of their ventures.

For over fifty years Bellevue Square has been home to one of the largest juried art fairs in the country. Each summer—and always the last full weekend of July—two hundred artists, selected by art experts, gather in their booths in the parking areas of the Square to show and sell the finest selection of art, representing the finest craftsmen in the country. It is always held this particular weekend—the three days of least likely rainfall in a region of year-round plentiful precipitation. It has only rained once or twice in that entire fifty years.

The annual Bellevue Arts and Crafts Fair was always one of the most contentious times with the merchants who didn't appreciate the fact that the fair had a tendency to keep the nearly half-million visitors outside of the mall, nor the fact that it used up all of the parking. In addition, most of the merchants were resolved that those coming to the mall for the fair were there to spend money on art, not in the mall stores. With that, I realized their decision had already been made: they weren't going to have any business; therefore, why try?

On the surface, they had every right to be concerned. However, during the monthly merchant breakfast meetings, we used to always try to remind them that they needed to think creatively to find ways to invite these people inside the mall. Some did, some didn't. But almost always, those who didn't try I can now link back to the Cain factor.

Faith allows creativity, where fear does not. Faith always finds a new idea to make things better, to grow and multiply. In a word, faith is creation. Fear holds back, shrinks into bitterness and stifles new ideas. Lost in envy and strife, fear ultimately produces failure and, in Cain's case, manifested itself into hate and finally murder. Faith loves and believes in the future, where fear covets and can only see the reality that exists in the present.

The secret to the success of capitalism and free enterprise is faith.

The secret to the failure of socialism and its children is fear.

These are the two primary distinct world views that shape our world. They have been here from the beginning. Fear and faith are as opposite as the light and darkness of this world. They are the true political antagonists, yet they are brothers.

Abel was successful and received favor from the Lord because he gave his best. Abel knew that he could offer the first and best of his labor, without worry of failure. Ultimately, Abel knew where his sustenance came from, and by faith he knew it would always be there, so he invested in it. His faith allowed him to see his reward.

Cain was afraid and only gave the minimum. He was only able to see what he had in the present. His fear blinded him and grew into envy, anger, and eventually hate.

In the book of Hebrews the author wrote, "By faith Abel offered to God a more excellent sacrifice than Cain." Faith was the missing link that caused Cain's failure and inability to strive for excellence. It is the missing element in socialism and communism that resulted in the collapse of the former Soviet empire and other socialist experiments. It is the missing element in the mind of the liberal-socialist of today and the reason for the discontent in political debates of our time. But faith is the prime factor in the success of capitalism and free enterprise as a governing concept. And its ongoing retreat in America today warns of impending tyranny.

"Kemper, do you remember that conversation between your dad and the merchant about the arts and crafts fair?" He did.

Before he passed on in 1982, Kemper Freeman, Sr., had once told me of one merchant who used to come to him every year complaining about the arts and crafts fair, and the fact that it hurt his business because people weren't coming into his store. In his view, people came strictly to shop the arts and craft exhibits and weren't interested in visiting the regular Square merchants. In those days, the old strip center had not yet been replaced by the modern mall of Bellevue Square of today, so the stores lined the parking area and each business was accessed from the street.

Finally, in one more tempered exchange, Kemper, Sr., finally told this merchant that, since this weekend also tends to be one of the warmest of the year, to try putting up a Kool-Aid® stand in the back of his store with a sign out front that read: "FREE KOOL-AID®." The merchant did this. People flocked in and had to weave their way between racks of clothing to get to the Kool-Aid®. He ended up having one of the biggest dollar-sales days of his year.

As I recalled the story, Kemper and I both laughed.

Faith cries out to innovation. It believes that even failure can be transformed into success, as long as you get one more shot at it. The key to the success of opportunity has always been faith. Fear cannot see opportunity, therefore it merely prophesies failure and, in the end, guarantees disappointment.

A recent book and movie entitled *Seabiscuit* is a sterling example of the foundation of true American spirit. This particular event probably had more to do with causing the rekindling of hope out of the ashes of the Depression than did any program from Roosevelt's New Deal. It is a true story about one of the most famous race horses that, after several owners had written him off as a loser, was purchased by a novice and his newly hired trainer. In the end, in a two-horse race, Seabiscuit, was pitted against the finest thoroughbred racing horse in America. As a two-to-one underdog, he won big. It sparked a revival in the American spirit in the 1930s, especially to Americans who were as depressed as the economy. Seabiscuit championed opportunity and gave hope to people when there was none to be found. The story exemplifies the true grit of the American psyche. At one point in the story, Seabiscuit's jockey says to another who will be taking his place in a race, "It's not in his feet." Pointing to his chest he says, "Its here—in his heart."

It was the faith employed in the rhetoric of his owner that sparked an old, but familiar trait of the great American spirit that forged this nation. The story is really about what the faith of one man, the horse's owner, did to change the lives of so many other people.

Faith is strength of heart where fear is faint of heart. Placed against fear, faith will always rally and find its way to victory. Faith always produces hope.

I've often watched in the media as all over America those of the mind of Cain attack the great visionaries, like the Freeman family of Bellevue. It's always the same story: he's a developer, an industrialist who is ravaging the countryside, pillaging the community for his own benefit. People like him, they say, are causing the depletion of the ozone layer, fossil fuels, and using up critical space by creating more and more commerce and offspring. These naysayers are the Chicken Littles of our day who run about proclaiming that the sky is falling. The contagious fear that follows them allows our legislatures to pile on more and more laws to assuage unwarranted fear often based on faulty science. This is what is leading us down the old familiar road to tyranny.

Bellevue Square today is no longer a center unto itself. The Freeman family has now expanded its development to another block, "Bellevue Place," and now the newly developed "Lincoln Square" across the street. It has grown into a destination shopping extravaganza called "The Bellevue Collection," attracting people from all over the northwest and British Columbia. The center now employs more than 7,500 people who make their livelihood in this place of their choosing. The grounds are finely groomed, and more than seventy thousand people a day want to come here. Wealth is created here as commerce thrives and faith abounds. The center has grown because faith always produces progress and fills a need. That is the heart of free-market thinking and what improves the standard of living for everyone.

Cain would have sided with naysayers of today. The truth is, however, it really has nothing to do with the environment, nor the space, the fuel, or the growth. It is simply the same old story of Cain. It is the long-running hatred of the have-nots toward those who have. They hate the Freemans and all people who create commerce because, if successful, the visionaries of today—those who are willing to make the sacrifice—are richly rewarded for having the faith to take the risk and make the investment. The Freemans are the Abels of our day. I so wish we could recognize that again.

Bellevue's Freeman family is a prime example of the kind of entrepreneurial, can-do spirit reminiscent of Abel and the primary ingredient in the long-standing success of this country. But he is becoming a dying breed. Kemper Freeman, Jr., became a mentor of mine because I saw in him the embodiment of vision and faith, although I was slow to recognize it at the time of our first meeting nearly thirty years ago. He took after his father in the same way that Kemper, Sr., must have also taken after his father, Miller Freeman. They could always see the silver lining in the dark clouds. That is the secret of their success.

Miller Freeman was instrumental in getting the Lake Washington floating bridge constructed in 1940—the bridge connecting the east side of Lake Washington to the city of Seattle. Without the bridge, and later constructed second bridge, The Evergreen Point Bridge, Bellevue would have never grown to its standing today. In fact, Miller Freeman and Kemper, Sr., paid the very first and last toll on the first bridge connecting two generations. With the help of a King County Councilman, Scott Wallace, Kemper, Sr., was instrumental in bringing about construction of the Evergreen Point floating bridge in the early 1960s, which then contributed even more to the growth and vitality of this region. He and Kemper, Jr., paid the first and last toll on this bridge connecting to the next generation.

Kemper Freeman, Sr., always saw the big picture. I remember after first starting my job at Bellevue Square how I would often go into his office in the early morning and have a cup of coffee with him. It wasn't the office I expected of a man of his caliber. An old military surplus-style metal desk was pushed up against a stark wall in the corner of the room. A metal chair sat to the side and I would sit.

"What do you think of your job?" Senior asked one day a few months after I started.

"I feel like a plate-spinner in a circus." I replied after a moment of thought. Senior laughed and nodded.

A year and a half later I was ushered into his bedroom to pay my final respects, as Senior would pass away just a few hours later. He could barely speak, and I wasn't sure he even recognized me at first. After saying a few words to him for a minute or two, I turned to leave and at the door I heard his voice softly, but distinctly,

"Keep those plates in the air."

Kemper Freeman, Sr., and now his son, understood what makes the world go around. And it was a big chance, to say the least, that Senior took to build the original strip center in the middle of strawberry fields in 1946 in what is now downtown Bellevue. Even the *Seattle Times* featured a huge, nearly two-inch-tall headline on the front of the paper one day that read "FREEMANS' FOLLIES," ridiculing them for their venture.

In those days there existed, too, an extreme jealousy and fear of the east side of Lake Washington becoming anything. In fact, it was Moss Bay—Kirkland today—that was supposed to be the real hub once the east side came to life. I remember Senior used to talk about the history of Bellevue Square and the east side often during the morning coffees.

There was no guarantee that the Freemans would succeed in their venture, or "folly" as the paper saw it.

"Do you know when I knew we were going to make it?" Senior asked me once.

"No, when?"

"In 1952, when Kirkland put in parking meters."

To this day, there are still no parking meters in Bellevue, which has a lot to do with why it ranks so high among American cities in retail sales and growth. And of course, parking is always free at Bellevue Square. But a look into local history reveals that the Cain factor has also been ever present in trying to stop progress here in Bellevue and remains so today, if not more so. It is especially prevalent within today's media culture, as they tend to look for the negative rather than the positive. Watching the city planning department of Bellevue over the past twenty-five years is a story of unprecedented growth of bureaucracy, whose vantage has become one of the socialistic methods of stopping growth, stifling business, and containing expansion. As stated in an earlier chapter, those are the hallmarks of socialism.

City planners are taught in college today to think like socialists. Thus, they plan for stoppage, not for expansion. They plan with all public transit in mind. You see, if we taught planners that liberty was the most important principle, they would plan with that in mind, rather than socialism. Or if they didn't believe the taxpayers had bottomless pockets, they would be honest enough to admit that mass transit schemes that cost countless billions, but move few people, are simply inefficient monuments to socialism and that's all. Those who run our colleges and universities, who for the most part are socialists, will not allow this to happen because it flies in the face of the Marxist socialistic-equality they seek to achieve.

In my hometown of Spokane, parking meters have been present since the 1930s. The original purpose of meters was to achieve what was known as "turns" in business, limiting how much time each car would be parked outside a particular business, so that another patron could visit. It was a necessity in the early days of retailing in downtown. But today in Spokane, revenues from parking meters now make up better than a million dollars in the city's operating budget, and now are a necessity for government.

One time, when attending a reception, I was talking to a city councilwoman about how things were done in Bellevue. She had no idea that any major town or city didn't have parking meters. I told her that much of the success of Bellevue as a retailing center was due to that fact. Over the past couple of decades, with the influx of various suburban shopping centers, the central business district of downtown Spokane has been dying because of outside competition where parking was free and easy. I told this councilwoman that what needs to happen is to do away with the meters, purchase a couple of lots to build ample free parking, and institute a few other cosmetic changes, such as eliminating some of the thoroughfare streets and turn them into pedestrian corridors. Then it will be inviting once again for people to come downtown instead of going elsewhere. She liked what I had to say, but really sparked up when I told her that sales revenue increases from the influx of people coming back would more than make up the meter deficit in the budget.

But socialism hates competition. It takes too much work and offers no guarantees. Bureaucrats think a lot like Cain. They can only see the bird in the hand. For some reason they can't seem to understand how business is good for government and can naturally increase their revenues without deliberately and forcefully picking the pockets of the taxpayers. But again, that takes faith.

The truth is free-market capitalism should be the eighth wonder of the world. It has been the primary economic governing system responsible for creating the wealthiest nation in all of history. The ninth wonder of the world would then have to be the prosperity capitalism has provided to America over the past two-hundred-plus years, not to mention how that has benefited most of the world.

The ongoing murmuring about the disparity between the rich and poor negates the fact that as the rich get richer, the poorer move up the scale also, to the point now where our poor are richer than the rich of the majority of foreign countries. Imagine living in England in the 1500s. Even the poorest of America would live better than the kings in that day. Better health care, food products, transportation, and endless choices of entertainment—all better than any king ever dreamed of by any royalty of old. VCRs, DVD players, incredible sound systems, cable and satellite television, washers and dryers, humidifiers, personal automobiles, computers, airplanes—an endless list of wonders of creation, creation born out of the desire to make life better and receive an achiever's reward. That is what America is about.

One of the obvious things we see when we stand back and look closely is that no matter what wars have taken place, no matter what natural disasters have occurred, life keeps on increasing on this planet—in every form. While liberal-socialists cringe at the thought, it is the way of God. He has always been a multiplier. He constantly challenged the Israelites in the Old Testament to test Him, to see if He wouldn't pour out wealth and blessings on them.

Through faith, death is overcome by life. Darkness is overcome by light. Lies are overcome by truth. Lack is overcome by increase. And fear is always overcome by faith. What could be a clearer picture of the Father? It is the real picture of how freedom began in America.

The God of the Old Testament—and the God of today— is a God of expansion, increase, and growth. His very first command to Adam and Eve was to go increase and fill all the earth. And it is because of those who have followed this instruction by faith that we can today feed an entire world without fear of famine. There are those who are willing to live by faith, rather than by fear.

Several years ago, teaching a church civics class, I used the following Bible story to simply paint a picture of how God views wealth and economy. It is story enveloped in faith and is a challenge to each of us as Americans to see as He does—so that we might see why we have done so well. This story and principle embodies the whole reason for our long-standing overall prosperity to date. In the story, Jesus gives us a clear picture of God's primary economic principle. Jesus was giving a sermon on a hillside. It was getting late in the evening, the crowd was very hungry and getting rowdy. His disciples had come out of fear and said to Him in Matthew 14:15–23:

> "This is a deserted place, and the hour is already late. Send the multitudes away, that they may go into the villages and buy themselves food." But Jesus said to them, "They do not need to go away. You give them something to eat." And they said to Him, "We have here only five loaves and two fish." He said, "Bring them here to Me."

The Marketeers

Then He commanded the multitudes to sit down on the grass. And He took the five loaves and the two fish, and looking up to heaven, He blessed and broke and gave the loaves to the disciples; and the disciples gave to the multitudes. So they all ate and were filled, and they took up twelve baskets full of the fragments that remained. Now those who had eaten were about five thousand men, besides women and children.

This single Bible story probably describes God as a God of increase more than any other Scripture, of which there are many. Interestingly, after feeding the thousands present (approximately 12–14 thousand) there was bread and fish left over. God doesn't just supply us with our needs, but more than we need, and this is the way it is in America today. We have far more than we need. Only a person seeing through the eyes of faith can understand this principle. Until that moment, the apostles still did not see this. On the hill that evening, until Jesus illuminated the apostles, they still saw as Cain did, from a fear-based perspective.

It is important to look and see as the socialist does—and as Cain saw. Imagine that there is no God in heaven, no plan, that we are just spinning off into the universe destined to turn into a dead and dying planet of desolation. Through the eyes of man, the future is bleak. He sees, as Cain did, that his share of the pie is shrinking. Every newborn child means one more mouth to feed, one more addition instead of subtraction of another consumer of the already dwindling resources. He sees his slice of the pie shrinking evermore and his possessions depleting—as did Margaret Sanger. In his refusal to acknowledge the God of creation, this is his view of the pie:

The pie in man's economy

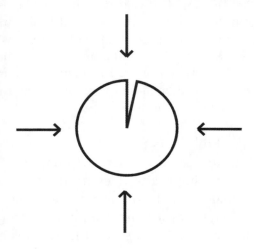

- **Always shrinking resources (Usage-depletion)**
- **Slices always grow thinner (population growth)**

Either that miracle happened that night on the hill—or it didn't. This is the crisis of faith for each of us today, right here in this story. If it didn't, then as far as I'm concerned, the rest of the book is a lie. But it did, and only in faith can we see it or understand that it truly is the foundation of our governing system. I don't know what happened that evening on that hillside. Perhaps a Chicken Delight truck backed up and opened its doors or maybe 125 Domino Pizza delivery vans showed up at that moment—I don't know. But one thing I do know is that those people's hunger was filled that evening. And it is a fact that can be only seen through the eyes of faith. It is an understanding that life is about multiplication, increase, and expansion. And the key, once again, is faith. With that faith in place, then we can understand God's view of the pie and why we are the richest nation the world has ever known.

The pie in God's economy

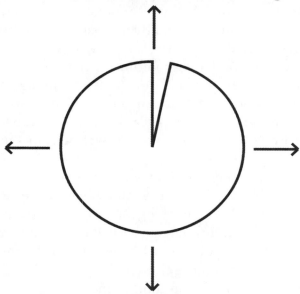

- **Always expanding, growing outward.**
- **Slices always grow larger from expansion (elongating)**

In this illustration, we can envision that as the pie expands, even if our slice becomes thinner, it become elongated; therefore, it still gains. In people terms, it means that as the population grows, as the pie grows, everyone's slices still get larger. How else do you account for an expanding economy that now delivers prosperity to nearly three-hundred million people—just in this country—with even our poor far better off than any other time in history? The economy had to expand and multiply to accomplish this.

And that is the heart and soul of the free-marketeer's view of the pie, life in general, and the marketplace.

We often have a nasty habit of viewing miracles as only happening in biblical times or only if tied to some kind of sci-fi channel on TV. But I've found that miracles take place every day and we miss them because we always end up giving the credit to man, rather than to God. Do you see it? The Great Conductor coordinates the timing of every event so that they coincide in His perfect timing, causing a multiple trillion events to happen in perfect harmony at exactly the right time and place. We miss it because we're almost always looking through the eyes of Cain—or we're off watching prime-time TV.

There is another factor in the success of America that is paramount. And it is tied to the difference in how the liberal-socialist views governing the world and how the free-marketeer views it. In a larger sense, it is also connected to a biblical thesis of mine, but I believe it is where we're at today in America and the church.

When I step back and look at the Bible as a whole, I see a God of the Old Testament who had a much more corporate governing structure than He did when He came in His Son. Mostly, in the Old Testament, God chose leaders and seemingly dealt with individual people through them or what we would call in the military, a strict chain of command. In the Marine Corps, for example, you could not go straight to the top, but had to go through the "chain of command," always going through the person above you and on up the ladder. In some cases, you could "request mast," which meant you could ask to talk to the man on top. But generally, it was frowned on unless you had a very important reason. There was good reason for the rule, which was efficiency of time for one.

In the New Testament, it is clear that Christ came to save the individual. He came as a "personal savior." That is where His focus was the entire time of His ministry and how we always refer to Him. Jesus saw it clearly as His Father did: the corporate can be no stronger than the weakest of the individual members. The strength of the whole body is as strong or weak as the overall condition of its individual parts. Any excellence achieved as a whole can only be as good as the excellence achieved by each individual. Our founders understood this principle in bringing forth our national principles. It is even inscribed on our currency: *E Pluribus Unum;* out of many, one. Do you see it?

The focus of society always must be on preserving the rights of the individual first, as the founders understood and as they established. If you violate the rights of one, then you have violated the whole. And government by its very nature has to dole out justice equally, which then dictates that the law or legal infringement on one applies to all. Nations don't have rights; individual people do.

Contrary to what the media and present day *edu-crats* are saying, America has become the most prosperous and plentiful nation in history because of the faith of our founders and so many who followed—and their understanding of these principles. The God of Abraham wants to multiply for us, both individually in our lives, as well as in our nation. All we are required to do is give Him the faith of Abel.

Looking for America

Attention needs to be paid to those who are constantly bashing free markets and to those legislators who are continually trying to find ways, via regulation, to tweak it, improve it as they see it. They're making it worse. Things have gotten so bad over the years in Communist China that its leaders began adding free-market capitalism to its socialism to make things better. Think they are learning here? Socialists always try to improve capitalism by adding components of socialism to it, regulating it to look out for consumers, all the while it gets worse. Perhaps that is because for many of them that is what they have in mind. Why is it that so many socialist countries try to mimic what we do when it comes to economics, but then fail? What is it that we do that they don't have or do? It's on our money—In God we trust. Trust means faith.

I always see so many examples where, left alone, the marketplace can accomplish wondrous things without the aid of do-gooder liberal-socialists. A case in point is the fast-food industry, and McDonalds in particular, who taught us all to clean up after ourselves without any government regulation having to be passed. It's good for them, and it's good for us as consumers. It costs them less if we get up and take our tray to the trash container and put the tray on top. In turn, that allows us a lower price for our meal. Others who do not wish to clean up after themselves can frequent other restaurants if they wish.

Actually, I had a friend once who joked about the advertising campaign that McDonald's ran all during this time while learning to clean up when we were finished eating. This was during the 1970s when McDonald's boasted "We Do It All For You." My friend said, "Geezzz, I have go order for myself, carry my food to the table, then clean up after myself. And they say they do it all for me?" We laughed.

But he ate there just the same and appreciated it for what it was.

Like Cain, socialists still can't tolerate what they see as inequities. To the liberal-socialist, in order to level or equal things, they must bring the highest to the lowest and excellence to mediocrity by removing the reward paid to achievement. However, that is really just an empty promise. History shows that those who run the show under socialism always elevate themselves to a higher way of living.

Certainly, a very limited amount of socialism has to be present in any economic governing system for mankind. Our founders understood this and spent a great deal of time discussing it during the constitutional convention of 1787. For example, our national defense is dependent upon all of us paying an amount of tax needed to fund the military. That is socialism, when we all pay a tax to provide one universal service needed by everyone: providing for the common defense.

"Kemper, I was recalling how a few people used to think that Bellevue Square was where only the high-class went to shop."

"Well, if we're going to have an image, I'd rather it be that than an image of low-class."

The success of free-market capitalism depends on the freedom of the individual to be able to create desired services and products in an uninhibited marketplace, to be the best they can be, offer the best product they can make or service they can provide—and then reap the personal rewards that come from the patronage for that product or service. If that potential reward is not present, the incentive to create diminishes and becomes low-class.

It bothers me when I hear negative comments about how politics is ruled by economics. To me, this is the way it should be. When the economic system is going to be altered and harmed by a proposed statute, it will hurt everyone. Free marketers understand this and want to curb it. Socialists understand it too, but they want to pass it. And from a taxing standpoint, this is the tool they use to tear down the better-off.

No system devised by man is a perfect system—but no system has served mankind better or improved the lives of countless millions more than free-market capitalism has done. But if we keep on riddling it with excessive regulations we will be just shooting the goose that lays the golden egg.

Once again, when free-market economics are coupled with faith they are an unbeatable combination. What Cain was really afraid of was that he wouldn't have enough. That was what kept him from giving the Lord his best. This is what the socialist is afraid of, running out of everything, as I discussed in chapter four. That is what the socialists see today when they see the world from the viewpoint of resources.

What would a robust economy really be like; how prosperous could we really be if we had more of our tax dollars left at home for us to spend and inject back into the economy? Would that not create more industry and jobs by creating demand? Would that not create private jobs for those displaced then out of government jobs? The reason why this cannot be in the mind of a socialist is, again, because it has only the guarantee of faith. They demand an equal slice through the guarantee of division of all fruits of labor. And they work very hard to get people to believe that the fruits end up only in the hands of the rich.

In the mid 1980s, I had the opportunity to serve for six years as general manager of the Washington State Dairy Commission, which is more commonly known as the Dairy Farmers of Washington. The commission, like many others in the state, are what is considered a quasi-state agency to serve a specific private industry, as requested by those industries. Commissions are created by the legislature, for the purpose of marketing their particular farming group, in our case, milk and dairy products.

When I was hired by the board of directors, I was told that they were looking for a fresh marketing perspective, that they wanted to break the mold and find new answers to increase sales of the state's dairy products. What I found was an industry deeply entrenched in old ways of doing things and in bed with the federal and state government—so much so, it had become very socialistic and really could not do things in a free-market fashion that would ever benefit them as farmers in the long haul. So, I told them exactly that. With about half the board, that did not sit well.

At the time, Washington State ranked tenth in the nation in dairy product production, yet was by far the number one seller of product to the federal government by its largest dairy co-op, Darigold. Wisconsin out-produced us by about ten to one, and California by about five to one, yet our state shipped more than both of them to the feds each year, under the federal dairy surplus program.

Co-authors Michael McMenamin and Walter McNamara's book, *Milking the Public*, details how this industry first became involved in federal support programs and how it has hurt dairy families, especially, but also the public through high milk prices. This high pricing in turn just keeps the industry from doing as well as they could. Although the dairy price support program had some rationale for its beginning a hundred years ago—namely the perishable aspect of dairy products and timeliness to market—it has far out-lived its purpose with the many ways product can be stored today. *Milking the Public* shows clearly that the dairy industry support program now is a puppet of government bureaucrats who need jobs and politicians who need campaign contributions. Many people may still remember the scandalous dairy lobby of the mid 1960s and into the Carter White House years, which had become the mainstay of doing business at the time.

Some of the large co-ops that exist dabble in marketing and advertising, but really do very little to market their product outside of direct sales to the federal government. In our state, Darigold is a prime example and the cooperative who sells the state's surplus dairy product to the feds. Compared to other companies its size, Darigold's advertising expenditures were pitiful.

Even now, I shake my head when I go into a grocery store in Washington and compare Darigold's prices with that of other name brands. For example, the other day I found Darigold selling their Half n' half for $2.58 per quart, which seems to be their regular everyday price at this time. Next to it on the same shelf was Western Family brand at $1.88 per quart. That is seventy cents less than Darigold's everyday price. And, Western Family buys their milk wholesale from the Darigold farmer co-op! What is even more peculiar is that out-of-state companies, like Oregon's Tilamook, well-known for superior quality, or Wisconsin's Land O' Lakes, can ship all the way here, and their prices are almost always priced under Darigold's product, or are at least very competitive.

While this seems strange to anyone in a very competitive business, it's not when you consider that Darigold had a protected market by being able to sell all they wanted to the federal government. Where is the incentive to market for them?

When I first asked this question to a Darigold sales executive one time, his answer was that people loved the Darigold product by name, and they had about a thirty percent market share, so they could demand the price. But the fact is, I found the company knew almost nothing about marketing and truly building name brand. Why should they care if people are gullible enough to pay $2.58 per quart for Half n' Half? If the customer doesn't buy it, no matter—Darigold can just turn it into powdered milk and cheese and give it to the feds.

I never worked for finer people than dairy families. Many are second and third generation, salt-of-the-earth people. But, in my opinion, they have been duped so long that they now live in the same fear of changing to a way of doing business that would require faith—and some hard work for companies like Darigold. But I also believe that the average farmer would be better off if he wasn't joined at the hip to a federal support program that is nothing but socialism parading as free-market. There were some dairy farmers that were horrible managers, who were being paid exactly the same for their product as other great managers. This will never change until they make the switch to faith and kick the feds out. At the end of the day, we're now seeing the coming extinction of the local dairy in favor of huge dairy milking complexes. I believe this wouldn't happen if the federal government was the one becoming extinct in the dairy industry. As for Darigold and others like them, they would never last a year in the private sector where the marketplace decides, as it should, the proper price and quality of a product.

The Dairy Commission style of marketing stands in stark contrast to the marketing and advertising world of Bellevue Square and highly creative free-marketeer competitors like them. I can't help but think of the comparison between the dairy industry that markets the whole as one entity allowing the bad manager, and a shopping center that houses many parts who compete with each other, eventually driving the bad manager out—which, in the end, improves the center for everyone.

Cain wanted a guarantee. Only with that will he give his best. But for a free-marketeer, there is no guarantee—there is only hope. And hope is produced only through faith. And Abel was rewarded for his.

I still remember when VHS players were released into the market in the late 70s and early 80s and the cries coming from Hollywood about how this would spell the end to moviegoers. Yet, it has only increased by leaps and bounds. The marketplace can take care of itself.

There is inherent risk in freedom. But today, a lot of Americans have come to mistakenly believe that it's government's job to take the risk out of life. We see it playing out in every corner of American society today. Civil litigation is chock full of suits beyond the scope of civil authority. Many are warranted; many others simply require the litigants to just grow up.

Another example is our legislation to take the risk out of the marketplace. Once again, we're trying to get government to do what we refuse to trust God for. Free enterprise and the American free-market system is not just a choice. It's the choice that most closely reflects the heart and personality of God—a choice our founders recognized. We cannot worship faith and fear at the same time. We cannot worship God and Caesar side by side.

General George S. Patton captured the essence of American free-enterprise in his famous speech from his movie *Patton*. His latest biography by Stanley P. Hirshon confirms that this speech did take place several times in front of several military units. Said Patton, "America loves a winner, and will not tolerate a loser." What Patton saw was the true spirit of America and the secret of our success on the battlefield, or in the marketplace.

Abel was a winner. Cain was the loser.

To the liberal-socialist, in order to level or equal things, they must bring down the winner to the level of the loser—excellence to mediocrity—and remove the reward that is reserved for achievement. Desire for equality, however, is really just a claim by the liberal-socialist. The major difference between free-market capitalism and socialism is that free market means choice, socialism means force.

The reason why the free-market has worked so well in America is not because we were a Christian nation by label, but because we've lived by the principles of Christianity of which the primary characteristic is faith. In other words, the system that we know as capitalism is a faith-based system. So, while capitalism is inherently risky, when you couple risk with faith, you inevitably get prosperity. Faith requires that you rise up, even out of the ash heap of failure again and again and assault the hill one more time. And for good measure, we've always included the golden rule. We're not a prosperous nation because we proclaim to be a Christian nation, but because we have inherently adopted the faith-based view of life and government.

Another primary characteristic of the Christian faith is serving. Jesus said in Matthew 20:27-28: "And whosoever shall be chief among you, let him be your servant." He went on: "I came not to be served, but to serve and give my life as a ransom for many." It is this principle in action that for over two hundred years has made this country the most prosperous the world has ever seen. There is a natural law that says when you serve, you will be rewarded.

On a trip to Mexico a few years ago, I was struck by one major difference between our two countries. That difference is service. Mexico depends on a vibrant tourist season to prop up its sagging economy, but its service to visitors is anything but accommodating. We were reluctant to tip at all in most cases, and when we did, we did so minimally, more out of sympathy for the plight of the disadvantaged people than for exceptional service.

In fact, some of the service was exceptionally bad, especially when compared to trips to Hawaii or other tropical resort destinations. Lying by the pool, more often than not we had to get up and go to the bar ourselves for beverages. In fact, our first evening in Mexico we guessed as to how much money was being lost due to the lack of attentiveness by servers, not just in tips, but in potential revenue to the establishment.

I don't want to sound uppity here; the Mexican people are a wonderful, lovely people and we could all learn a lesson from their humbleness. But I'm not writing about the wholesomeness of a people but, instead, to remind us of what I've always believed was the prime ingredient of America's success and prosperity. And that ingredient is serving!

The Marketeers

Serving comes in many forms, from pampering hotel guests with beverages by the pool to the resourcefulness that invents products and meets consumer needs. Serving competes and meets challenges. It always seeks new heights and a greater excellence. America's success since its birth is due primarily to an economic system that rewards those who serve. It is interesting that when our founding fathers separated from the British crown, they chose a more pure free enterprise approach governmentally—in a limited form and scope. They believed people might reach their individual potential (pursuit of happiness) more freely with as little interference as possible.

As Director of Marketing for the new Bellevue Square in the early 1980s, I learned a great deal from watching the growth of Nordstrom into one of the most successful chains ever. Anyone who knows the story of Nordstrom knows that their entire company philosophy is based on service. During recessionary times when discount retailers were touted as the new wave in retailing, Nordstrom was the fastest growing major department store in America. Yet their prices reflected the opposite of discount. I will always remember an old Bellevue Square photo I found from the early 1960s. Dwarfed next to the huge Frederick & Nelson department store was this little tiny shoe establishment, about the size of a convenience store. Its name was Nordstrom-Best. That was the beginning of what is now the largest anchor store in the mall and one growing throughout America. Frederick & Nelson is no longer.

The most successful people and organizations I have ever known had hearts of servants. Contrary to today's social whiners, most wealthy people didn't come into their money by inheritance or theft. They were made rich by a willingness to produce, meet needs, and serve their fellow man. They are willing to work the extra hour, give the extra effort, look for a need to be met, and they keep an eye out for an opportunity to serve. Prosperity is not a right—it's a privilege. And that privilege is earned.

So if you're looking for a tip, there are two ways to get it. Do the minimum and get the minimum. (Maybe a tip for sympathy.) Strive for excellence and receive a true reward. (Maybe even a bonus.) That is the American way. That is the spirit of the Marketeers.

After beginning to understand more thoroughly the principles of free-market ideology, and understanding it was the choice of our founding fathers, my mind began to change on a lot of issues. One of those things was Santa Claus. The movie *Polar Express* stunned me as I saw it the first time with my granddaughter. After remembering how children react to the whole subject of Santa Claus and Christmas, I couldn't help but think of when Jesus had the children about Him and on His knee, and what He said to the scribes and Pharisees of his day, who all donned the face of Cain as they stood around him. He said this: "Lest you become as one of these, you cannot see the Kingdom of God."

With children, faith is easy. They want to believe. And with absolutely no understanding of where the presents come from, they know intrinsically that they come by believing in Santa Claus. We must return to that simple faith that allows the fish and bread to multiply again, to be able to see why we prosper. So, now in my 50s, I found out my parents lied to me. There is a Santa Claus—and I do believe.

Without economic freedom there can be no liberty. Without liberty there can be no freedom. And there can be neither without the faith and free marketeers.

For Cain and his offering, the Lord had no respect. So Cain became very angry.

"Why are you angry?" The Lord said to him. "And why do you look sad? If you do well, don't you know that all will be well with you? But if you don't do well, sin crouches at your door, waiting to consume you."

Cain couldn't accept this. Then he met Abel in the field and killed him.

Scottish Nobles

The Nobles are the key to Scotland.
Give them lands and titles in Yorkshire.
Make them too greedy to oppose us.
                    —King Edward (Longshanks)

It was the first day of presession week and the speaker
of the house stood to address the House Republican
Caucus. Both Republicans and Democrats have their
caucus rooms located just off the floor of the house where
the members gather to take a break from floor voting and
to strategize the passing—or killing—of bill proposals. The
new legislative session would open the following Monday,
and this week was used to acclimate new members and
prepare them for the start of the upcoming session.

I had been hired to work within the caucus in support of
all the new members elected in the huge Republican sweep
of 1994. Washington State had seen the biggest turnaround
in its House of Representatives across the nation from
Democrat control to Republican; gaining thirty-three new
members, nearly reversing the Democrat majority from the

session before. Having been the campaign consultant for nearly a third of those new members, this job was more or less my reward, although Republican leadership understood that I knew and was trusted by these members. Since my post never did have a title, I made up one that I felt was fitting: *Concierge*.

Although I reported to the speaker's office, I was pretty much on my own to assist all of the new members in becoming familiar with how the legislative system functioned. In hindsight, working so closely with these legislators was an incredible learning experience. Until near the end of session, I would retire with them to the caucus, and I was able to get a taste of what it was like to be a legislator and see things from their vantage. As the session progressed and things began to heat up, I felt what they did—and would eventually find myself mired in much of the controversy to come.

As we waited for the speaker to begin, there was a near giddiness among all the new members, an anxious expectation. Relishing their newfound power and positions, the newly elected caucus leadership displayed confidence and experience. Now in the majority, the Republicans controlled all of the legislative committees and the speaker position, which controls the floor of the House. It is likely the second most powerful position in the state after the governor.

After welcoming everyone and making some opening remarks, the speaker took a few questions.

"What are we going to do about the Democrat legislative staff?" came one question. Whichever party is in power gets to hire the research and other legislative legal staff that serves both caucuses. It is a very central and important part of being in the majority, and it is common for the incoming majority to clean house, so to speak. The reason for this is that most of the staff is partisan in their philosophical views.

So, it is important for either party to have the right-thinking staff to assist in pushing their agenda forward.

"I have met with the Democratic minority leader and we have decided to go ahead and leave much of the staff in place." I couldn't believe my ears. This was the first thing to come out of the speaker's mouth indicating the direction of the new Republican majority—perhaps more importantly, his leadership capability. Oh well, I thought, maybe it will be OK. It wasn't.

Next, the speaker introduced the chairman of the Health & Human Services Committee, who came to the front to speak. He began by announcing the overall direction he would take as chairman of that committee. The session before, the Democrats had made great strides in socializing the state's involvement in health care. It was our opportunity as Republicans to reverse the direction and reaffirm the market-driven forces spelled out in our own party's platform.

I sat in shock as he spoke very clearly that he wanted to "tweak" and more or less improve what the Democrats had done. Although I didn't see it as clearly as I should have at the time, this was where I began to see how many Republicans will espouse one thing to the voters on the campaign trail, then do another after getting into office—in this case, taking the majority. Moreover, and remembering that it is about political warfare, Republicans never reassault the ground they lose. They merely concede it. Although I didn't know it at that moment, it was going to be a long session.

In understanding how government really works, it is extremely important to understand that government is force or power that is fueled entirely by money. Every law and regulation passed has to be enforced, and that enforcement costs money derived from tax revenues. Until working for the House Republican Caucus this year, I never understood just how important the proposed state budget was in being able to achieve what it is you want as a legislator. As with everything, the majority party gets to write the budget. In Washington State, the budget is written either by the House or the Senate in alternating fashion every other biennium. This year it was being written by the House Appropriation Committee, of course now controlled by the Republicans.

Throughout the prior two years when the Democrats were in power, the Republicans would hammer them in the press and on the campaign trail for passing the largest tax and spending increase in our state's history. There was no doubt that every new member I knew in that caucus at the beginning of this session had it as an intention to roll back the spending, as well as make tax reductions. It is a simple matter to any true Republican that reducing taxes stimulates the economy, naturally increasing revenues from existing tax rates as commerce increases.

Several weeks into the session the appropriation's chair presented to leadership and then to the caucus as a whole a new budget of $16.3 billion. The Democrat budget from the prior cycle was $15.3 billion. As stated earlier, that Democrat budget represented the largest tax and spending increase in state history, a point we had just used as one of the primary issues to bludgeon them at the polls. Now, here we were proposing, not to reduce that, but to increase it! It's true that much of this increase came from naturally occurring revenue increases, but not all of it. A huge fight was brewing that no one saw, not even leadership.

In addition, one of the most repressive taxes to Republicans is the Business and Occupation tax (B and O), which takes right off the top of gross revenues generated by business, rather than from the net. To small businesses, especially those just starting out and many of which do not make any profit to begin with, it is a debilitating tax and keeps many new businesses from growing and hiring new workers—if they can stay in business at all. Before the start of the session, one of the things also touted on the campaign trail by Republicans was a repeal of this tax. Now we were being told that we were merely going to propose a fifty percent reduction in this particular tax. Things were slipping badly as the session droned on.

As I look back now, I see that many in leadership did not understand the real earnest drive behind the conservatives who joined their caucus that year. Nor did the conservatives recognize the lack of drive in a majority of those Republicans who had been there for a while. It was a mix that was going to be explosive before the session ended.

It didn't take long before various new members were coming to me as a confidant to ask what they should do in their opposition to the increased budget proposals. Although I felt the same as they did, I was unsure exactly what to tell them. After all, being on the inside was new to me, too. Finally, the tact I adopted went like this. "Let me ask you this," I would say. "What did you tell the voters in your district on the campaign trail?" It was somewhat of a trick question, since I had written so many of their campaign materials. They had spoken very clearly that, not only did they say they would work for smaller government through lowering taxes and reducing overall government spending, they said they would never support tax or spending increases. I would then conclude with "So, if you feel compelled to vote for this budget the way it is, then you need to find a way to justify that vote to the people back home." A rebellion was in the making.

During this session, I was sharing a house with two of the new legislators and it became the headquarters for the conservatives in the caucus to meet off campus and discuss important issues, primarily this budget matter. One day a few weeks before the end of session as the time neared to bring the budget out of committee and to a full vote, a meeting was called at the house to discuss what could be done to bring the budget under control—a budget that had now increased to $17.3 billion, which now represented increases larger than what the Democrats had passed the session before. It was ludicrous to these conservative members. With their mounting opposition, they had been told by Republican leadership to come up with ideas of just how to cut the budget. They did exactly that and, that evening, they had come prepared with over a half-billion dollars in cuts.

Earlier that same day, I was approached in the halls by one of the Republican members in her second term who informed me that I was being accused of "locking up the budget." She suggested that I hightail it over to the speaker's office to clear the air. I arrived a few minutes later and sat down at the large round table in his office.

"What is going on here, Doug?" came the question. I replied by telling him what I was telling these new members when they came and asked what they should do. He knew that many of them trusted me and so he was careful in his approach. Just the same, he told me I couldn't tell them that. I knew then that I would anyway. *I'm not going to get into the habit of lying for anyone,* I thought at the time. *Nor would I make up some hodgepodge to help this crowd.* I suggested to him that he come to the meeting at the house that evening to hear them out. To his credit, he agreed and came.

That evening, besides the speaker, there were twenty-one members who came to the house. Earlier, we recognized that there was a great effort going on around them to get them to acquiesce to leadership, so we had drafted a pledge sheet that each would sign as a commitment to not vote for the budget unless it was reduced. I can still see it lying on the coffee table. One of the questions asked of the speaker was what he thought would happen if they voted "no" on the budget. His answer startled me. "I think if you do this, most of you will not come back here." He was referring to his belief that if they refused to vote for this budget they would not be reelected in their perspective districts. I couldn't believe what I was hearing. All of sudden, all the things that we stood for, all of the things that we had said during the campaigns, were now reduced down to being reelected. In other words, to the speaker, these things were simply unrealistic and immature rhetoric that was unachievable. At that moment, I realized that he was not a true conservative. What difference does it make what you believe if you don't stand for it?

Finally, came the question that is etched in my mind forever. I can still remember the look on Joyce's face as she asked in earnest, "Mr. Speaker, if we agree to support this budget, what assurance do we have that it will not continue to grow?" His reply was quick and steadfast. "I can promise you this. We will be having a lot of barbeques at my house in July because I'm not budging."

Session normally comes to an end 105 days after it starts, putting the close around the end of April. What he was saying was that he would not allow a budget to come out of the House that was any higher than it was on this day. His reference to having barbeques in July was that, if it came to a confrontation, he would not allow it to pass, then requiring the Governor to call for an extended session. It was a courageous statement, but one that would never be lived up to. I think he knew it.

The next morning the budget grew to $17.3 billion. A few days later, it grew to $17.6 billion.

One week after this night's off-campus meeting, I was expelled from attending the caucus meetings. The liberal members of the caucus began to see me as a threat and had gone to the speaker to have me removed. He agreed to do so. Among other things, this showed me his true allegiance. This was the beginning of a rift between him and me that would turn into an outright war over the next few years. Many times he tried to put me out of business as a consultant with Republican candidates. In reality, he failed to see that all his hostile assaults against me did were to merely galvanize my relationship to conservative Republicans all the more.

Admittedly, at the time this took place during session, I made a conscious decision to help these members come to the right conclusion as I saw it—and as I know they saw it. When they came to me, I knew it wasn't for my advice. They knew the right answer. They just wanted someone in this place to tell them that what they believed was OK. I did that.

At the time of this budget battle, there were sixty-one Republicans and thirty-seven Democrats. In order to pass the budget on the floor takes a simple majority. Therefore, in this case, out of a total of ninety-eight House members, the Republicans only needed fifty "yes" votes. So, they could lose no more than ten votes of their own members, without falling below fifty. If they don't have enough votes out of their own caucus to pass their own budget then, in essence, the Democrats get to write the budget. Because in order for them to find the votes, they will then have to cross over to the other side of the aisle and get members from the Democrat caucus to support it. In order to do that, they will end up having to agree to demands made by the Democrats.

What the Republican leadership was telling the budget holdouts in our caucus was that if they voted against it, then the budget would even increase further because the Democrats would insist on adding many of their spending priorities. Although this wasn't really true, it seemed to make sense at the time. But the fact is, the speaker could have gone to the so-called mainstream or middle-of-the-roaders of the Republican caucus who were really responsible for letting the budget grow to its present state anyway, and insist on them bringing it down. Experience has taught me that these members rarely stand on principle and are much easier to get to change. To me, it showed he simply didn't have the will.

It is easy to say with all confidence that there is no other vote taken that is more serious than the budget vote. As said earlier, government is fueled by taxes, and its size and scope is completely strapped to the budget. If you want to shrink government, you have to shrink the budget. If you want to grow government, you must grow the budget. No greater pressure comes upon a member than over the budget vote. And in the case of the budget this year, it was turning into a nightmare for a lot of the members whose convictions would not allow them to vote for it. It is something I will never forget. I watched as Republican leadership would corner these twenty-one members and pick them off one by one, knowing they simply had to get the twenty-one whittled down to ten, in order to pass the budget off the floor.

One particular member who was stalwart really took a beating. I felt for her. She struggled with all of the "common-sense" reasons why she should support the budget coming from leadership. One night, I drafted this letter and gave it to her.

Dear Cheryl,

From our discussion, I thought I might share some further thoughts on the matter of the current House budget and the question as to "what is the right thing to do?"

That question, "What is the right thing to do?" is really the only question that needs to be addressed in this entire debate. If each member of the caucus will ask themselves that question and answer it honestly, then you will all do the right thing—whatever that may be. It cannot be what I think, the speaker thinks, or what anyone else thinks; although all of those opinions are certainly helpful.

I found it interesting during many of the caucus meetings this year, that everyone was encouraged to "vote together as a caucus," and of course I understand the importance of that as a general rule. Yet, at various times, when it came to so-called "sensitive issues" (such as abortion), the group was told they could—and should—vote "their conscience." I guess I have to ask myself what is more important than taking people's money (their property)? Except, certainly, sanctity of life.

Another point is that if you see things differently, and want to vote another direction, you're then warned of "dividing the caucus."

I heard the following argument again today:

"Well Doug, if the budget comes in at 17.4, or 17.5, it really isn't going to make that much difference . . . The people really don't know one from the other, anyway. Besides, we can have pretty good reasons for it back home."

In other words (as Rush always says about Clinton), "How can we fool 'em today?" or "What they don't know won't hurt them, right?" Isn't that what we always objected to about the way the Democrats did business?

The flaw in this kind of thinking is obvious. It didn't pass the first test—asking the basic question, "What is the right thing to do?"

Another argument often heard (and laced with some truth) is: "You can't do it all in one shot. You have to do it slowly, over time." (I will address this more fully, later on.) But let us consider some other questions that may aid in answering the initial question concerning "doing the right thing."

To begin, let me lay out for you what I believe was the basic "overall" message of the Republicans last fall. (Keep in mind also, that nearly 75 percent of new Republicans that won here and throughout the country would be considered "conservative" in their views. In fact, the majority were also "pro-life," which dispels the liberal myth that only pro-choice Republicans stand a chance.)

It could be said that the message that won the election was both a "morally and fiscally conservative" one. Overall, we told them:

1) We will vote for less government.
2) We will cut spending.
3) We will vote for fewer taxes.
4) We will get tough on criminals.
5) We will get back to fundamental, basic academics in education.

And, we told them in that order. And they told us, in overwhelming numbers that is exactly what they wanted. The fact of the matter is that the only way you can cut government, is by moving to the second item—*cutting spending*. The important thing about the first year of the biennium is that it's all about the budget. And everything else you want to accomplish is tied to that budget.

The bureaucrats and liberals have created a monster. In order to keep it alive, they must feed it. In order to kill it, you must stop feeding it. Have you done that?

So, now ask yourself the following questions:

1) Why did I run for office?
2) What did I tell my voters?
3) Am I doing what I told them?
4) On the campaign trail, am I going to hear more of what I heard from the Democrats at 4 A.M. the night we passed out the budget at 17.3?
5) Am I going to do the right thing? Or am I just going to try and fool'em?

Frankly, the question isn't just "Can you vote for a budget over 17.3?" But, also "Can you even vote for a budget as high as 17.3?" Somewhere in all the flutter these past few weeks, that question was lost. The Democrats have already reminded you that, at 17.3 billion, you've just passed out the biggest spending increase in the state's history! (Which is what we thoroughly thrashed them for last year). If I were a legislator, I would surely be having trouble voting yes at the current level, which makes the rest of this moot.

Scottish Nobles

Two months ago as the budget was getting ready to be presented, there was a *Seattle Times* editorial that praised the House for its budget at *16.7 billion!* They didn't even realize it had gone up before their ink had dried. Why?

Bob Williams [Evergreen Freedom Foundation] made a wise point that one evening, when he said that the budget process is always done backwards. Instead of working the process first, you must first pick the right number. Then you make the process fit. Otherwise, the process will eat you alive.

For all the beating the Republican caucus is taking, they should have started at 16.3. The beating wouldn't be any worse. (Remember who's doing the beating, by the way. It's not those who sent you there!)

Everyone knows where I stand on the budget issue. I make no bones about it. And, I tend to view things from the political perspective in how it will play out back home. As I spoke of earlier, the question as to whether this all can be accomplished over time, rather than all at once needs to be addressed.

First of all, do you think we as Republicans are going to have the time the Democrats have had? If not, how much will we get? Is the electorate going to give us time? And secondly, this argument has been used over the years, but the Republicans then never stayed in power long enough to come back and do it right. Or, they simply lost their vision next time around. I'm just finishing reading a book titled *Dead Right* by David Fromm. The basic question of the book is whether or not conservatives will, this time, come through with what they said they will do, in terms of downsizing government.

Finally, is your vote, or those votes of the other true conservatives who are deeply concerned, needed to pass the budget? The truth is if the budget goes up high enough, the Democrats will be overjoyed to vote "yes" on it.

Cheryl, is this another time for "government as usual"? Or is this a time for drastic changes in the way things are done?

In closing, I have to remind you again that this is all my own opinion. Each member must decide the final outcome. I'm very proud of the new conservative members this year. I'd be proud to work for any of you again.

Warm regards,

Cain and Abel are the two players on the field. They always are. It is the two of them who shape the way the world goes. It is and will always be a struggle between these two personalities and worldviews, but there is one other element—that is those who go through life not caring one way or the other. Cain despised God, or else he wouldn't have done what he did. Abel loved God.

Never before had I seen or understood the division in Republican ranks until I witnessed it firsthand working for the caucus. It was shortly after this stint working in the Republican caucus that the movie *Braveheart* was released. In that movie I saw portrayed the essence of what is happening politically in America, especially within the Republican party. In the movie there were also three factions at play. First, you had King Edward or Longshanks as was his nickname. He was the most ruthless king in England's history. Longshanks was a tyrant who ruled over Scotland with an iron fist.

Next, you had the commoners who lived under that oppression. One day, following a series of events, William Wallace rebelled against the king's soldiers stationed in Scotland, and a revolution began. Finally, the third faction in the story were the Scottish nobles. They were the ruling class of citizens at the time and were forever cutting deals with King Edward to keep the people from rising up. Even though the nobles always claimed publicly that they wanted the same things as the common folk, in the end, they sold William Wallace over to King Edward. This is what happens constantly in the Republican party, and why I always encourage people to review the voting records of their elected officials to see if they are who they say they are.

Interestingly, William Wallace and his followers had King Edward on the run. They would have obtained freedom a lot earlier had it not been for the Scottish nobles who constantly undermined them. Such is the same with the Republican party today in America. Conservative ideals—the very heart of the party's platform—are being sold out for "lands and titles" as were the Scottish people by those nobles who speak well but really don't stand for anything. Victory in politics is, supposedly, gained through the art of compromise. And it's a trading game. In some cases, being sold out is a better characterization. But the factions portrayed in the movie show me that what we're up against today is the same age-old game that never changes, but must continue.

Several years following this budget debacle in the Republican caucus, I remember having a conversation with a state senator who was there at the time in the House. I asked her if she had ever considered what the state, or even

America, would have been like had the conservatives held on that point. She hadn't. Conservatives were told that they would lose not only their own coming races, but other races for the Republican party because of their being stiff-necked about the budget—especially if that budget had failed.

But here's the truth. Over time some of these members lost because they didn't hold that day, and in other cases they lost heart and ended up becoming part of the problem. And the Republican party candidate losses in races since have increased for the same reason. Had this lowly group of well-meaning conservatives held on that budget vote in April of 1995, Washington State would be a different place today. Abortion funding would have been out of the budget for the first time, taxes would have been lowered, which likely would have spurred the economy. Government growth would have, at the very least, been contained holding back the riptide of regulations choking all of us. And, most of all, the great exodus from the party would have never happened—the exodus of those who were giving up on the party, many who have never returned. They simply don't believe what Republicans say anymore. Finally, the election for a new governor of Washington was held in 1996. It is possible that race could have been won by Republicans had they not sold out one too many times before.

Courage is what rallies people. The Republican Party in my view does not understand the difference between needed compromise and selling out.

When being interviewed now by the press, Republicans are cornered easily by the leftist interviewers because they are being asked why Republicans are not doing "Republican" things, like tax cutting—those bread-and-butter things that the GOP is expected to stand for. The GOP has conceded the ground for the things in its own platform now to the point where less than a third of Precinct Committee Officer (PCO's) positions are even filled in the average district. Republicans now spend their time explaining why they no longer truly defend the core principles of their party. For example, instead of talking about privatizing Social Security anymore, Republicans have abandoned that battlefield as a party and are now talking of "protecting Social Security" along with the Democrats, for the sake of saving the next election. To the GOP, if the majority of Americans don't favor privatization of Social Security, then why should they pump bullets into a dead horse? What is the purpose of defending a position that will ultimately lead to their demise as a party in power? But what we must begin to see is that this is the kind of thinking that is not only destroying the party, but our nation. What Republicans are really asking is, "Why try and do what is right if you can't win anyway?" If I have to answer that, then the reply would be meaningless.

Cain thought that way. He had done what was asked of him, but the reward went to his brother, Abel.

Undoubtedly, the biggest betrayal in my time, as a Republican, came in the 1998 legislative session. Most of the leadership that was in control in 1995 was still in place, although by now the GOP had messed around and lost the majority in the Senate and was on the way to losing the House. At the beginning of each session, many of the conservative organizations come to town to meet with the true conservative legislators and staff to work out a list of priorities to try to get done legislatively. We always met in a room in the legislative building and would bring sack lunches.

During this particular meeting in 1998, after the agenda had been completed and most folks were about ready to leave, I raised my hand and asked if anyone was keeping their eye on the proposal coming to have the state fund a new Seattle Seahawk's football stadium. One of my close legislator friends, and a candidate as well, who was leading the meeting nearly laughed out loud when I brought it up. Two years earlier, the Seattle Mariner's football franchise had maneuvered their way through the legislature and received a new public funded baseball stadium. I was involved that year in trying to get the Republicans to realize how silly it was for them to do such a thing in the face of their own platform stands, such as keeping government out of the private sector or, maybe, less taxation? Since when is it the place of government to fund any private enterprise? Occasionally, such as with an issue like this one, you may find yourself in the same foxhole with the liberal lobbyists who agree—if not for selfish reasons, like not wanting another slice taken out of the pie they are vying for. This was the case in this situation

Nevertheless, most in the GOP went along with the Mariner's Stadium, many of them taking a brutal beating when they faced their more conservative (and some liberal) voters back in their districts. It was a lesson most people thought the GOP had learned. They were wrong. And it became another striking blow against Republicans regaining control of the majority in either house.

So, now comes 1998. No one in the room that day took me seriously when I said aloud, "You wait, this Seahawk Stadium is coming to a committee near you!" Several days later it did just that. However the stadium itself is a minor story. For conservatives, the real prize this year was getting partial-birth abortion passed. Everything seemed in place to achieve victory.

Scottish Nobles

Concerning the Seahawks' stadium, I still cannot understand why the Republicans ever considered such a thing. Once again, it was the true conservatives who stayed strong throughout the fight. But why would you want to publicly fund a private stadium where the owner is a multi-multibillionaire, anyway? I love football and I love the Seahawks. But this was wrong for Republicans to do and was a betrayal of their own party platform. And again, I believe it cost them down the road. What is even worse is that when other stadiums were being considered by other states, the sticker price on theirs was all about $100 million less than ours. After doing some research, I discovered that being wrapped into the finance package was the old Kingdome, prior home to the Seahawks. The present governor, Gary Locke, had left a $100 million debt as King County Executive before running for governor. I smelled a rat, but could not get anyone to listen. Why would anybody that has a fundamental understanding of the role and parameters of civil government ever support such a public project? The answer is in the question. As Jonathan Swift once said, "It is impossible to reason a man out of what he was never reasoned into."

Coming to life in the session was a bill in support of outlawing partial-birth abortion. Agreements had been made with the Republican ranks to tie the bill to a referendum, which would automatically send the bill to the next general election ballot for the voters to decide. As social-conservatives, we knew that it was an easy fight and would pass fairly easily when put to the voters. Who would know that this measure would get tangled up with a football stadium?

During negotiations with those who wanted the Seahawks stadium bill passed, a decision was made to put the Seahawks stadium to referendum as well, to let the voters decide. Another deal had been struck to accept an offer from

Paul Allen, Seahawks owner, that he would privately fund an election to be held in June of that year, approximately five months from then. Now the partial-birth referendum and the Seahawks referendum were on a collision course because Washington State law requires that any referendum approved by both houses of the legislature automatically goes to the next general election ballot, which now was being scheduled for June to accommodate the vote on the Seahawks stadium. The reason for the partial-birth abortion ban bill to go to referendum was that a referendum goes directly to the ballot, never stopping at the governor's desk. In this case, Gary Locke would have vetoed the measure had it come as a normal bill passed by the legislature. In this case, a referendum cannot be vetoed by the governor and goes straight to the people.

As soon as all of this came to light, another partial-birth abortion ban measure was introduced in the House. This bill proposal did not have the referendum clause, so even if passed, it was dead because it would be required to go to the governor's office and face a sure veto. This was probably one of the most disingenuous moves by the squishes in the Republican party I have ever seen. All of a sudden, you had all the middle-of-the-road House GOP caucus members clamoring to support this bill, as if they were supportive of banning partial-birth abortion. This is the crowd that runs every time anyone even mentions some social issue coming forward as a bill.

Here is why this new bill introduction happened and is important Anybody with any political savvy knew that—following the lessons learned via the Mariner's stadium two years prior—getting the Seahawk stadium referendum approved by the voters was going to be rough going. Since conservatives as a whole would oppose such an effort, the last thing any stadium supporter wanted was the partial-birth abortion ban to show up on the same ballot with the stadium. If it did, it would draw out hoards of conservative voters who would overwhelmingly cause the defeat of the stadium. So it was important to them to get the partial-birth abortion referendum bill killed and bring up the new one, the Trojan horse, behind it. What was amazing as I worked this bill along with others is how, to the squishes, it was perfectly OK to use the argument that the people should have a choice with the stadium proposal. But they changed tunes when it came to the referendum partial-birth bill.

But that's the way it goes inside the GOP these days.

I don't think I ever remember legislators and outside lobby efforts stronger on anything than trying to keep the referendum alive and passed. To me, it seemed to be going well. Then on the last day, all hell seemed to be breaking out. Those who were our friends seemed to be changing to our enemies. Finally, came the moment in committee when it came time to for the executive committee to vote one of the two bills out. After taking counts, we were positive that we had the votes necessary to bring the referendum bill out and to the floor. To my astonishment, the chairman called for the regular bill, the vote was taken and the bill passed.

I could not believe my eyes. The executive committee vote was taken verbally. The "Partial-birth Abortion" bill—without referendum—passed committee and was now on its way to a floor vote. In this situation, many liberal Republicans disingenuously voted for a piece of legislation they knew would never become law. It was the biggest sell-out that I have witnessed yet in the GOP, and would be a catalyst for my leaving the GOP that same year.

I stood up to leave the hearing room, once again feeling the sting of betrayal. I was dizzy from anger. It wasn't that I minded losing so much—although that was bad enough. What I found so troubling, so disheartening, was how people in our own party played the game. Some who professed to support the ideals of the party's platform—including eliminating something as horrifying as murdering fully-developed fetuses by sucking their brains through a tube—used deceit and manipulation. I was enraged. I needed to leave before I threw up or threw something.

I had that panicky feeling of wanting to call my pastor—someone—anyone—to sound the alarm! A horse, a rider, a shout that the enemy was coming! But in a moment, I knew it was futile. At this moment in time, nobody wanted to hear it.

I jumped in my car and left the Capitol. It had stopped raining as I drove along Interstate 5 toward Tacoma and the Puyallup turn-off. It would occur to me later that I wasn't half as mad at the situation at hand as I was with myself and my own failure again this day. We had come so close to victory. Yet it seemed that the closer we got, the faster it would slip down that long corridor where the door at the end just seems to move further out of reach.

I couldn't believe the profanity coming from my own mouth. One of my biggest carryovers from my service in the Marine Corps has been using profanity when I get angry. I changed lanes to take the exit as the rained-soaked pavement reflected the lights from the oncoming traffic ahead.

This present situation of coming so close to victory seemed so familiar to me, but I couldn't put my finger on it. The darkness, the rain, it seemed so familiar. Then I remembered . . .

Scottish Nobles

. . . that chilly monsoon midnight flight out of Marble Mountain south into Arizona territory. It was hot and humid on the ground, even during the monsoons, but the climb to three thousand feet left you cold. The lights of DaNang faded to the rear as darkness swallowed the two choppers moving toward the target zone somewhere in the Que Son foothills. This was an emergency extraction, of infantry Marines. The zone brief revealed a *Condition One,* meaning they were presently taking fire. Dropping into a zone where a firefight was taking place was never one of my favorite things to do.

"Gunners lock and load! Cleared to fire! Left gunner, fire to your side!" His message was wasted. I had already released the safety on the machine gun before he spoke. My body felt lighter as the bird began its descent, banking left as we circled down. My hand gripped the door frame. The fear was invigorating to my senses, and the numbness that was Vietnam faded for a few moments as the shot of adrenalin rose above the fear. I checked to see that my bullet-bouncer was strapped around my chest. My heart thumped in rhythm to the rotor-wash. Soon, I knew it would start, the tracers from enemy guns streaking though the blackness in search of us.

We flew closer, now within a few hundred feet, as I began to see tracers welcoming us. I waited for that sound of rounds piercing the thin metal skin of the choppers that you can hear even through your helmet. One hundred feet. Fifty. Ten. Finally, down. I began a short, controlled fire burst into the darkness through the tall elephant grass off to my side. My own tracers now answered those coming in our direction. The chopper's skin flexed in and out violently from recoil of my machine gun. The ramp to the rear lowered and several Marines scrambled quickly onto the back of the chopper. A nearby Cobra gunship raked the grass and jungle off to my side. A few brief seconds later my knees buckled as the powerful main rotors gripped the heavy night air and we lifted rapidly out of the zone into the night sky. Still rising, the VC tracers receded, and I knew I had escaped danger and death one more time . . .

. . . The drizzle on the windshield began to mix with the tears in my eyes, as I passed the sign to the Puyallup exit off I-5. I relaxed and pictured the scene in my mind over again and again. Then I realized—I had almost forgotten—*It's always this way in war, Doug; your adversary always fights fiercest when you are nearest your objective.*

The way it turned out a few months later, without the partial-birth ban on the ballot, the conservatives stayed home and the stadium passed, albeit so narrowly that it took three weeks to wait for all the mailed ballots to come in to be counted. In addition, Paul Allen, Seahawks owner, had spent several million dollars on advertising in support of the measure, while, ironically, the only public opposition to tax-dollar funding for the Seahawks' stadium came from a Democrat senator. To his credit, he made up his own placards and went down to sign-wave on some corners in his own town. To my knowledge that was the only monies spent in opposition: whatever it cost to make up the placard and for gas to get to the corner. It passed, barely getting the needed fifty percent.

Scottish Nobles

I have contended for some time now, that the biggest threat to our country, politically speaking, is not those elected on the left or right but, rather, those in the so-called middle. They always seem to stand for the least and are always the most likely to betray and run in the fight. They are the cowards that are selling us out of our very inheritance.

I believe that the reason why we are in the current state of affairs in this country (runaway national debt, deficits, crime, and a multitude of other societal illnesses) is because of theses middle-of-the-roaders, or squishes as they're known in Republican conservative circles. These people are gutless. They refuse to take a stand on anything, On the campaign trail, they talk the walk, but once elected they fail to walk the talk. They fool the voters by convincing them that they are "balanced." (If they really were, wouldn't we have a "balanced" budget?)

Even as a staunch conservative, I'd rather see a real liberal elected; at least his true colors show in his voting record. The squishes in the middle are all over the board and then drum up gobbledygook excuses for their votes as they head home.

For example, everyone knows liberal-socialists love to spend money. And generally speaking, deep down they believe the government owns all wealth and property and merely lets us keep some. Liberals always get blamed for the high taxation and deficit spending. But I believe they have been unjustly blamed, at least partially. Let me explain.

Rarely, if ever, have the Democrats been able to pass tax and spending increases—either nationally or in the state of Washington—without the help of Republicans. And it's not the solid conservatives giving in, but the so-called *moderates* in the party—the squishes. I saw this firsthand this session inside the House Republican caucus.

Many good conservatives fell prey to the voice of reason and were sucked into joining ranks with the squishes to pass the largest spending increase ever. (The only saving grace was that if the Democrats had been in the majority, it would have been much higher—maybe).

But Republicans, as well as Democrats today, are convinced they must hide their political philosophies to win favor—in part, because many have no intention of living up to them anyway. In fact, with the GOP, since power politics have taken precedence over principle, it has become a regular strategy now to simply *out-Democrat* the Democrats to win votes. For example: The GOP philosophy (reflected in the platform of previous years) believes that benevolence (welfare) by the state is not a legitimate function of government or under its jurisdiction, either constitutionally or morally. To most conservatives in the party, and reflected in the platform, charity belongs to the individual or to the church. But, since GOP leadership no longer believes that they can win carrying that banner forward, they have capitulated and conceded the ground to the liberal-socialists. So, today, the debate no longer reaches the table. Consequently, most people never hear this side of the issue and the critically needed public debate on this principle or a hundred others like it. It has become another major battle we've lost in the war, as we continue our slippery-slide into socialism and despotism. With other issues, such as education, the Republicans—out of fear—have also conceded with the white flag of surrender.

I've always wondered if Abel fought back in the field that day or if Cain drew him into the field and ambushed him.

Scottish Nobles

Once, when I made a point about the importance of getting runaway government reigned in, I had a legislator say to me: "Doug, don't you understand? We can never get back to where we were; where you want to go. It is simply too late." My answer to him? "If that's the case, we've already lost. So, what are you doing here?" I told him he should just go home, because when we assume that posture in the fight, then we've already conceded defeat and are merely wasting time—but for what purpose? Republicans have done just that. That's why we're dropping behind on all of the issues important to Republicans in our platform. I always ask my friends to show me where we've gained any ground over the past three decades, even when Republicans have held majorities, both here in Washington State, as well as the other Washington.

The so-called *mainstream Republicans* when challenged on this point will always claim that we are "holding our own." In other words, we are not letting things get worse. They do this constantly with arguments over government budgets. Personally, I've come to subscribe to the General George S. Patton way of waging war, in this case, political warfare. Often, when speaking to his troops, he would tell them, "I don't want to get any messages saying that we're holding our ground. We're not holding on to anything. Let the Hun do that. We're advancing and not interested in holding on to anything—except the enemy."

The truth is we're not holding our own. We're losing ground. As stated earlier, with almost every major issue— even when Republicans have been in the majority—we've lost significantly: taxes, growth of government (which equates to loss of liberty), property rights, and individual rights—you name it. We've slipped badly. It is very likely, if not assured, that the many tenets of the so-called "Patriot Act" will never go away. Anyone who pays attention knows that few government power usurpations are ever rescinded.

Perhaps this point of concession by the GOP has never been made more succinctly clear than by Howard Phillips, founder of the Constitution Party, formerly the U.S Taxpayers Party, and president and founder of the Conservative Caucus. As head of the Office of Economic Opportunity under the Reagan administration, Phillips saw first hand what was not getting done by Republicans. The following are a portion of Howard Phillips remarks shared at the outset of a debate held in 1994 that addressed the question of whether or not it was time for conservatives to leave the Republican tent.

> Gerry Ford, in his first presidential address to Congress on August 12, 1974, just a few days after he inherited the presidency from Dick Nixon, summed up the core beliefs and the consistent strategy of the Republican Party leadership throughout my lifetime, when he said to Tip O'Neill and his colleagues in Congress: "I offer you a banner of consensus, compromise, conciliation, and co-operation"—in other words, a white flag of surrender.

> The liberals will not surrender power without a fight. We have got to be ready to spill some blood, theirs and ours, too. There will be casualties: lost battles, lost elections, and indeed, lost lives. But, without a fight, we cannot win.

> The strategy of the conservative movement, following the leadership of the Republican Party, has been to lose as slowly as possible—that is, to merely slow the rate at which the liberal agenda is enacted, rather than to oppose that agenda on principle. There is no Republican plan for winning, in the sense of changing the direction of public

policy. Both parties, the Republicans and Democrats, are headed in the same direction, albeit at different rates of speed . . .

In my view, Howard Phillips understands the correlation between political warfare and that of physical warfare. I'm not saying these things to convince good conservatives that it's time to leave the Republican Party. Personally, however, I think it is. Because if a person thinks they're getting anywhere in the Republican Party, based on decades of evidence, in my opinion this has about the same chance of happening as one boarding the Titanic to get to New York. Howard Phillips says it this way:

> As long as the GOP successfully plays Pied Piper to wishful thinking conservative donors, workers, and voters, we shall surely remain *en route* to a national drowning. Like the Pied Piper, the Republicans play a sweet song, even as they guide us on the path to destruction. They have even persuaded most conservative GOP activists that conservative language in the quadrennial platform is equivalent to changing the direction of the country. But our job is to capture the *government,* not just the platform.

As I mentioned earlier, when most elected Republicans abandon their own party's platform, it becomes betrayal—intentional or otherwise.

When in the minority, I constantly hear from Republican leadership that there is not any point in fighting or standing firm on any issue until they get the majority. But each time they win a majority, I then hear the same reasoning for why we can't take the offensive—only then it's for fear of losing the majority. Today, I simply do not believe them anymore and experience has taught me that they will never tackle the tough issues. They simply do not have what it takes—which brings us back to character.

At the outset of this past election cycle, I had the leader of the State Senate Republican Caucus and their consultant request a meeting with one of my incumbent state senators and myself. My candidate was facing some very serious media trouble, and the purpose of this meeting was to warn us regarding "talking about any hot-button issues," namely abortion. After listening to a solid ten minutes about how Republicans always lose when they start talking about moral issues, I finally interrupted and said this: "Of all my candidates over the past twelve years, not one has been less than openly and solidly pro-life, without exception. I've won eighty-five percent of these races, and with those who lost, never did it have anything to do with the fact they were pro-life. So, please tell me again about this being a losing issue."

The fact is, Republicans are losing races, not because of what they talk about—they're losing races because of what they won't talk about. They miss the fact that Americans are hungry to hear people of courage and conviction stand to their feet and speak with character, those who will get up and talk in plain English—and then do what they say. As I told this same Republican senate leader at another time: "I just wish you guys would spend as much time worrying about what you should say as you do with what not to say."

In his case, he was a former Democrat who had switched parties when he saw that his district was beginning to swing more Republican. Party leadership is always glad to have defectors, whether or not they are in any way Republican by character. This alone proves that they are merely interested in power, not in principle.

When we do what is right because it is right, not because it is pragmatic, when we hold on to strong principle without being distracted by the fear that grips us, when we check to make sure we are not calling our fear wisdom, and when we take it all unto faith—then He comes to our aid and we cannot possibly lose.

This is one reason I've found that Republicans, as a group, always lose. They spend all their time on defense. The Democrats are much better at political warfare and have far better generals in their ranks. Politically, they are ruthless, and they win. They know how to fight. I admire them for that. Republicans will never get into a fight that they aren't sure they can win ahead of time, and that is why they will continue to fail.

The point of having a political majority is to carry forward an agenda approved by the greatest number of voters. That's the game and the very intention of our system of government in America. When selecting leaders, voters are telling their legislatures of the overall direction they wish to go in. That then becomes the opportunity you have as an ideological entity to implement the ideas you shared with the voters on the campaign trail. I have discovered a long-standing reluctance with Republicans to uphold the party banner once they gain power. They want to be liked too much.

During the campaign season, they talk the walk but, after arriving in the majority, their fear of losing that majority overwhelms them, and they lose their vision. They go cross-eyed, and they no longer remember what they are doing there. Democrats get it; Republicans don't. I've often wondered if the Democrats sit in their caucus on the other side of the House and Senate floors and snicker to one another behind closed doors. I know I would.

Republicans conduct political warfare in much the same manner the nation prosecuted the Vietnam War. And, believe me, the party is full of anti-political war activists. Imagine what would have happened to the Marines assaulting the beaches at Tarawa during World War II if leadership had not been willing to sacrifice for victory. Twenty-five hundred Marines fell in the lagoons that day in order to defeat Japan and retain freedom. You never plan to lose, but you cannot win unless you are willing to lose first.

Another point in the art of political warfare that Republicans miss is this: as with physical wars, the public has little stomach and patience for prolonged warfare. If you're going to fight, you must commit yourself totally, holding nothing back. If you flinch—if you hesitate—you lose. Republican leadership always flinches—they always choke—and they almost always lose. They just don't get it. One undeniable thing I've discovered in this business of elections is this: America is dying for some true leadership, those with the courage to tell the truth and stand by their convictions.

I always tell my candidates that if the public doesn't like what you say, then they deserve what they get. If you have to lie or hide what you believe to get a vote, then you aren't serving anyone but yourself. If you lie to the voters to get their vote, you're simply hurting them and the entire cause. Your own hunger for power has now become more important than telling the truth. You just lost. Tell them the truth; if they can't handle it, let them vote for the other person. They get what they deserve. It isn't your place to save them—especially if you have to lie to do it! There is a general philosophical worldview that motivates legislators, a difference that we need to understand. We cannot rely solely on a few stands on issues they may take. As voters, we need to understand their more global view of life and government. The devil is always in the details.

But for us today, it's Cain who is beginning to rule. As a nation, we are now frozen in *his* headlights, paralyzed by fear rather than driven ever forward by faith, now overwhelmed by the Cain Factor.

I'm reminded of Patrick Henry's famous oratory at Richmond Church in Virginia when the colonists were in serious debate about separating from the crown. I like Patrick Henry. If he were living in America today, he would be considered a right-wing fundamentalist. I would be in good company. This was the tail end of Henry's famous speech:

> We shall not fight our battle alone. There is a just God who presides over the destinies of nations; and who will raise up friends to fight our battle for us. The battle, sir, is not to the strong alone; it is to the vigilant, the active, the brave . . .

> Is life so dear, or peace so sweet, as to be purchased at the price of chains and slavery? Forbid it, Almighty God! I know not what course others may take; but as for me, give me liberty or give me death!

Heroes and Villains

No arsenal, or no weapon in the arsenals of the world,
is so formidable as is the will and moral courage of free
men and women.

—Ronald Reagan

The traffic is bumper to bumper and nearly at a
standstill heading south on Interstate 5, just north
of Seattle. I'm on my way back to Olympia from a
meeting with a homeschool group in Snohomish County.
Although it's just a little past noon, it is nearly dark from
the heavy, thick, dark cloud cover that is spewing rain
over the region. Most of the cars in front and in back of
me have turned on their headlights, now reflected on the
rain-soaked pavement.

As I pass under the 45th Street overpass, a glance over
my left shoulder reveals my former office in the university
district. I also spot the Meany Tower Hotel across the street
and recall the day that so many things changed in my life,
that early morning breakfast when I met him.

He was a remarkable man. His eyes set narrowly on his face, with high, wider-than-average cheekbones that testify to his Norwegian descent. His once-sandy-blond hair was now graying in a salt and pepper fashion. He shook my hand warmly as he took his seat at the table. Later, I noticed a striking resemblance between him and George Washington, not only in facial structure, but in physical stature as well as in character.

At first, I thought I could see the politician in him. But I soon found out that there was great depth and substance to him. This breakfast meeting was a favor to a friend who wanted me to meet this man running for the United States Senate. I first fidgeted with my watch, anxious to get this over with. I despised politics. But the fidgeting soon ceased. Little did I know that the next three hours would change my life.

For me, Leo Thorsness became the example of what our founders had intended as character traits for those serving in public office: a person's ability to uphold the underlying principles of good government and a great nation. Testing a man or a woman was proof of their ability to stand in the face of pressures of the legislature or from an unrelenting media that scrutinizes every last detail of a public servant's life—especially those who take firm positions. I have since concluded that leadership truly begins with one's ability to overcome adversity. Leo used to say, "I have been tested, and I came back with my integrity intact." I soon discovered that his integrity was his single most prized possession after his lovely wife, Gaylee, and daughter, Dawn.

When I met him this day in Seattle's university district, Leo Thorsness was completing his first term as a Washington state senator from a district where no Republican had ever won before. It was the 11th Legislative District of southeast Seattle, a predominately black and impoverished area of high crime and low self-esteem. People here were less likely to vote, but when they did they tended to vote Democrat. It was common for the Democrat incumbent in this district to take better than two-thirds of the vote or, many times, simply run unopposed.

But Leo did win, albeit narrowly, by a mere few hundred votes to become the first Republican senator from that district in the history of the state. He did so based on his character and his record. And what a record it was.

Leo Thorsness was born in Walnut Grove, Minnesota, in the town that was the true setting of the television series *Little House on the Prairie*. Enlisting in the Air Force at eighteen years old, Leo eventually entered Aviation Cadets and flight school becoming a fighter pilot.

Serving as a major in his first tour of duty in Vietnam from 1966 to 1967, Leo was flying F-105 fighter missions out of an airbase in Thailand, when in early April 1967, he found himself in a situation where a critical life-or-death decision had to be made. After flying an aerial combat dogfight against Communist MIG fighters over Hanoi, both Leo and his wingman had run critically low on fuel. After taking out one last enemy fighter, and with only one refueling tanker in the area, Leo ordered his wingman to head for the tanker out over Laos. Even while critically low on fuel himself, Leo gained altitude and began the long flight back over Laos and into Thailand knowing he probably would not make it. It was Leo's hope that, after climbing to a very high altitude, he could pull back on the throttle and somewhat glide the aircraft slowly down until reaching the base's runway. He couldn't have timed it any more perfectly, for just at the point of touchdown, Leo's F-105 ran out of fuel. For his sacrificial and courageous acts of that day, Leo would eventually receive our nation's highest award: the Medal of Honor.

But Leo Thorsness would not receive his medal—or even know about it for six years. Eleven days later, on another similar combat mission over downtown Hanoi, Leo's aircraft took a missile "up the tailpipe" as he described it later, and Leo's aircraft immediately started to disintegrate. Ejecting from the aircraft at over 675 mph, (well over safe ejection speed), Leo's lower legs were blown straight sideways up to his knees. Once on the ground and captured by NVA soldiers, he was unable to walk without his legs buckling.

Nearly six years in the infamous "Hanoi Hilton" would leave this man to never be the same again. "Three years of torture and three years of boredom" was how Leo would characterize it to me when we would talk about it on many road trips that we would take around the state together during the long U.S. Senate campaign to come. My own year of duty in Vietnam was a vacation compared to what Leo and several hundred others like him had to endure at the hands of their merciless Communist captors. I realized later that his life experiences didn't give Leo all the answers concerning issues of governing. What it did give him was lack of vanity, an open heart and mind, as well as humility with which to be able to see the truth. I learned from him that a clean heart produces a clear mind.

As strong conservatives, Leo and I agreed on most issues, but not all. Hardly an issue went unspoken on many of our trips together. I remember one particular campaign outing as we were driving between Pasco and Yakima, Washington, when the conversation became so heated over the issue of a vote Leo had taken in the state senate on the controversial "hate crimes" legislation that he pulled the car over and we both got out to take a breath of fresh air. Leaning over the top of the car facing each other in frustration, the talk continued at a slightly elevated pitch. Finally, I said something that I do not now remember. But, in an instant, Leo became silent. He paused, and then said, "I hadn't thought of that." With that, we got back into the car and on our way. Every campaign stop we made from then on, when that subject came up, Leo would tell the audience that his hate crimes vote was a mistake. That's the kind of man he was.

When I argue, I never expect the other guy to back down. I never expect anyone to admit defeat. I wouldn't, so why would they? Therefore, I didn't know how to react at that moment. I was ready to slug it out for as long as it took. But I learned something from Leo that day about not needing to always be right. He taught me that I might be right, but I must be willing to learn.

Finally, the traffic is moving again. The rain has stopped, and the university district is fading in my rearview mirror as I approach the Lake Union Bridge. Seattle's Space Needle looks almost out of place in its architecture all these years later, following the 1962 World's Fair. Once towering over the city, it's now dwarfed by the many office buildings towering throughout the downtown area.

Looking back now, I see that character is everything in leadership. Without it, voters are left far short of what they deserve in their elected representatives. Leo would have made a great U.S. Senator. Not because he would have gone to Washington, D.C. with all the answers, but because he would have gone with the right heart—and a teachable spirit. Only in that spirit are we able to find the right answers. The citizens of Washington State don't know what they missed. Most politicians are deathly afraid to admit a mistake for fear of losing confidence and votes. I watched closely, and at every stop when Leo would share that mistaken vote on hate crimes, the opposite happened. Voters were so taken by his honesty that there is no doubt in my mind—he gained votes. Leo never stepped in front of a crowd with the idea of manipulation. He was the real article, and people swarmed to that. I know now that God had this campaign with Leo in mind for me personally, as I began my own full-time journey into the political arena. I think He wanted me to see some real character before I became swallowed by the "go-along-to-get-along" mentality so prevalent in the halls of our legislatures.

Leo's narrow loss was a bitter defeat and hurt that would take me years to get over. Now I understand that often we must lose over and over again, or as long as it takes, to build into us the character we need in order to truly appreciate the real cost of victory when it does come. For His people, God will not allow it any other way. I don't know that I would have understood that then. I do know this: if we could do Leo's campaign over now, we could do it better—and we could win. And I would trade all of the victories I've enjoyed since then if I could go back and win just that one. But it seems I am far more interested in victory than God is. He is more interested in character. And I've discovered since, that when I pay more attention to that principle it is then that I receive my reward. Ultimately, true victory only comes when His character is instilled in us. Any other victory is hollow, and in reality, merely defeat in disguise.

There was an irony in Leo's U.S. Senate race for me personally. Leo's strongest, primary opponent, who was also the leading contender, was a four-term congressman whom I had actually done some work for in his initial race in 1982. My employer at that time, Bellevue's Kemper Freeman, Jr., a former legislator himself, asked me to help lay out the candidate's media and broadcast plan for the campaign because of my broadcast and advertising background. Although I was relatively backslidden at that time in my faith, I still felt better about doing the work for this particular candidate because I knew that, at the time, he was publicly pro-life.

Ironically, now, eight years later, I came back to work— this time against this man—as Leo Thorsness's campaign chairman. The congressman was also now running for the U.S. Senate along with Leo in what was a three-way Republican primary. As an incumbent congressman, he had now spent eight years in Washington, DC, and had suddenly become pro-choice, which often happens to many in office that lose sight of themselves and slip into the beltway reality of political correctness. It is what often happens to those who don't have the right character to begin with. And it happened to this man who went on to win the primary election in this Senate campaign, but who eventually lost in the general election.

It was an amazing thing to watch as Leo would speak to large and small groups around the state how the crowd would warm to him. He wasn't a particularly good speaker, and even had a gravelly, somewhat hoarse voice, but he spoke plainly and honestly with nothing contrived. His heart shone through, and the crowds responded to that. He didn't hide his feelings on any subject, and it was crystal clear where he stood on every issue and in his support of traditional moral values. But, it was here that Leo's life's trials were evident to anyone listening. The sincerity of the man came through and would always excite the crowd. Leo never planned it; it was merely natural and accidental.

On the other hand, Leo's opponent was a former radio announcer and television anchorman in Seattle with lots of experience at public speaking. At first, this opponent's speeches were the same old *say nothingness* that has come to characterize political speeches of both parties today. But as our opponent's campaign consultants began to watch Leo come away from each and every public appearance with the usual eighty percent or more support, over time the congressman's speeches became more "me too" in nature in an effort to try to stop the hemorrhaging of his support. I will never forget this, because it showed me the kind of character that most Americans are crying out for. It was on their faces, in their eyes. I'm convinced it is still the same today—perhaps more so.

My real baptism of fire came about three weeks before the end of the primary campaign for Leo Thorsness when the National Republican Senate Caucus, then headed by Senator Phil Gramm of Texas, arbitrarily decided to weigh in on behalf of Leo's congressman opponent. The caucus had gotten "soft-money" from major donors allocated to this congressman to the tune of more than four hundred thousand dollars. It was an unprecedented event and one which would bring about our loss. The spoken and unspoken cardinal rule in Republican politics is that the party, its members and organizations, never, ever, get involved in or take sides in a primary election.

This would be the first of many such Republican betrayals that I would witness over the coming years, which would eventually drive me from the ranks of the Republican Party. Funny thing today is that I probably get more respect standing outside the party ranks working for solid Republican conservatives than I ever did on the inside. For years following the 1994 Republican sweeps, many in the party's leadership, including the House speaker, tried tirelessly to put me out of business by telling candidates if they hired me, they wouldn't get any caucus financial support. In the end, their efforts only galvanized my standing with conservative candidates all the more. Of course, the threat was a bogus lie, anyway. As I told my candidates, the only thing you ever need to remember as a candidate is that the Republican Party needs you—and the seat you seek—far more than you need them. It was true, and following primaries, which we always won, the money would flow to my candidates as well. In the years since, the party's hatred of me has never outweighed their greed for power and obsession to be in the majority. It is from this hatred and quest for power that I find my own security.

Following the primary election, in which Leo narrowly lost, we were able to see that this soft money given to his opponent had made the difference and had cost us the election. It was apparent the congressman's camp had done a voter survey late in the campaign (which I discovered a few years later), and found out Leo was gaining so rapidly that this congressman was beginning to lose badly with conservatives to the point where he was likely to lose. Leo's message and character were gaining momentum. So, the three-term congressman had gone to the Republican establishment for help, and they did so, gladly.

The saddest thing of all is that Leo was the only candidate who could have beaten the Democrat in the general election almost on his credentials alone. Some believe that, since the Democrat was running unopposed in the primary election, a lot of rank and file Democrats were free to cross over in the primary election and vote for the congressman who made a better opponent for her in the general election. At this time, in Washington State, primary elections were a free-for-all, not requiring any party declaration. Nevertheless, this is another area where I believe the Republican Party is so busy listening to its own mantra, it doesn't have a clue as to what truly motivates the average American voter.

This is the thing I have come to dislike the most about the Republican Party leadership: I've seen in the past fifteen years, the good-old-boys club that breaks the rules whenever it suits its personal whims. In this situation, I would come to see this as the standard operating procedure for the left wing of the GOP. It did not like having a candidate like Leo Thorsness, who they knew had the courage to do what is right, even in the face of overwhelming pressures. Leo had been beaten so severely in POW captivity that anything the party wimps could dole out wouldn't faze him. GOP leadership always likes the candidates whom they can manipulate for their own legislative agendas, those who will dance to the Pied Piper. But Leo had been tested. He couldn't be bought, and they knew it. His opponent's voting record from both the state legislature and Congress was all over the board, clearly showing that he had either been bought or had no idea of what Republicans really stand for. As was becoming the norm in the mid '90s, he was running from the party's platform.

This U. S. Senate race was also my first exposure to the disease I now refer to *as reelection-itis* where getting re-elected becomes more important than doing what is right. It has become the black plague of politics. "Don't you see?" they say. "We must gain the majority in both houses before we can win any battles." But when they do achieve the majority, the GOP must continue to *not* do what's right in order to keep the majority. It's the voters' sucker game, the cats that chase their tails. They never catch them, but they're satisfied as long as they're still in view—just out of reach. They can at least continue to play the game.

Heroes and Villains

Another example of a serious betrayal that Americans who were paying attention were able to witness took place during the 1996 presidential elections. Pat Buchanan had won major southern primaries, the New Hampshire primary, and then went on to win the all-important Iowa primary, much to the chagrin of the GOP status quo establishment. One evening, a day or two following that victory, former HUD secretary, Jack Kemp, and Reagan man, Bill Bennett, appeared on *Larry King Live* to speak out against Pat Buchanan in front of millions of Americans. Their sole purpose was to stop the growing exodus of Dole's ranks over to Buchanan that they knew would only increase if he won again in future primaries. To Larry King's credit, he at least had the courtesy to ask them a pointed question about what he viewed as hypocrisy.

Following their filleting of Buchanan, King said: "Gentleman, I must ask this question. Your party has what's known as the Reagan 'Eleventh Commandment,' which, as you know, says 'Thou shall not speak ill of another Republican.' In light of that Republican cardinal rule, why do you come here and speak against Pat as you are?" Their answer was the telltale of true Republican politics. Mr. Kemp and Mr. Bennett told King, in essence, that Pat Buchanan was dangerous for America, and this point to them, overrode the intent of the Eleventh Commandment.

I couldn't believe my ears. This became one of many staples of betrayal that began driving me from the Republican Party. I've found this type of betrayal happening time and again here in Washington State. Whenever the rules don't fit the establishment's agenda, they simply break them.

This isn't about Pat Buchanan. It's about people who put themselves above the rules; rules which they demand the rest follow. It is the pinnacle of arrogance. Today, I tell my candidates to never sign the "Eleventh Commandment" pledge that the state party requires of all candidates who run under their banner. Once again, leadership threatens my candidates with the promise of no support should they not sign. But, as always, when it comes down to winning the primary and moving onto the general election, the party's need for the seat will always outweigh whether or not a candidate signed this pledge.

Besides, primaries are to show voters differences between candidates. Again, this is a character question. There shouldn't be an "Eleventh Commandment." The Golden Rule will suffice. If you have the right character, then integrity and honor among men and women will keep your remarks about your opponent focused on revealing where he stands on the issues, or his voting record in the case of an incumbent.

A few years ago, I had a candidate with an opponent who was extremely liberal and, in reality, was a Democrat. She had received campaign contributions from one sitting Democrat state legislator, another former Democrat senate candidate, and from many other usual Democrat supporting organizations. Because of some confusion in Republican ranks in this district as to who was the real conservative, I had written a fund-raising letter to my candidate's supporter list to set the record straight and calling our opponent out as a liberal and exposing her contributions. There was nothing personal, demeaning, or name calling in the letter, other than use of the label "liberal."

That letter found its way to the Washington State Republican Party chairman, who contacted my candidate to express his concern over "speaking ill" of another Republican. In a letter to the state chairman, I told him that when Reagan made that Eleventh Commandment statement, I understood him to be speaking of personal, demeaning types of attacks between candidates. I sent him copies of our opponent's contributions showing clearly that she was a Democrat, a wolf in sheep's clothing, and being supported by Democrats (which, by the way, is a common problem in Republican ranks). Then I went on to remind him that the purpose of a primary is to show the differences, politically, between opponents. Surely, Reagan knew that. And, finally, I told him that if that wasn't what Ronald Reagan meant then, in my opinion, the former president was wrong on that issue. The fact is the Republican Eleventh Commandment gives more help to the liberal candidates than it does to conservatives, because it becomes a silencing tool against exposing the real character or ideologies of candidates. Voters need choices.

As a consultant, I have yet to lose a primary election between a candidate of mine and a liberal candidate in a legislative race. I believe this is because we clearly show the difference between us as conservatives and them as liberals. Most Republicans understand the fundamental tenets of the party's philosophy and will gravitate to it when provided the facts. We didn't call this woman opponent personally demeaning names; we merely said she was a liberal and a "socialist." I told the party chair in my letter that we would surely welcome her referring to my candidate as a "conservative." In this case, I knew full well that the chairman, who is a liberal "mainstream" Republican himself, did not like my candidate. In the end we won the primary and went on to win in the November election.

To say what you believe in a campaign implies commitment. A candidate who refuses to answer where he or she stands on any issue is not worthy of my vote. The campaign philosophy of the Republican Party today is simple. In their heart of hearts, they believe that a vast majority of Americans no longer agree with most elements in their party platform, so they've abandoned many of those positions and then try to hide from the platform. The Democrats are now faced with a similar situation. Some candidates in the GOP out-and-out run from the platform, as Bob Dole did in 1996, in order to get elected. It didn't work in Dole's case, and he took a shellacking. More often than not, candidates who play hide-n-seek in a contested primary lose when they run. Voters—especially independent voters—can smell a phony who wants to be all things to all people. As the old saying goes: If you don't stand for something, you'll fall for anything! One attorney friend of mine once reminded me of a remark made once by Harry Truman who said: "If you have two Democrats in a race, the voters are smart. They will always vote for the real Democrat." I still do not understand why the GOP cannot understand this.

I'm not oblivious to the realities of campaigning. The one overwhelming factor in winning a race is name-familiarity. A huge majority of Americans select their vote almost entirely on that factor alone. This is unfortunate, but true. It is even more prevalent the lower you go in major races, from presidential on down to local races. After looking for party identification, people look next to a name they have heard. In state legislative races, I've always tried to tie that name, in everything we do, to a positive theme or idea I can plant in the minds of my candidate's voters. Usually, that theme is connected to an ideology that, after surveying voters, I find will play well with them. But always, we keep it honest.

It's the same with many other issues. Think about it. How many times has a Republican leader on the news said that the party will work for lower taxes, less government spending, less bureaucracy, less regulation, and so on? We know this is the primary philosophy of the GOP. But we never seem to get there. In fact, even during times of Republican majorities in Congress and state legislatures, over the past two or three decades, the opposite has happened—in most cases—with Republicans growing government even more! There are several reasons for this.

First, some people do mean what they say more than others. Other candidates don't mean it at all, but say it anyway. Still others don't know what they believe or what to say, and end up saying whatever some consultant tells them to say to get elected. More often than not, the basic philosophical foundation is there. What's missing is the character. It's from the character that a person finds the courage to take the tough vote.

Over the years, I've given up on simply drilling a prospective candidate on where they are on the issues. Although I still insist on a certain litmus test in deciding who I will work for, I spend more time these days dialoguing with a candidate to assess where he or she is in the character department. This has become another bone of contention between me and Republican leadership. I've developed a reputation for being unwilling to work for some candidates who I've felt were not solid enough in their views. In several cases, I've also fired candidates who wouldn't work or started to sell out on the issues. I've found that if they can't work on the campaign trail, they certainly won't have the character to do the right thing on the floor of the House or Senate. It makes no difference what you believe, if you don't have the courage to stand in the fire. The fact is, if people say they believe something but won't stand up for it, then they really don't believe it. Voters need to spend more time following their elected representatives' voting records to see if they are who they say they are. Believe me, there are plenty who are not.

The second reason for the doublespeak is ignorance. I have found many well-meaning legislators who have what I call "good conservative instincts" but no informational or educational background to back up those instincts. When faced, say, with a floor debate in the House or Senate, many a good freshman Christian conservative stands to his feet to speak, only to be verbally sliced-and-diced by a liberal-socialist who can smell a freshman legislator high on adrenalin but low on substantive knowledge. The problem then becomes that, lacking the understanding of why they believe what they believe, they become discouraged, begin to drift aimlessly, and become no good to anyone.

If I was setting the pace and agenda for the party, here's how I would do it.

We take a solid stand on all issues in our platform. We fight each and every time our issues comes to the floor. This is the intention of political warfare and, as stated earlier, when political warfare fails and tyranny is the result, the war moves from the legislative floors to the battlefields. That is the only true course of history. If we lose the majority and are unable to prevail because voters reject our ideologies, then voters get what they deserve. It's as simple as that. We must stop trying to fool them into electing us. It is disingenuous and merely slows the train on its way to hell, anyway.

"Doug, don't you understand that politics is the art of compromise?" I don't disagree, so long as you're not the only one compromising and that it doesn't include compromising away bedrock principles. In an earlier story, I shared how Washington State would be an entirely different place today, had the House Republican caucus held out on voting for the budget in 1995. Once again, that would have been a principled vote, the principle being two-fold: not going against commitments made to voters and, secondly, by remembering Republicans are the party that believes in lower taxes and less government. How can you vote for a budget that does the opposite? Here again, Republican leadership told the group of conservative legislators who were initially withholding their votes that they needed to support it this time so that they could be re-elected and come back and fix it the next time. But history now reveals that, even over two subsequent bienniums in which the Republicans reigned as the majority party in the House, they never attempted to accomplish this. In fact, they created and supported larger government and increased budgets.

It's a character issue. Say what they may, but the evidence refutes what leadership claims. The fact is, our political adversaries know what we're made of. They know that we've bought into their promotion of compromise and getting along. We want to be liked too much. We're not willing to be accused of being aggressive. I'm looking for candidates today who understand the situation in front of us. I'm looking for the candidate who is more interested in principle and standing tall, regardless of personal consequences; the candidate who disregards the prestige and perks; the one who says, "I will do what's right in this term. If I'm not re-elected, then so be it."

Looking for America

One of my candidates who irritates both Democrats and Republicans is a senator from southwest Washington. Don has long had a reputation of being aggressive and a fighter. He has been especially ridiculed for this from the Democrats and their left-leaning press, but also from the weak-kneed members of his own caucus who are generally not there to accomplish anything, anyway. In addition, some conservatives avoid Don, because, in my opinion, they too have a misunderstanding of how to wage political war.

But I love Don. The more I study history and the more I understand the character of our founders, the more I see a lot of it reflected in Don. If he had lived in revolutionary times, he would have been a Patrick Henry. In my book, he is a champion. He's not there to play games or enjoy the prestige. He's there to move the ball and win the game. That doesn't bode well in this day of "Hey, can't we just all get along?" Don most deliberately pokes the opposition in the eye at every opportunity.

I've had many a late-night conversation with Don and listened to his broken heart over losses he realizes could be victories if his caucus had some leadership with backbone. Others, who know Don well, know him as a man with a big heart. Val always calls him, "The big teddy bear in disguise." It's true. And I've always found these kinds of fighters are the ones with the big hearts. They're the ones who truly care enough to fight the fight. Don sees the sum total at the bottom of the page and is not willing to sit idly by while the country is sold out by cowards and squishes. In Don's case, as with others, it's a huge sacrifice for him to serve in the state Senate. It has hurt his personal business and been extremely hard on his family—a family whose children missed their father a lot over the ten years Don has served.

Personally, I've learned a thing or two from Don. Never have I met a person who moves forward and succeeds on pure will and adrenalin quite like he does, I'm convinced that if Don wants to accomplish something badly enough, he can't be stopped. He has the fighting spirit that will contribute to the success of the conservative agenda. Is he perfect? No. If he has one problem, it's that he takes on too many fights, and he knows it. But, champions do that. And Don is no different than anyone else; it's easy for him to stray if someone like me is not snipping at his heels. He's taken a few bad votes for which I've gotten into his face.

If we're ever going to move the needle, if we're ever going to make progress in reigning in this runaway government, if we're ever going to curb the tide of growing socialism, then we must begin grooming candidates who have the character to wage the kind of political warfare necessary for victory. The problem in America today is a character problem. What the Republicans did to Leo Thorsness—and to many others who have followed—proves to me that they really don't want change. In the end, they are really no better than the more prominent socialists of the opposing party. It works like this: If you believe exactly the same as I do but won't raise a finger—then you are my adversary.

Today, I have finally come to the point as a campaign strategist where I will not work for a candidate who will not take the "no tax" pledge. Republicans as a whole have been bought off by power and prestige. They want to be liked; they have bought into the political correctness of the times that says peace is more precious than liberty. And they have forgotten that on every principle they compromise, they lay a heavier burden on the coming generation in its quest to maintain freedom, along with an increasing likelihood of life in tyranny for Americans.

I always ask potential candidates if they believe the people are taxed enough. They always say yes. So, then I ask them under what circumstances they would support a new or an increase in taxes. If they squirm, I know I'm in trouble. If they decline the pledge, then they simply do not understand the problem today, nor will they ever be able to do anything other than vote for increases if they are elected.

I can't help but think of Dan, a House Republican from the 39th Legislative District, and his lovely wife, Janis. Next to Leo, Dan is my prized candidate, friend, and another true man of character. I've learned so much about what I lack in the character department just from watching Dan. He first ran in 2000 for the Washington State House of Representatives. Over the past five years our families have become close friends. He is quiet, but strong. I like that about him. He has the strength of Don, but the peace of Christ. He's well liked on both sides of the aisle—but he's solid as a rock. Early in our discussions the first time he ran, Dan had decided to take the "no-tax" pledge, probably largely due to my prompting, but he quickly understood the importance of this single objective and how it related to everything else he cared about in government. We spent many hours discussing the principles behind the issues.

I will never forget once after guiding the initial campaign meeting with Dan and his team and setting in place the plan, I had written their doorbell piece to be handed out at each door he visited throughout his district. I then e-mailed it to them for review. One night about a week later, I had a call from both Dan and his wife, Janis, who was on the bedroom phone. They had called late in the evening, following a campaign meeting with their team. Their voices conveyed concern. A new man, who had recently moved out to the west coast from Massachusetts, had joined their team and this particular meeting. They had showed everyone present at the meeting the draft proposal of the doorbell piece that Dan would use when doorbelling his district. I had written into it the pledge that Dan would never vote for or support any tax increase. This new campaign volunteer, who had some experience on Republican campaigns, had expressed strong concern over making such a pledge. The rest of the meeting turned into a discussion about the pledge.

By the end of the meeting, based on this man's points, not only was the team convinced, but Dan and Janis had also become convinced that such a pledge was ill-advised. As I listened to them share their heart over what this man had shared, I realized it was the same pragmatic talk I had heard so many times before. What if this, or what if that, what if a nuclear war breaks out—then what?

Republican leadership hates it when a candidate takes a no-tax pledge. When it happens, then leadership loses control over them or the possibility of getting a vote for a higher budget, as happened in the 1995 session that I spoke of in the previous chapter, or to use the budget for leverage on other things. Anymore, Republican leadership has joined the club and loves to pay off different groups in the same way the Democrats do. That takes money, and when it's all gone to feeding the burgeoning bureaucracy, more is needed to make the payouts. They can't do that if a majority of their caucus members are on record with no new tax pledges. Dan was given the same pragmatic arguments that this man on his campaign team did by the House Republican campaign group when they saw what I had written for him.

I listened as Dan and Janis both made a heartfelt case for removing the pledge from the doorbell piece. Ultimately, it was their decision. As we talked, I reminded them again that if Dan didn't take an oath to his voters now, my experience shows he would never be able to hold in Olympia. That is the reality. But they held that they wanted the pledge removed. In their final statement, Janis spoke and reiterated something they had said earlier in the phone conversation. "Doug, once again, it's just that we just think that this man was right. You can never say never. You just don't know." My frustration began mounting as I saw again the spirit of fear and pragmatism overtaking the moment. We were now down to whether or not I would print the piece the way it read or change it. It was scheduled to go to print the following morning.

"OK, Janis, let me ask you, is that statement true? We can never say never?"

"Yes, we believe it is. And we have counseled couples in marriage counseling in this way," she answered.

"Oh really," I responded. "Janis, let me ask you this. When Dan asked to marry you, did he say he would never cheat on you, or did he say he would try not to cheat on you?" Several moments of dead silence followed, then Janis spoke.

"Print it!" she said clearly.

The three of us laugh when remembering that night now. Dan did take the pledge. Not only did it not hurt him, it has helped him. The lobbyists who constantly hound legislators clamoring for a yes vote on some tax bill leave Dan alone. They know he took the pledge and will not bend. They recognize he's a man of principle and conviction. Republican leadership hates me for that. Other candidates I've had over the years have taken the same pledge. To Republican leadership, it seems character is an unneeded commodity in the art of politics. In any case, until the party is willing to make this commitment, voters are really given only a small marginal difference between what they get from the Democrats or the Republicans. I will say this: we will never see any substantial changes for the better in government at any level until voters demand elected officials make steadfast commitments.

Perhaps faltering marriages today really is a good analogy in this discussion and a reflection of what we see happening in our legislatures. Now, over fifty percent of marriages fail. It's interesting to note that the traditional marriage vow of commitment is also gone in a growing number of weddings. Until we begin looking for legislators willing to commit to not cheating on us, rather than just saying they believe in not cheating—until then, we will forever see larger and larger government budgets, more and more regulations (that take taxes to enforce), and a never ending depletion of our personal wealth and liberty.

To all of this, liberal Republicans would tell me I'm unrealistic, that these types of efforts will keep the party from gaining the majority, which is needed to steer the bigger picture of government. To that I say, first of all, no Republican ever lost an election because he refused to raise taxes—not ever! The past three decades prove that the GOP no longer has the character to win the fight—even when they are in the majority. The Republican Party desperately needs to understand that if they have to lie, manipulate, and sneak up on voters in order to win an election, then they can never get anything done once they gain power. What

Republicans are really saying is this: a majority of Americans agree with the Democrat agenda. But, if that's the case, then why would we lie to the people to get elected and then do the opposite of what we said? If we have to say "me too," echoing what Democrats say, then we may as well let the Democrats have it if that's what the public wants.

Again, Republicans would tell me that the campaign materials they write for their candidates never say much of substance anyway, so as to keep from saying anything that will irritate potential voters. And to that I say, I have been writing conservative messages of lower taxes, reducing government's size, and the other entire prominent bread-and-butter Republican platform issues for years—and my candidates are elected on them. The truth is: Americans support lower taxes as well as reducing the size and scope of government. By and large, so do a lot of Democrats. What Republican leadership doesn't seem to understand is that the voters just don't trust them anymore. The Republican Party has lost its heart and soul. The party that rose to power in just six short years championing abolition of slavery, today can no longer muster enough courage to fight for the life of the innocent unborn that is an integral part of its platform. Instead, some of its leaders run in embarrassment from the platform. Incredulously, the GOP has become fear based in its election decision making. They have become the party of Cain.

In addition, they refuse to be held accountable. The candidates I've worked for know full well that I will be there following the election to hold their feet to the fire, reminding them of what they espoused on the campaign trail. During one election a few years back, I remember once being asked to write an attack brochure on an opponent of a Republican woman I had once served as campaign consultant. Not long after she was elected, I saw what a mistake I had made. She had no more idea of what a good Republican should be than Stalin did about being a capitalist. After doing the research on her opponent's voting record and comparing it with hers, I called the state party chairman back and told him we should do the hit piece on her! She was a Republican, but her voting record was worse than many Democrats. There is nothing worse than tolerating this kind of behavior. But watching the types of Republican candidates the two caucuses in our state recruit to run for office, it proves that being in power is what they are really after. A majority of these people will never move the platform of the grassroots Republicans forward. Many of them are really Democrats who can only win in a district running as a Republican.

Once, Val mentioned to me during a discussion that even when her own senate caucus held the majority, she was amazed that they couldn't get anything done.

"Val, that's because you have never really been in the majority," was my reply.

When the party's caucuses are sprinkled with Democrats with "R"s after their names, that isn't a true majority, especially when they consistently cross the aisle and vote with the Democrats. If the Republican Party is supposedly the party of conservatives, then voters have been misled. Worst of all, conservatives who always get drawn in to vote for many of these liberal Republicans, are the ones made out the suckers.

As I contended in the previous chapter, the Scottish nobles in our midst are the real problem. William Wallace had Longshanks beat. But in the end he lost only because he was sold out by the nobles in order to keep the peace—and to secure more benefits for themselves.

Finally, on the issue of character and conservatism, I heard that one very good lady in our church had voted for Ralph Nader in the last 2000 presidential election. I'm sure many other Christians did, as well. While I understand the frustration of not wanting to vote for either a Republican or Democrat—not wanting to vote any longer for the status quo—I still squirmed in my seat when I heard this. Ralph Nader is not pro-life. How can you vote for a man—entrust your life to a man—who has no respect for life? A man who leaves the matter of murder up to the individual?

For all the tests Mr. Nader may pass in this lady's mind, he flunks the most important. Our Declaration of Independence lists life as the first and foremost important ideal of our society and then affirms that its government's job to secure that right to life. How can you trust people who declare to be pro-choice (pro-abortion) knowing full well that they are already violating their oath of office, in which they must swear to uphold the Constitution? Remember that the Declaration of Independence contain the stated values from which the Constitution was drafted. It was the stated purpose for which our founders split with Britain and went to war, the very reason they pledged and sacrificed their lives, fortunes, and sacred honor.

If we buy into the media hype that civil government has no place in deciding the moral issues of right and wrong, then we need to go back to the Scriptures and rediscover God's purpose in redemption, which was redeeming all of the physical world, as well as men and women. Further, if we think that the Constitution is just some antiquated document, I pray that we will have the decency to establish a new set of rules before we continue to violate the old set. If we disregard the law because we don't like it, then we're no better than the socialists we oppose; we are simply lawbreakers. Even if people don't agree with some things in the Constitution, they have an obligation to abide by it until it's changed, otherwise their own security under the law—any law—is in jeopardy. If civil government's foremost purpose is not to protect innocent human life, then we are all in serious trouble. If the primary job of government isn't to punish the wicked, thereby holding them accountable to a set of unchanging principles, then we are doomed to tyranny.

The most important thing in choosing a legislator, at any level of civil authority, is in determining whether or not that candidate has a correct understanding of the jurisdictions of God's various governments, in this case, civil government. Too often, I've come across potential candidates who understand some of the dicier moral issues, such as abortion or homosexuality, but have no idea of where to draw the line after that. Proper jurisdiction in consideration of such things as property rights, taxation, and many other functions of government are imperative for a conservative legislator to know. There are two ways of finding out. First, we need understanding of the whole of God's Word, applying it to every aspect of government. Second, we need to study the founding documents and historical writings to discover what the founders intended. If you want to know what to do with what you've got, you have to go back to the manufacturer—which is God first, then our founders.

But the one primary ingredient missing that keeps our leaders from being the statesmen who lived in our founding era is character. Even as a nation today, we celebrate

Hollywood celebrities as heroes. Now you even see this played out in our national institutions.

For example, it used to be that we had pretty high standards as a nation when it came to choosing those individuals to use on our postage stamps: faces of great people and presidents that appear on literally hundreds of millions of letters each year. In fact, not just faces, but symbols of our freedom and cherished traditions. Eagles, Old Glory, national monuments, Independence Hall, among many others. These were the constant reminders every day of what we stood for and where we came from. And, all of these things symbolized something deeper than what met the eye. They spoke to our values and served as common threads to weave us together in common purpose. It was merely preservation of a cherished culture.

Marilyn Monroe was an actress. Her life was a tragedy and ended so. I doubt seriously that anyone would want their children to aspire to the likeness of Marilyn Monroe. Whatever she represented certainly doesn't compare to those early Americans who gave so freely of their "lives and sacred honor" or to the monuments. They give us future and hope. That isn't to say that Marilyn Monroe didn't contribute anything. I just wouldn't put entertainment in the same class as freedom and liberty, even though Hollywood likes to.

If the earlier faces and symbols on stamps represented the true values and overall condition of America at that time, and the ones of today represent our current health and spiritual well-being, then we're in trouble. Where the earlier symbolized honor and the birth of a nation, this current one symbolizes the death of a nation. I mean, the early Americans died for causes we don't talk about much anymore. Marilyn Monroe died from drug overdose and sexual exploitation. So did Elvis and Jimi Hendrix, both of whom also have stamps. So, the next time you see, or use a Marilyn Monroe U.S. Postage stamp, think of it as a symbol of a culture gone wrong; a culture that has worsened since her death. Show it to your children as an example of what to guard themselves against. You may want to save a few of the old stamps to give them something to aspire to. Those old ones may not be around much longer. They'll probably be replaced by a Kurt Cobaine special edition.

As to character, I cannot forget the legislator who came out of his office door one early morning in Olympia in 1995. We were only a few weeks from the end of the session.

"Psssssst, Doug, got a minute?" It was about 7:30 A.M., and I had just walked past his door. He was one of the new Christian conservatives whom I didn't know on the campaign trail. He was from Puyallup, a teacher, yet as brave and as steadfast as anyone I had met down there. I walked into his office. There was an immediate difference in that Grant had set up a little oval table in front of his desk with a small couch on one side and chairs on the other. He told me he didn't like sitting behind the desk and having people in a chair in front of him as it felt like he was intimidating them.

"What's up, Grant?" I spoke as he closed the door and we both sat on either side.

"You know what?" he started. "Every day, since the beginning of session back in January, I've had Judy keep my calendar clear in the mornings, like now, so I could just spend some peaceful, quiet time in the Bible and prayer." I could see tears welling up in his eyes.

"But, well, you know the pace around here. The last couple of weeks I haven't done that. But today I could, only because my early appointment cancelled." I nodded as Grant continued.

"So, I'm sitting here this morning praying, and all of a sudden I realized something. You know what it is?" He looked into my eyes. "What is it, Grant?" I asked.

"I'm starting to like it around here. You know, the prestige; having the doors opened for me everywhere I go. I like it." He was in tears now. I started to smile—wider by the moment. I was almost ready to laugh.

"What in the world is so funny, Doug?"

"Listen, Grant." I sat up and leaned over. "I'm not worried about you. You just proved that you figured it out. You're OK. It's some of these other people I'm worried about."

As I observed with so many during that entire session in 1995 working for the House Republican caucus, I can see why the attraction to the power and prestige is so alluring. It's everyone, Democrat and Republican. Val, one time when introducing her husband, Keith, to me the first time, said this while he and I shook hands. "His job is to keep me humble." She wasn't smiling. And he does.

It is this kind of down-to-earth humbleness and self-examination that I find in all the people I've been chosen to work for over the years

I love them all. Val, Dan, Mike S, Mike P, John, Lois, Bill, Joyce, Cheryl, Joe, Lynn, Larry, Harold, Steve, Bob, Grant, Leo and Gene. I salute them. Character, regardless of what the media or academe say or how hard the present age tries to redefine it, it's really still the same as it's always been. They all would have made good Marines. They had the courage to stand and sacrifice. If I ever have to go to war again, I want them in the foxhole with me.

I'm reminded of Engels' writings on Marxist Leninism when he spoke of waging war, both politically and on the battlefields. His view of political warfare, he said, was the same as physical warfare. Said Engels, "Thrust your sword into them. If softness you meet, plunge forward. If steel you meet—retreat."

To conservatives who love this country and who see the road in front of us, Don't lose heart. Let them find steel!

The Clergymen

"You have done nothing for which to be ashamed."
—Benjamin Martin's sister-in-law in *The Patriot*

"I have done nothing. And for that I am ashamed."
—Benjamin Martin's reply

Hey, Doug, what happened? How did the homosexual bill end up passing in the legislature?" came a recent question from a friend of mine in my home church. He was asking about the same special-class protection bill that has been proposed for the past twenty-nine years in the state legislature. It's not unusual to get this type of question from people who know what I do for a living. I was somewhat surprised years earlier, though, when many people in this same church—including some pastors—never even knew there was such a proposal.

I turned to face him. As I did, a vision of so many years flashed before me and I realized just how long this one fight, among so many others, had been going on. But as I stood there looking at him, the standard reply just wouldn't come. Instead I remembered all of the fine legislators whom I had watched stand their ground over the years facing enormous pressure from their colleagues, having their names and reputations dragged through the press, many times in such slanderous and demeaning ways. A lot of them were gone from home for so many months out of each year while their kids grew and their family was strained without them. A lot of these people make such huge sacrifices that most will never understand.

I thought of Mike and how his marriage was tested to the limit as he carried out what he felt the Lord had called him to. I remembered how he had gone through three or four jobs in just two legislative terms in office. Serving in office puts a tremendous strain on employers, too. Many legislators who have their own small businesses get hurt the worst. Some come home to find it all but withered away. The salary legislators are paid is a pittance of what most people confuse with congressional salaries, but most in the church do not know that.

Selfishly, I also remembered the first three years my wife and I had not only gone unpaid but used our own savings to stay afloat for the privilege of serving the church. And all that time, not one time did anyone in my church, pastor or otherwise, ask to find out if we were doing OK financially. It had a huge impact on our marriage too, as I would often be gone weeks at a time, for months on end. The financial strain caused us to pull back at times to survive, and to do less than what I wanted.

"Do you want the truth? Or do you want me to sugarcoat it?" I asked my friend after my daydream. For me, something has broken. I realize now that we are seriously running out of time in America. Even at a Christian writer's conference recently, I was told many times how you must speak nicely, use short sound bites, don't be harsh, give them a takeaway—something they will like, sugarcoat it. I heard how the best-selling books for Christians are now romance novels. That's how we sell in America today. That's how we sell in the church. Make it taste and feel good—or it won't sell. As long as we don't swear in it or get too sweaty and direct in our love stories, then it's OK. In other words, just wash the sin in bleach, and it will be more palatable.

The truth doesn't sell well.

"The truth is, Carl, we lost because you don't care. That's right, Carl. It's because of you and countless other lazy, self-absorbed Christians who don't have a clue what is going on over in Olympia or in Washington D.C., nor do you care to? Want me to go on?"

"Sure." He says. What else is he going to say now, anyway?

"You watch the network news occasionally, and you think you're informed. You're not. You are being lied to. Tell you what, Carl, let me ask you a question. How many candidates have you ever supported financially with a contribution?"

"None I guess." He's getting sheepish now. I almost feel guilty. He tells me he has put up a sign sometimes in his front yard. Such sacrifice.

"I've been to your house. I see that you have a lot of the latest electronic toys and gadgets. In the summer you and the family take nice vacations. They and you are all well-dressed. You drive a nice car." I'm leaning in heavy now.

"Look, Carl. We lost this fight because you didn't show up for it, that's why. You know, it's not that hard to figure out, Carl. Bad laws come from bad legislators. If you don't like what is coming out of there, then you have to change who is sitting in the seats. Don't you get it?" I'm mad now.

"Well . . ." Now he's getting defensive. "There are a lot of things for Christians to get involved in, the first of which is my family. That comes first with me." I see the great escape coming.

"I've got news for you, Carl. All the things you want for your family are tied up in civil government and the liberty it is supposed to guard. If you don't want your daughter getting pregnant in high school, then you had better pay attention to the fact that they are passing out condoms there—and in junior-high—which is the same as promoting sex. If you don't want homosexuality to be taught as an acceptable lifestyle in your son's classroom, then you must fight to keep it out. Don't you see, Carl? If you raise your kids in a world of filth and decay and tyranny, then what good did your quality family time in front of the TV do you?

"So, it's like this, Carl. Until you sacrifice something of value, some comfort, some toy, and make a substantial contribution to the cause, you're going to see more of this."

"Well, why doesn't the pastor make a bigger deal out of it, then?" Carl asks. Here it comes—the buck-passing now.

I can't help but think of those who spoke of going to war against King George. It was not a friendly debate, as I understand it now. There was great division on the point. But, so many times the warm and cozy don't want to hear how cold it really is outside or to go out and bring in the wood. Patrick Henry today would be considered a fanatic. This is what he had to say on the matter and, specifically, about the truth.

"For my own part I consider it as nothing less than a question of freedom or slavery . . . It is only in this way that we can hope to arrive at truth, and fulfill the great responsibility which we hold to God and our country . . ."

The truth, is we don't care. Yes, we don't understand it all, either. But the fact is, we don't care enough to find out the truth. And Carl is right about one thing—most pastors don't care enough either, which then brings the whole story back to the beginning.

Alex de Tocqueville, in his travels diary, *Democracy in America*, made the following observation following his three-year journey through America in the early 1800s:

> I sought for the key to the greatness and genius of America in her harbors . . .; in her fertile fields and boundless forests; in her rich mines and vast world commerce; in her public school system and institutions of learning. I sought for it in her democratic Congress and in her matchless Constitution.
>
> Not until I went into the churches of America and heard her pulpits aflame with righteousness did I understand the secret of her genius and power . . . America is great because America is good, and if America ever ceases to be good, America will cease to be great.

Passing out condoms to our kids and force-feeding them in school that homosexuality is an OK lifestyle is what I would call "ceasing to be good."

Author, speaker, columnist, and former pastor of thirty years, Chuck Baldwin, made this observation in a recent article in *Covenant News,* entitled "America Has a Pastor Problem."

A pastor is never "off duty." He is literally on the job "twenty-four seven." For example, I cannot remember the last time my wife and I took a real vacation. It is even hard for me to remember the last time that I had a single day away from work, much less an entire week.

In addition, a pastor's work is, for the most part, vastly underestimated and underappreciated. And on the whole, his pay is barely adequate. His wife and children live under microscopes and virtually everyone lays claim to his time. Furthermore, pastors are some of the most criticized and denigrated people on the planet! They constantly find themselves at the butt end of jokes and sarcasm from unbelievers and are even castigated and harangued by people within the church. Therefore, it is no wonder that pastors are leaving the ranks at record numbers and are wandering from church to church like gypsies. No wonder so many pastors' children turn out bad, and no wonder so many pastors are having stress-induced heart attacks.

The first time I read Mr. Baldwin's article, I couldn't help but think he was talking about those brave, but worn out, Christian legislators who serve so tirelessly on the front lines of government. The description is exactly the same. But I realized he is right. The fight they are in is exactly the same one. The same things happen to legislators, too. They either get battle hardened or they get battle fatigued and fall out of the fight. For the most part, the church has vacated the battlefield and left many of the troops alone on the field.

Mr. Baldwin went on:

With all of that said, however, it still behooves me to very frankly say that America's basic problem today is a pastor problem! Our nation is collapsing from within because pastors are sitting idly on the sidelines, refusing to be trumpets for truth! With all of the duties and responsibilities associated with the pastor's job description, no duty or responsibility is any greater than that of being God's watchman! Unlike any other, the pastor stands as a voice for truth in the midst of a cacophony of lies and distortions.

Remember, too, that John the Baptist went to prison and eventually lost his head, not for preaching the Gospel, but for boldly denouncing Herod's adulterous relationship with his brother's wife. Furthermore, the boldness of men such as Isaiah, Jeremiah, and John the Baptist has been the pattern of genuine preachers throughout history. Men of God throughout the ages have possessed the same sort of grit and character as was found in Moses, Elijah, Jeremiah, John the Baptist, Simon Peter, and the Apostle Paul. They were courageous, uncompromising men! They feared no man, be he politician or potentate! They attempted to please no man or group of men! They were untouchable, incorruptible, indefatigable proclaimers of truth! When Germany and Switzerland needed reformation, there was Luther and Zwingli. When Scotland needed liberation, there was William Wallace, supported by numerous Scot preachers. When England needed someone to help rid it of slavery, there was Wilberforce and his band of committed clergymen. America, especially, has enjoyed a plethora of firebrand preachers. In fact, the American revolution would never have taken place but for the preaching of Jonathan Edwards, John Witherspoon, John Leland, and hundreds like them.

So, what has happened to the current generation of preachers? How is it that there is such a dearth of leadership from America's pulpits? Where is the loud, clarion call for truth? Where are the preachers who are willing "to root out, and to pull down, and to destroy, and to throw down"? Where are the courageous, fearless, undaunted men who would rather die than compromise?

Instead of championing truth, today's pastors champion political parties. They cater to wealthy contributors. They wiggle around controversy and grovel before government bureaucrats.

Of course, it doesn't take a brain surgeon to figure out that today's avant-garde preachers are being cheered on by a host of friends and supporters. After all, look at the "big" churches in America today. What do you see? Do you see "big" pastors marching in pro-life rallies? Do you see them carrying placards outside of abortion clinics? Do you see them rushing to the side of Terri Schaivo? (In this regard, the Rev. Jesse Jackson was willing to do what not one "big-name" evangelical leader was willing to do. Amazing!) Do you hear them challenging President Bush when he refuses to assist Alabama Chief Justice Roy Moore or when he increases federal spending for abortion providers or when he appoints numerous open homosexuals to high public office?

I could not count the numbers of people who have privately told me how much they appreciate my public stand for this issue or that. They have slapped me on the back and said, "Go get 'em." But, where do they attend church? Where do they give their financial contributions? At the "big" church where the pastor won't say "boo" to the devil.

As Martin Luther said, "If I profess with the loudest voice and clearest exposition every portion the truth of God except precisely that little point which the world and the devil are at the moment attacking, I am not confessing Christ, however boldly I may be professing Christ. Where the battle rages there the loyalty of the soldier is proved. And to be steady on all the battle fields besides is merely flight and disgrace if he flinches at that point."

I truly believe that if enough preachers would decide to be the courageous proponents of truth, as were our ancestors, and would determine to preach the truth without fear or favor regarding any person or political party, they could turn our ship of state around post-haste! I further believe that if they don't do it soon, it will be (if it's not already) too late.

Furthermore, if and when the funeral wreath is hung on the door of America, historians will correctly record that it was our pastors who let her die. Solve the pastor problem and America's basic problem is solved.

One time, I was privileged to teach a civics class in my home church adult Sunday school class. This particular Sunday was the seventh week of my eight-week course. Having been explaining to this group of about a hundred-fifty or so church friends about the importance of civic involvement, I decided to find out how many had ever been intimately involved in an election campaign.

"I'm not asking the following question to embarrass anyone, but just to learn myself about an opinion I carry. So, it's OK. Please just answer honestly." I knew the answer before I spoke, but I still hoped it would be different. "How many here have ever made a financial contribution to a candidate for public office?"

Two hands went up. I was afraid of that. That's less than one percent. No wonder we're losing.

And now I see so very clearly that our pastors are the gatekeepers to the most powerful entity the world has ever seen. Sometimes I am totally amazed that pastors don't see the power they truly wield and were entrusted with by God. As I stood there with only two hands to count, knowing how my own pastors were unplugged from the civil arena as well, it struck me. The American church is in disobedience and has missed its assigned duty. Or, as we used to say in the Marine Corps, the church is simply AWOL: absent without leave. I knew all about that.

. . . It was just a few days before Christmas 1969, and I had been out of trouble for a while. Lieutenant Colonel Lavelle told me to stand at ease and then asked me if I knew what the three pieces of paper were lined up on his otherwise completely clear desk.

"No, sir," I said, although I had a hunch what one of them was, because the night before, Jerry and I had been bar hopping in Santa Ana. We had changed our military identification cards so they would show our birth dates one year earlier. We were twenty years old at the time, but you needed to be twenty-one to drink legally in California. Passing back through the gate, I was nabbed by the Marine guards when my military ID card didn't match up with my Washington State driver's license. They rarely checked, but this was the luck I seemed to be having in these earlier days in the Corps.

"This one is a meritorious mast for the fine work you've been doing in your section," LtCol. Lavelle started. "Along with this second one—a meritorious promotion back to PFC," he continued. "Seems as though some people around here think you're a pretty good Marine. And this one," the colonel stood up and pointed to the second sheet from behind his desk, "is your leave paper to go home for five days at Christmas. And, now," the colonel looked back down to his desk top and picked up the last piece of paper. "What is this, Simpson?" he barked, now pointing to the document from the previous night's outing—the paper report writing me up for illegally changing my military identification card.

"Sir . . .," I started to explain to him what we were doing, but he silenced me with a simple wave of his hand.

"I know what you were doing, Marine," he said more calmly now. "But don't you understand we can't have people running around making up phony IDs for obvious reasons."

"Yes, sir," I followed.

He paused momentarily, and then sat down slowly. He looked up straight into my eyes. "Private Simpson, to me your life seems a book of contradictions," he spoke in a genuine fatherly tone. "One minute, I can't find a finer, more competent and outstanding Marine, and in the next moment you've got one foot back in the crap again," he stood up, his eyes never leaving mine. "Son, it's time to grow up. You're a good and capable young man; now it's time to live up to it. You may not think much of yourself right now, but there are a lot of people who think you're a pretty good man." He paused once again.

The results of my earlier courts martial for being AWOL included 120 days hard labor in the infamous Camp Pendleton "red line" brig. But after spending just four days there, I was released late one night and taken back to El Toro Marine Corps Air Base. I found out later that Lt. Col. LaVelle had gotten me released, yet without any explanation whatsoever. He didn't agree with the outcome of the trial and knew there were other extenuating circumstances that I had refused to talk about, even at my courts-martial. I never knew that he was aware of the truth.

"OK, here's what we're going to do," he reached out to hand me my promotion warrant and shake my hand. "Congratulations on your new stripe," he smiled warmly as he shook my hand. "Have a nice time at home," as he handed me my leave papers. "And we'll take care of this third item when you get back," he said, pointing to the paper charging me with the previous night's infraction, which remained on his desk.

But we never did take care of it. Nothing ever came of that paper that I know of—at least in terms of me "standing tall before the man," as we called it in his office. But within a week of returning from Christmas leave, I received combat orders for Vietnam.

I would never forget his words to me that day. Another day, three years later, just prior to being released from four years of active duty in the Marine Corps, I happened to run into him at Camp Pendleton. I was now a sergeant. I thanked him for those earlier words. It would've been easy to believe that my orders to Vietnam were the punishment he foresaw. Later, I came to realize that it was not the punishment that Lt. Col. Lavelle had in mind, but rather, the opportunity for a lost and immature young man to find himself. He knew that only in a tough situation might I rise to a new level. He saw something that I couldn't in those earlier days.

I had been told by the courts-martialing officer a year-and-a-half earlier that "It is likely you will never see lance corporal in this man's Marine Corps." Yet, in Vietnam, I had received two meritorious field promotions and was selected for another field promotion to sergeant before returning home, including several air medals and three meritorious commendations. It was indeed a contradiction. It would be an event that would change my life forever and set me on the road to my destiny. Lt. Col. LaVelle had put me on my way to regaining my self-respect and discovering who I really was. All I knew at the time was that I wanted to make up for my misdeed, that of being AWOL.

In due time, as a church, we will all stand before the Man, as I did. And we will be held accountable for being AWOL. Sometimes we get so caught up in living the good life day to day that we forget about the past and the tomorrow coming so fast. We forget that our actions today will affect so many after us. There are literally millions of people in the future who are counting on me to fulfill my life's obligations today and every day. Often, when that reality strikes me, I'm nearly brought to my knees. But, who am I?

Cain, forgot the consequences of his failures. Cain wanted the promise of the present, trading all of the future for the reward of God at that moment. In doing so, he also traded away the moment.

The church in America today is a paltry shell of itself when compared to the pastors of the founding era and the role the church played. In many ways, it has now become similar to the church in Christ's time. The modern church, too, has sold out to Caesar.

In America, we have legalized being on the take with the beloved federal 501-C3 tax exempt status for churches that choose to stay out of politics. If they don't they become subject to the same tax burden as everyone else. And, of course, there is the Social Security tax exemption for any pastor who chooses to take that personal tax advantage, plus other hefty deductions the rest of us don't get. But I'm sure they also had a cut in Christ's day. Wasn't that one of the reasons why He overturned the tables in the tabernacle?

The liberal-socialists know exactly when to pull the chain. Several years ago there was a bill proposal here in Washington State to revoke the tax exemptions of those churches that get involved in elections. It was (House Bill) HB-1929 titled "Changing the Tax Exempt Status of Non-profit Organizations." It was being proposed by a Democrat representative from southwest Washington. The Democrats don't fool around. They go for the throat. Flushing out the meaning of the title here; "non-profit" means "churches." And the true reason for the bill behind the façade was to keep churches from distributing voter guides recommending specific candidates and encouraging churchgoers to vote for them.

Although the bill died a timely death in committee near the end of that legislative session, it is likely that few church pastors were even aware of the bill in the first place, simply because they are just not paying any attention, nor are the countless people warming the pews who are sedated by *Seinfeld* at 6:30. The fact is, as I tell any pastor who will listen, a law such as this would probably never pass muster in the U.S. Supreme Court, anyway. And, it is doubtful that the government would ever try to enforce it because of that. But it's a moot point because the liberal-socialists are well aware of the present impotence of the church. In any event, there are many reasons for the church to stay uninvolved.

It was during this time early on that I began to discover that tax exemptions are rendering the church useless in the civil arena. I am also acutely aware that it becomes a convenient excuse to avoid the conflict altogether. The political fight is a tough one and not for faint of heart or the lazy minded.

After I lobbied against HB-1929 for a short while, I suddenly stopped and came to my senses. One day when I stood to leave after visiting with a legislator from Spokane on another matter that year, he asked me, "Doug, tell me how you feel about HB-1929." I turned at the door and thought for a moment. Then I responded, "Oh, I hope you pass it." He looked surprised. "Are you telling me the churches you represent would approve of your support to remove their tax exempt status?" "No," I said. "But they aren't here, nor are they even aware that I'm here. So, until they show up, we'll do it my way." He looked baffled. "But I will tell you this," I continued. "The day you actually pass this bill and revoke their exemptions, well that is the day they will finally come to town."

The Clergymen

With that I turned and left. A few days later the bill died in committee, of which this particular legislator was chairman. Later on, I realized I shouldn't have said that to him. It just might have been the very thing that killed the bill. The last thing the liberal-socialists want is for the church to come to town. In the legislature, you must never lose sight of the bigger picture.

My own church leadership all but ignored what I was trying to do. I used to meet with my pastor whenever I could get his attention, but other than a slap on the back and a heartfelt "go get'em," his mind was on other more important things. At breakfasts I had with him from time to time, if I went on about it too long, it seemed his eyes began to glaze over. So, I stopped doing that. I've found that it really is true that we do only invest in the things dearest to our hearts. It's an old story, really; liberty has always been taken for granted.

As with other churches, a steady parade of foreign missionaries came and went from our church. I began to see that so much of the church as a whole today is so busy playing church, we've missed the assault taking place inside our own camp. As in the church of Christ's day, we have elevated Caesar to a pedestal and have rendered ourselves powerless to deal with him. Don't misunderstand me, Sunday schools, foreign missions, and other programs are important. But, without a strong home front, churches have no platform from which to launch their missions. Any military commander understands that the most critical aspect of winning a war starts with defending your own home ground.

I see the same structure in much of today's American church government as I do in American government. It is my opinion that oftentimes many pastors end up seeing the structure of church government the same as the Old Testament methods from an overview perspective. In other words, as I mentioned in an earlier chapter, pastors view it from a corporate worldview. Oftentimes, I think the individual gets lost here as well.

I remember once visiting the old Christ Church in Alexandria, Virginia, that was originally built in the mid-1700s. I was struck by the fact that the pews were "family" pews structured so that the pews in each were facing to the middle, so that the persons sitting in a particular pew would be facing each other, rather than the front. In other words, the emphasis was on family, not the pastor. They were big on families praying together in those days. The pastor's perch was a spiral staircase that elevated him to a place so the sermon could be better heard. The focus here was definitely on individuals. Today, all of our pews face forward; the focus is almost always on the pastor and his associates in a governmental fashion. And the benevolence that was once up to the individual has now fallen to a board within the church.

I've often told friends that I believe that anything that happened or happens structurally in American civil government, likely happened in the church first. In other words, the move from individual to a more corporate view of government happened first in the church. I think a study of American church history shows this. Benevolence is a prime example. Historically, at the same time this mission was being turned over to the civil arena, it was being passed up to the top in churches, too.

Today, the church sees itself as a victim of government, rather than understanding they were intended to be on top.

The Clergymen

It has become just another in a long line of whiners. I can't help but see a leadership in the church today that dreams of a time when they will stand before the true King and be able to exclaim: "Lord, Lord, look what they did to me." Unfortunately, I believe that what they will hear for an answer is: "No, look what has happened because of your lack of stewardship. Look at the tyranny and despair caused on the succeeding generations because of your lack of stewardship, you slackers! What have you accomplished with what I gave you in establishing my Kingdom on earth?"

In the past two decades, I've been involved as a member of two churches and watched as both have come apart. In both cases, I believe it was due to bad governmental structure. The shame of it all is that they were both churches that recognized the importance of passing off the baton to the next generation and worked toward that end. But both churches had all but eliminated a governmental system of checks and balances or accountability to a set hierarchy and, to a great extent, created a monarchy for the pastor. Church leadership began usurping more and more power from parishioners and the whole thing started to unravel. Much like civil government, they saw a void in some situations and tried to fill it. Well intentioned as it might have been, as I've said before and have come to understand, if it doesn't fall under your jurisdiction, it will fail no matter what you do.

When I go to church, I want to be challenged. I don't want to be saved over and over again every Sunday. I want to grow. I want to know what my life is supposed to be about. I want to be pushed forward to complete my destiny. Is it really any wonder why kids today are bored to death in most churches? For the most part, today, they are left with the belief that they're just another member of a group of souls that accidentally happened along this planet in this solar system at this time—a big cosmic accident imagined by the liberal-socialists. They are told, sometimes unspoken, that the object in life is to get through it all and sin as little as possible so that you can pick up your gold watch and check out at the other end, all with "fewer black marks on your heart" than the guy sitting next to you. We've even turned this into a spectator sport now.

What we so desperately need to tell them is that they are individuals specially designed by the Creator with a very specific purpose. Their life has been planned for them by a great and merciful God who loves them and will clear the road in front of them as they become aware of Him and the task before them. We need to tell them that they cannot possibly lose. We need to tell them that their sins of the past, present, and future have already been forgiven so that they never have to question their redemption again. And, finally, we need to tell them that they need to fight sin in their own lives because, not out of fear of becoming guilty again but, as with Job, it is a snare, a trap to keep them from reaching the prize of their destiny. They are God's plan for the future.

There is one—and only one—entity in the world today that has been given all authority on earth and that is the authority that was given the church. Either we didn't know or have forgotten that *only* the church has authority. In fact, it is the church's moral authority in the political world to-day that escapes the lips of most pastors. Ironically, it was the church that set the perimeters of this nation's original blueprint, without which we would have been nowhere near the city on a hill we became.

Perhaps another way to characterize it would be to say that the very freedoms we enjoy today, as well as the unprecedented prosperity we have enjoyed as a people, are a direct result of this nation's willingness to follow God's governmental precepts in the first place—ever since the sailing of the Mayflower.

If the foregoing statement is true then, in terms of God's grace on this nation, I believe that today we are living on borrowed time.

In my view, our nation's future successes and prosperities are predicated upon what the church does or doesn't do—and not any other factor of society. It really is that simple. The day the church retakes its rightful place of authority in the political arena is the day America will return to its greatness—not a moment before. What we are witnessing today is nothing new. It is the ongoing struggle between the kingdom of darkness and the Kingdom of light, right and wrong, good and evil. For the original covenant by the Pilgrims of Plymouth Plantation was simply a dedication of this land and its inhabitants to the Lord God Almighty. Let us remember that those one hundred and two passengers aboard the Mayflower came here for one purpose—that of liberty from sin through the freedom of worship. When that is lost, then America will be lost.

I always remember the scene in the movie *Braveheart*, as the men of the Scottish village were discussing what to do after Longshanks had broken his word and killed all the men and pages who came to the meeting. Later that night, there was a lot of chatter as they sat about the campfire trying to decide what course to take. Finally, one man spoke up: "There are too many of them to beat them."

Came the reply from Malcom Wallace, "We don't have to beat them, we just have to fight."

Today, once again, many of the evangelical leaders, and some I view as self-purported prophets, are again calling for a revival. I love revivals. I've been through a few. And revivals always call for prayer and fasting, and I'm all for that. But I've come to see a troubling pattern about this phenomenon and its use by churches. Too often, the effort of the church stops with prayer and fasting and fails to extend to action. In every case I can think of in the Old Testament, revivals of fasting and prayer almost always produced significant change and preceded war and action by God's children. These revivals caused a course correction in the world in which Israel lived.

In America, in the past forty years and following several revivals, things have only grown worse. And I believe that is due in large part because too many church leaders like to blow the trumpet but fail to rally the congregations behind them. Thus, in my political walk, I've become very skeptical of these cries for revival. It takes money to win political warfare and money takes sacrifice. Yes, let's get a million people to pray and fast for days on end. But the real revival comes when that million people are changed in that revival and rise up to carry the banner forward.

We cannot lose. As Christ hung on the cross in the latter moments, He saw it for us and proclaimed, "It is finished." With those words, He left us with all we need to complete the mission. Again, it's a crisis of faith. We must turn from our deistic views of an uninvolved god and see again the great, active, and magnificent God standing before us. We need to see as Abel did. Abel knew he could not lose and gave his best. He knew that giving his best was his only choice. And God held him in regard for his choice.

The Clergymen

Pastors, you have the most powerful weapon on earth! You have all the wealth at your disposal. At a moment's notice, all the battles of the legislature can be over tomorrow. You are the commanders of the greatest army ever assembled. But we need to be careful not to succumb to the same mantra of the Republicans: that we will not take up the fight unless we know for sure we can win.

I remember an old black and white western movie one time when I was a kid. All I remember is that there were three or four cowboys on horses fleeing from about five hundred Indians on ponies. These cowboys made the mistake of taking a wrong turn and found themselves pinned into this canyon with the only way out being the way they had entered. So they sat on their horses facing away from the entrance at the sheer wall in front of them and the approaching Indians behind them. Finally, one of the cowboys—seeing that they were trapped and finished—says, "Well they've seen our backs. Now let's show them our faces." So they turned and charged this huge army of Indians. Well, in typical Hollywood style the movie ends there. And we know that they perished.

But, what struck me about that movie is the courage—even in the face of complete futility. We need that in the church today. We don't have to beat them, we just have to fight.

A Patriot

"If ye love wealth greater than liberty, the tranquility of servitude greater than the animating contest for freedom, go home from us in peace. We seek not your counsel, nor your arms. Crouch down and lick the hand that feeds you; may your chains set lightly upon you, and may posterity forget that ye were our countrymen."
—Samuel Adams–father of the American Revolution

Following the end of legislative session, almost every legislator, staff member, and lobbyist leaves town in a rush to get some rest and recreation. The grueling pace and stress has caught up with most people by this time, and the marble hallways around the capitol are all but deserted the day following *Sine-die*.

Me too. My family has planned a week's cruise to celebrate my great aunt's 100th birthday and are catching a plane in Seattle bound for Los Angeles and, eventually, Ensenada, Mexico, via the Carnival cruise ship lines.

"You will have to step over here with me." The woman speaking wore a starched white blouse with the large capital letters TSA on the back. Her green slacks, wide black belt with walkie-talkie and one small leather case attached give her the appearance of being law enforcement. I think the idea is to provide a sense of security for the masses. It may for some, but doesn't for me. This security agent had randomly picked my great aunt for a more in-depth search as part of the new airport security measures under the Patriot Act recently passed by Congress.

"Would you like to sit here to remove your shoes?" The woman asked my great aunt who, at one hundred years old, has all but lost her sense of balance. Towering at four-foot, ten inches on her toes, she weighs just over a hundred pounds. Her hair is totally white, and she can barely hear, so I guide her into the chair and try to explain more than once that she will be searched. She looks a bit uneasy.

We had already taken everything out of our pockets, placing them in the plastic container, along with our shoes. All keys, loose coins, and everything metal had already been cleared to the other end of the conveyor, and security was now going through my great aunt's carry-on luggage.

"What is this?" The security agent asks, looking at my aunt and holding a miniature set of antique nail scissors. *Her question is a bit overzealous,* I thought. I answered for my aunt. "I'm sorry, but you cannot take these," she informs us. My great aunt has had these tiny heirloom scissors all her life, given to her by her mother. The security agent tells me the only way to be able to keep them is if we return to the main terminal and find somewhere to mail them back home to ourselves. This is now impossible, because the time we've already taken to clear security has eaten up any excess time before the flight leaves. We left them there.

A Patriot

My great aunt is now asked to stand, legs spread, so that they can run their wand all over her, up and down each side, up the insides of her legs, and completely around her. She stands with her arms up in the air, teetering with her loss of balance at her age. *She appears slightly intoxicated and like a criminal being frisked after some bank heist,* I think, as I watch this travesty.

"It is for your own good." I am told by those who defend this process by authorities under the Patriot Act. To which I say—even if I agreed with that statement—searching a hundred-year-old woman who can barely walk, hear, or see is not reasonable by anyone who has watched the events unfold since the attack of 9/11. More than once I have received e-mails that clearly list every single terrorist attack since the Munich games of 1972. Every single one, with the exception of one totally disconnected from middle-east terrorism, was perpetrated by Muslim males of middle-eastern decent between eighteen and forty-two years of age. So whom, by any common sense, should the TSA be looking for as the most likely culprits?

Common sense is a problem today in government. We have traded it in on political correctness that says we must not discriminate—even if it kills us. So, in this instance, we will fool around and humiliate little hundred-year-old ladies rather than focusing on the proven demographic of potential terrorists. We want to appease those who might think it is wrong to focus on those who are proven likely to commit a heinous crime. We are now more afraid of offending someone than we are of facing the prospect of another terrorist attack that might claim multiple thousands more lives. That is not reasonable, nor is it American. Any legislator who approves of such bidding is not our friend.

Once again, it is Cain. It is the coveting of equity that overrules plain logic.

The fact is, procedures such as this new airport security—and much of the Patriot Act as a whole—have nothing to do with security. It is mostly a giant federal public relations program to make people think they are more secure—sort of a sedation of the masses. And, perhaps it also has to do with adding 175 thousand more people to the federal payroll. Does anyone who understands history think for a minute that we will ever see the end of this?

I have found one thing true about bureaucracy, which is that once bureaucracy solves a problem, it will usually either deny the problem has been resolved, or will create another, in order to remain attached to the tax nipple. Already the combined weight of federal, state, and local government makes government the number one employer in the land. As some have warned, with more than fifty percent of the workforce now employed by government and with around fifty percent of our income going to some form of taxation, it is hard to say we are not already a full-blown socialist country. Even the briefest look at history, shows it will only grow worse. It is important to remember that government is not a producer, it is a consumer. And most of the needs we receive by government can be done cheaper and far more efficiently in the private sector.

The real price to liberty came fairly early on after the 9/11 attack.

"This war against terrorism we are now engaged in will likely last decades," came the response from the Secretary of Defense—who was repeating President Bush—when asked about how long the war on terrorism will last. I was horrified. Any historical study of our founding fathers shows their clear warning of becoming involved in "foreign entanglements," as it was called by President George Washington. In most of their writings, we find a further aversion of fighting protracted wars of attrition that they understood would simply sap our wealth and economy, and drain our sense of well-being as a nation.

Today, however, we have become the police of the world, now fielding a military presence in over 147 countries, to which most Americans paying attention, I believe, are growing weary.

Americans are now under surveillance twenty-four hours a day outside their homes and, in some cases, inside their homes. Views of concern expressed by many in Congress of both parties over the extent of powers granted under the Patriot Act are certainly warranted.

As a Vietnam War veteran, I couldn't help but wonder if we had learned anything after that devastating ten-year war. My concern was not the question of whether or not we should have been in Vietnam in the first place but, rather, the way in which the war was conducted. Many people will remember it was at the outset called a "police action." It only became a war after it had become so obvious that it could no longer be sold otherwise. There are so many resemblances to what we are doing now it is eerie. If I'm sounding "anti-war" here, please read on, so that you know it isn't so. I just believe there is a specific time and way war should be fought.

A short time following the attack of 911, I wrote the following op-ed piece for the local paper, having been asked to do other articles in the past. They refused to run it, of course. And it needs to be remembered that within two weeks after the attack, nearly all media deliberately stopped running video footage of the planes attacking the Trade Towers in Manhattan. I believe this was because it was enraging an easily-led public who, in their growing anger, would have supported more than what was then being offered by the Bush administration in retaliation. What we were told at the time was that many psychologists felt that watching the attack in such graphic display was damaging to the American psyche.

I think that not watching is more damaging.

A Declaration of War

As I watched those planes slam into the Trade Towers and Pentagon, I wondered even then if we would truly grasp what was happening to us. Pearl Harbor resulted in only half the casualties of this attack, yet we had no problem understanding what had just happened to us as a people at that time and no problem declaring war. Are these people any less a threat than Emperor Hiroito or Adolph Hitler? Bin Laden and Islam have openly pledged our complete destruction, which is their declaration of war on us. What is it we are missing here?

Since September 11, I have seen in the press this growing notion that we can find Bin Laden and company, arrest them, and bring them to justice in some sort of world court of law. What shall we try them for? Murder? Kidnapping? Hijacking? Flying without a license?

Since World War II, the United States has yet to issue a declaration of war for every conflict in which we've been engaged. We have also lost every conflict in which we've been engaged. Is there a connection here? Less

A Patriot

than appropriate responses by American leadership have consistently left our commitment to resolving conflicts half-hearted. I remember only too well the lack of national will with regard to my own experience in Vietnam and the effect it had on all of us serving there, as well as those at home..

This most recent assault on our nation was the most outrageous act of war against the sovereignty and people of the United States of America—ever! It was not the murder of 3,500 persons. It was their death by a declared war, by an avowed enemy and as such, requires a like response. Breach of civil law requires law enforcement; an act of war requires a response of war. This is not an issue that can be settled by civil courts, because it stands in direct defiance of all law perpetrated by a people who reject the very law of God.

In these situations then, it is only war that can reestablish and reaffirm the law and its basis—not the other way around. And what is wrong with those in our nation at present who are running around soul-searching, trying to figure out what it was we did wrong to make these wonderful people so angry at us? I've got news for them: these people hate us and will not be bought off!

During a foreign policy discussion recently, someone said to me that we didn't lose in Korea, Vietnam, or the Gulf. According to their reasoning we merely compromised and walked away. But isn't stopping short of victory the same as defeat? And every time we've pulled up short, we've simply deferred the inevitable pain to a future generation for resolution. The problem simply grows worse.

This present crisis began ten years ago when George Bush, Sr., pulled up short 125 miles south of Baghdad before the fight was finished. Now it's come home to roost. And I'm not sure Junior is up to the task.

Bin Laden and company do not share the political correctness of the liberal elites in our country who say that nothing is worth fighting or dying for. They proved that during the first few seconds of the attack. If you turn the other cheek to these folks, you'll end up dead. This attack on the United States was entirely without concern as to civilian deaths. Incredibly, they used American civilians as weapons. During the Gulf war, we began spoiling the world into believing that war can be fought in a surgical manner of high-tech weaponry with pinpoint accuracy inflicting few civilian or "innocent" casualties. So what we've done now is create a situation wherein world opinion will no longer tolerate collateral damage on the part of America in military conflict.

The Geneva Convention is a great concept; it's just that nobody but us is abiding by it. Don't misunderstand me; I'm not advocating its abolishment or senseless carpet-bombing of innocent women and children. I'm merely saying that it happens that the innocent die in war and always will. To think that war is only fought between those in uniform is to deny the facts of what just happened to us or other peoples throughout history—including America's own war for independence. We cannot separate citizens from their government in the assignment of responsibility; nor should we.

Our nation's charter is predicated on the belief that the power and ultimate responsibility for civil authority rests on the shoulders of the people. So how is it, then, that we can believe that it's different for any other people? It's not different. If it's a true principle, it's true for all. And the only way any people will rise up and take responsibility for their country's government is when they pay the price for their government's irresponsibility. If that wasn't the case, then America would have never been born in the first place.

War is a messy, ugly thing and, as cruel as it sounds, that's how it's supposed to be. In the end, when victory is achieved with truth and righteousness reaffirmed, only then is peace produced. But war is uncivilized, and we need to quit trying to civilize it. That is why it should always be the last resort.

I couldn't help but take note of the recent public statement by the Taliban supreme leader, Mullah Mohammed Omar, speaking of the radical Islamic terrorists:

"The situation where we are now, there are only two things: either death or victory. To those who are fighting and bombarding us, they should understand the Afghan man is a fighter willing to die for Jihad."

That might be pretty scary stuff until we remember what General George S. Patton had to say about fighting when he assumed command of the Third Army in Europe. He said that "No[body] ever won a war by dying for his country. He won it but by making the poor dumb [person] die for his country.

So much for inspiring Islamic rhetoric.

What we are now witnessing is the result of decades of shortsighted American foreign policy. It has been a schizophrenic policy that put Suddam Hussein in power in the first place, replaced the Shah of Iran with the Khomeni, and is even somewhat responsible for the present Taliban. It's been a helter-skelter policy based on short-term material gain and no pain that now sees our troops facing some of our own weapons in the hands of our enemies across battlefields.

Regardless of what long-term mistakes we've made in foreign policy as a nation, or what course corrections may be needed, there can be only one response to what just happened to us. And that's a formal declaration of war by our Congress. Short of that, our total cumulative national will won't be any better than it was in Vietnam and will very likely end up the same way.

If I sound a bit "dovish" here, let me say it more clearly. Until such time as future generations of our present enemies recall with horror in their eyes the terrible price they had to pay for violating our liberty and freedom, Americans will be relegated to living without that liberty and freedom. Because the only other option is to close down our borders, surrender our civil liberties, start frisking citizens on the street, and leave soldiers posted in our shopping malls. Even then, all we've accomplished if we leave these whackos with any remaining ability to wage war is to leave our children in a graver danger than what we face today. Benjamin Franklin said it best: "Those who would trade liberty for security deserve neither security nor liberty."

This is not a situation that requires the hiring of Mafioso mercenaries to capture murderous pirates on civil charges and international warrants. It is an American war! With less than a declaration of war by our Congress, with less than the fullest of retaliatory response on those directly and indirectly responsible, we leave our people without the unifying tie of a common will left us constitutionally by our very wise founders.

At the moment I watched those two planes strike in New York, I had this thought: If we do not have an equal or greater resolve than those nineteen imbeciles who threw their bodies into those buildings—we will lose.

There has been much debate about the war in Iraq. I've more than surprised many of my conservative friends because I have not been supportive of the war. But it's not war I'm opposed to, it's the way in which it is fought. In this instance, I can't help but believe we are following an historic pattern of fighting that will, once again, continue to sap our strength and leave us short of victory. Quoting General Patton again. "The trouble with politicians is that they always pull up short and leave us with another war to fight." In this instance, those raising red flags about the war in Iraq correctly point out that we are advancing from one reason to another reason for our actions looking for a reason to be there. We have gone from a stated purpose of finding and destroying weapons of mass destruction (WMDs) to, now, building democracy. And our president himself chastised President Clinton for "nation building" when first campaigning in 1999.

I'm not interested in building democracy in the world. (If I was, at the very least, it would be republics I would establish.) It is none of my concern what kind of government other people choose to rule. That is their business. I want to trade with them, be friends with them. But it is up to them to decide whether or not they want to. Yes, there is the problem of dealing with the Stalins and Hitlers, and other questions of pre-emptive strategy. But I don't think that was the case here, nor have we as a nation settled on the right method of dealing with that. The closest we came I think was under President Reagan, which was a strategy of deterrence—the right answer in my view.

"Boy, it must be hard on you to see the welcoming the troops are getting when they come home today," a friend said to me recently. He was speaking of his remembrance of how badly returning Vietnam veterans were treated when coming home from the war. At first, his question caught me off guard, and I had to take stock. But it was easy and sudden.

"Actually, I cried and was elated for them. You know, in a way, it was vindication for me. I felt like I had come home too," I replied.

My pride in serving in the United States Marine Corps should be obvious to anyone reading this book. What it gave to me as an immature man has been invaluable to everything else I've ever done or accomplished. And I am tremendously proud of our armed forces today. But I just never want to expend one life or one shell until we have a complete plan for victory—not a guarantee of victory, but a plan based on victory, one in which its decision-making process is free of governing by political public relations and reelection strategies to stay in office.

As stated throughout, we must find people who are committed to doing what is right, not what is politically feasible in order to hold power. I have always told my candidates that doing what is right should always be paramount to getting re-elected. Anything else is the shortsighted strategy. Just what do you want your legacy to be: true patriot to your country or to your political party?

So just what is it that makes a patriot? How would we define it?

In America over the past decade or more, the media culture has so damaged the word patriot that many people today are afraid to be called such. Definitions of words are changing rapidly today. Today, if you call yourself a patriot you're automatically labeled "far right."

Noah Webster's 1828 dictionary defines the word patriot this way: "A person who loves his country, and is concerned for its best interest." Webster went on to define the word patriotism as this:

> Love of one's country; the passion which aims to serve one's country, either in defending it from invasion, or protecting its rights and maintaining its laws and institutions in vigor and purity. Patriotism is the characteristic of a good citizen, the noblest passion that animates a man in the character of a citizen.

A Patriot

I can't help but believe we've lost our understanding of "the love of country" in this past generation or two. Probably not since World War II has there been a real sense of true patriotism. I sense that some of this loss may have come from the Vietnam era, from which I'm still not sure we've fully recovered with any sort of national healing.

Words are being re-defined in our present-day media culture, such as changing the word *homosexual* to *gay*. Who made that decision? In the same way, the word *patriot* now carries a somewhat negative connotation.

A few years ago, pastor and historian Steven Wilkins clearly delineated the subject of patriotism in an address. He began with a look at the word government, both in Noah Webster's dictionary and present-day dictionaries. When you look up government in Noah's 1828 diction-ary, it lists the different arenas of government, and in his initial description of the word Noah writes: "Men are apt to neglect the government of their temper and passions." He also went on to say that government is "the exercise of authority by a parent or householder. Children are often ruined by a neglect of government in parents."

Then he goes on to list the different forms of govern-ment, such as self, family, ecclesiastical or church, and fi-nally civil authority. But when you take a look in a modern dictionary, such as the *New World Dictionary*, you get an entirely different definition. It describes government this way: "The authoritative administration of public policy and affairs of a nation, state, or city."

Do you see what's happened here? In modern day defini-tion, there is not one mention of the other legitimate God-ordained forms of government. We have totally lost our understanding of what God intended as the jurisdictional arenas of government. Civil government is a God-ordained government, and I would never say otherwise. But it is one of several and never intended to be sovereign over any of the others. All were intended to fall under the sovereignty of God. That sovereignty of God is the only guarantee we have that the other governments will not become tyrannical.

If we ask an attorney, we will find out that all law really comes down to this question: who is in authority, in whose jurisdiction is a particular issue? And today, as we have discussed, civil government has declared its sovereignty in so many arenas that it was never intended. And the greater problem? We don't even bother to argue it anymore.

As Wilkins states, "The state now directs the education of our children, regulates our business dealings, subsidizes the arts, and manages the health care of all our people." These things must be done, but I would certainly question the legitimacy of the government directing them. One thing I always tell legislators is this: if you take away people's responsibility, all you get back are irresponsible people.

There are five characteristics of a patriot Rev. Wilkins laid out that I want to share here.

A real patriot honors the government of the Lord Jesus Christ above all governments. He understands that when Christ is on the Throne, all other governments fall at His feet and into their proper order. He understands that there is only one true king . . . King Jesus. He is no friend to his country he who does not honor the sovereignty of the Kingship of Christ. Do you understand that Christians were not persecuted in Rome because they were Christians; they were persecuted because they would not acknowledge the divinity of Caesar. The true patriot understands that liberty is a gift from God . . . not government.

Second Corinthians 3:17 states, "Where the spirit of the Lord is, there is liberty." To me, that means it can be found nowhere else. Wilkins goes on to the second characteristic:

> The patriot understands this and seeks to keep his country close to God and his commandments because he knows that all prosperity and hope only exists in the liberty that comes from God. The true patriot will never allow the government to assume itself to be the giver of liberty. A true patriot calls his country to accountability. Why? Because, as Webster said, he loves his country and is concerned for its best interest. He knows that if his country strays from its submission to God, that it is doomed to tyranny. There is no middle ground, and we must begin to understand this. There is either liberty or there is tyranny, freedom or bondage, that's it . . . and we need to know the recipe of each.
>
> The true patriot is unafraid of public or media scorn when it comes to crying out when his country is wrong. And the patriot knows he must oppose his country when his country opposes the things of God.
>
> The patriot is quick to repent; both of himself—and for his country. He knows that the only way his country can get back on the right path is through true repentance. He does not make excuses for his country. He knows and understands that national repentance begins with personal repentance. Proverbs 14:34 says: "Righteousness exalts a nation, But sin is a reproach to any people."
>
> He knows that there are more important things than winning elections. Tell me why do we keep electing people who consistently sell out on the things we hold dear; these people who keep compromising away God's Word for the sake of political expediency? Victory that is won through compromising God's principles is not victory—it is defeat! The patriot is quick to repent and humbles himself before the living God and begs for

mercy for himself and his country. He knows there can be no other way.

Finally, the true patriot never loses heart. The patriot never grows weary of investing in his country and answering the call. He knows that his country requires a personal investment from him. He knows that he must pass on his country's great heritage to his children if its legacy is to be preserved. He knows that he must fight for it!

Wilkins concluded with this:

Patriotism is honoring the Lord and His covenant with us. When we do . . . He blesses us. He even causes our enemies to be at peace with us. He comes to fight for us and defeats our most powerful foes.

But, if we ignore Him, He says 'I will desert you' and will give you over into the hands of your enemies—and that's what has happened today. We have ignored the true King and therefore He has allowed tyrants to rule over us. We have ignored His word . . . and He has given us rulers who have ignored it as well. We have refused to truly worship Him and now are obliged to worship a godless state. And, we have refused to exercise mercy and charity, so now we must submit to robbery by the state and are coerced into the redistribution of our wealth. So, today there are many forms of patriotism but only one true Biblical Patriotism. All others are idolatry.

We must understand that socialism only comes when we do not obey God's tenets in the first place. We *will* give. The only questions is to whom: God or god?

A Patriot

To regain a true sense of patriotism in America today, we must start by reinstilling honor back into politics. Howard Phillips once said, "Your vote is the currency of your virtue." We have allowed the American media to trample politics and politicians to the point that they are viewed as less honorable than the used car salesmen of yesteryear.

There was a time in America when it was not only common, but important, to refer to an elected representative, in public or in print with the salutation of "the Honorable Senator," or "Honorable Representative." Today, we seldom refer to them that way. As has happened with nearly every other institution in America, we are dumbing down and eroding the respect of public office and especially those holding public office—politicians. In America of late, we have allowed the media to do our thinking for us too much of the time.

We must get back to the fundamental understanding that politics is a vehicle, just the same as political parties. It is simply a means to a public policy end, no more, no less. It is the way for us as Americans to affect our country and our future. It is the method left us by our founders to guard those things we hold dear. And it is no uglier and no more corrupt than we make it or allow it to become. In the same way, we know that fear is a hard taskmaster. We must not allow the vileness in which our elected representatives are regarded by the media culture today to capture us and our children anymore.

We must begin again to hold our elected representatives in the highest regard—with honor—regardless of their political bent. Frankly, we must do this even for the ones we don't like, because it is we who are responsible for their being there. We get what we deserve. And maybe—just maybe—if we begin to regard those we hold in contempt highly and with honor again, maybe we can get close enough to change their hearts. Scripture tells us in Proverbs 16:12, "It is an abomination to kings to do evil, for the throne is established by righteousness." Therefore, as a church especially, we must begin treating the American political arena and our politicians with the respect they are due.

Referring to the question of whether or not the church should be involved in politics and civil government, I have two quotes to share: the first is from John Quincy Adams.

"The highest glory of the American Revolution was this: it connected, in one indissoluble bond the principles of civil government with the principles of Christianity."

Adams knew that the founders in styling government had just given Americans the most freedom and liberty any people had ever known. And he knew that it would be so only as long as we maintained that indissoluble bond.

President George Washington said, "Of all the dispositions and habits which lead to political prosperity, religion and morality are indispensable supports. It is impossible to rightly govern the world without God and the Bible."

Perhaps Proverbs 29:2 says it best. "When the righteous are in authority, the people rejoice; but when the wicked rule, the people groan." So, are we groaning in America today? We should be—this is if we are basing it on the moral health of the country and the future that it brings.

I'm addressing this because I believe, if we're going to survive as a nation over the long haul, we must re-establish honor in our public elections and the integrity of holding public office. As is typical of the media culture that we're a part of today in America, we have succumbed to the belief that politicians are all crooks of which none can be trusted.

We have participated in the brutal verbal lashing of elected officials to the point where we have begun to "self prophesy" our own state and national shortcomings on the part of office holders. I would even go so far as to say that when we tell politicians over and over again that they are crooks and no good, that is in fact what they've learned to live up to.

Thus, it could be that part of the apathy that exists in the country today toward politics stems from this attitude of disrespect that each of us has accepted on an individual basis.

As a campaign strategist, I've gained a tremendous amount of respect for any person who runs for the state legislature or any public office. Running for the legislature is grueling. If you run—really run—for the state legislature, you soon find out what the definition of work is. Most candidates have to hold a forty-hour a week job and still get out and ring 15–20,000 doorbells by election day, not to mention a full slate of other activities.

I've found that most people who run for public office run out of conviction, regardless of their political beliefs. But, looking back at early history again, there was a time in America when politicians were held in the highest regard, certainly compared with today. So why is that?

For one thing, in those times, people understood the issue of authority in a godly perspective and had high respect for the rulers placed over them—or the ones they allowed to get into office. Secondly, I think that early on, public officials were viewed as the gatekeepers to the rights, liberty, and deeply-held convictions of Americans. Soon after fighting a very ugly and brutal revolutionary war, Americans put a lot of stock in its politicians and the responsibility that went with public office. They understood the preciousness of their newfound freedoms and liberty. They knew their elected representatives were the ones charged with guarding the inalienable rights spoken of in the Declaration. They were, and still are, the protectors of the faith of the original covenant and, frankly, the very religious freedoms that we enjoy. What could be more honorable than that?

Once we return to understanding the importance of political participation, once we have retaken our place in the marketplace of political thought, once we reinstitute our belief that politics and religion are inseparable, once we begin to sacrifice to wrestle control of the civil arena in America, and once we learn to understand government as God intended it, then on that day we will then be able to truly stand as patriotic Americans again. Any less than that, as Steven Wilkins stated, simply spells idolatry.

The bottom line is that today we as Americans are being asked to surrender our freedom and liberties to those who do not understand the very purpose of, or the proper role of civil governing, and who do not understand the fallacy of trading away liberty for security.

I'm reminded of the words of Frederic Bastiat, French statesman, economist, and author in *The Law,* and his comprehension of the term liberty. Said Bastiat in his concluding paragraphs:

> God has given to men all that is necessary for them to accomplish their destinies. He has provided a social form as well as a human form. And these social organs of persons are so constituted that they will develop themselves harmoniously in the clean air of liberty. Away, then, with quacks and organizers! Away with their rings, chains, hooks, and pincers! Away with their artificial systems! Away with the whims of governmental administrators, their socialized projects, their centralization, their tariffs, their government schools, their state religions, their free credit, their bank monopolies, their regulations, their restrictions, their equalization by taxation, and their pious moralizations!

A Patriot

And now that the legislators and do-gooders have so futilely inflicted so many systems upon society, may they finally end where they should have begun: May they reject all systems, and try liberty; for liberty is an acknowledgement of faith in God and His works.

The morning was cold in Plymouth Harbor as the men began moving over the side and onto the net, climbing down to the longboat below them. As they moved away from the sanctuary of the mother ship and moved along silently through the still shore water directly for the beach, each mind focused on what lay ahead. As the hull of the longboat scraped the first rock and sand of shore and as their feet touched ground, they gathered together to kneel to give grateful thanks to the Lord Jesus Christ for safe passage and to dedicate this new land to His purposes. For centuries God had preserved this land and held it in safekeeping for a people ready to make a covenant with Him.

Epilogue

November 20.

At 0320 hours, the men began their climb over the sides and onto the cargo nets, climbing down to the waiting boats below. The rising sun silhouetted the ships a half-mile or so off the reef. The unusually low tide would become a factor a little while from now.

As they moved toward the beach away from the sanctuary of the mother ship, each mind focused on what lay ahead. As the hulls of the LVT's and Higgins boats began crossing over the jagged coral reef . . . all the forces of hell rose up to greet them.

The few who survived that first volley of shells on their landing crafts huddled together finding new sanctuary along the coconut wall that protruded above water. Many would never survive the two hundred or so yards that still lay between them and the beach. From every direction, smothering machine gun fire mercilessly riddled the boats from the beach and the lagoon. Armor-piercing rounds began ripping and penetrating the thin skins of the LVT's, cutting some of the men in half. Waves of mortars began scoring direct hits on the landing craft transporting this initial wave of the Second Marine Division, U.S. Marines, to Red Beach One, dozens dying at a time. This was the island of Betio in the Tarawa Atoll.

Only minutes into the landing, a dozen landing craft floated listless and afire with red pools starting to form around them. Of the 125 landing craft moving the Marines inland, only fifty remained afloat by days end.

Less than a third of the initial wave of Marines moving through the surf to cross the reef would ever see the beach, much less the end of this day. Most who reached the beach were severely wounded, many of them dying after crawling from the water. The second wave of Marines coming up behind was faring even worse.

Never in the history of warfare have men been asked to face such withering fire before them with only the cold sea behind to which to retreat. But the Marines kept coming.

Caught in a most vicious cross fire, the clear south-Pacific waters of the lagoon began turning crimson from the carnage. Those able to reach and move forward along the long wooden pier did so stepping on the submerged bodies of their fallen comrades just to keep their heads above water.

By day's end, hundreds of bodies bobbed in the surf, and hundreds more lay lifeless, scattered about the beach onshore. The few Marines managing to reach shore hunkered together less than fifty yards inland, trying desperately to reorganize the little that remained of various units cut down by the waiting defenders. It was a tenuous beachhead at best, with their commander reporting to Pearl that "the situation is in doubt." But when dawn arose on the second day of landing, the hell continued and they moved ever-forward through the surf.

Inch by inch, the Marines moved onward and began securing the beachhead. Casualties continued to mount and by day's end, the cost to the Marines was over a thousand dead with two thousand more wounded.

But by the end of the second day, Colonel Shoup, Commander of the Marine landing forces, radioed a new report: "Casualties many; percentage dead unknown; combat efficiency—we are winning."

The Marines continued advancing, bleeding, and dying for yards, slowly driving the enemy from their positions. These defenders were the emperor's finest Imperial troops, chosen especially to repel this attack on this important tiny atoll.

Of the sixty-five hundred Japanese defenders, only seventeen would survive. One of those taken prisoner was asked later if and when there came a doubt in his mind that the Japanese would be able to hold. "Yes," he said, "when the dead and dying Marines just kept coming and coming."

It is 9:45 P.M. Friday evening, as I pass the last exit to Sprague Lake. Almost home. From here, it's thirty-five miles in to Spokane. Over my left shoulder, the rolling hills of the Palouse are silhouetted below a rapidly dimming blue horizon of the western sunset. I love this time of year. *It is fitting,* I think to myself, *that completion of the legislative session coincides with the entrance of daylight saving time,*

spring, and warmer weather. Funny, how a positive always follows a negative.

I know the fear that gripped those Marines in the LVT's and Higgins boats chugging toward the reef and shore at Betio that day. And I know the amount of faith it took to overcome that fear in order to produce victory and preserve liberty. I know them. I am so very grateful for the sacrifice they paid that I might remain free. I'm so glad they arose to do their duty. Now we must also.

I think back on William Bradford's writings in *Of Plymouth Plantation*, and the fear the Pilgrims felt in the storm—and the months that followed as so many died around them.

It was a Democrat President who got it right, I think as the Bull Pines come into view on the horizon. Franklin Roosevelt, faced with the very real task of getting a nation that was behind the times to catch up with a world already at war, said, "We have nothing to fear, but fear itself." Most historians agree that had Japan not attacked until, perhaps, a year later and had we continued to avoid the inevitable, there is a very real possibility we would have been too far behind and unable to win in World War II.

It is the same fear of the future that keeps us from warring against tyranny and sin. It keeps us from going the distance, always settling for less than total victory. It is the fear of Cain that threatens to destroy the very core of our being as individuals and as a nation.

Fear produces cowardice; faith produces courage.

I realize now that until we begin to move forward, willing to make the sacrifices necessary for victory, until then, we will continue down the slippery slope of despotism, eventually realizing a worse hell that the one we wish to avoid. Jesus said, "Whoever loses their life for my sake will find it." The sake of Christ was liberty. And He died to give liberty to all mankind. If we're going to preserve that liberty, we must always be willing to do the same. To the naysayers, those who seek peace, to them I say: the great paradox is understanding that real peace always follows war—war that reaffirms and reestablishes the law of God and nature. Only then can there be real peace or liberty. For as the Bible says in Eze. 7:25: Ruin comes; and they shall seek peace but none *shall be.*

I watch as a plane reaches the airport runway off to my left, and it occurs to me just how much I've learned in the past ten years of my political involvement. As I pass the Garden Springs exit, I recall the many great warrior friends I've made working in the legislature and the campaign con-sulting business. And tonight I'm especially grateful that many of my questions have been answered.

I do remember the question, and now I know the an-swer to Rodney King, to Robin Hood, to Karl Marx, and to all the other God-haters. It is Cain who haunts us and divides us. It is Cain who drives us to accept tyranny as a surrogate of liberty. And it is *his* father's sin that crouches at the door seeking to overcome us. Now I know what that sin is. It is fear. It is the opposite of faith and the root of all other sin.

But as God told Cain that day, "you must learn to rule over it."

As I began the final descent of Sunset Hill, I realize *he* is still with me. But so is his brother Abel. Today I must choose between the two.

By faith Abel offered God a better sacrifice than Cain did. By faith he was commended as a righteous man, when God spoke well of his offerings. And by faith he still speaks, even though he is dead.

—Hebrews 11

To order additional copies of

Looking
for America

Have your credit card ready and call

Toll free: (877) 421-READ (7323)

or order online at: www.lookingforamerica.org